Get off the Bus

(Bulls!t Undermining Your Success)*

Written By

L. A. WALLACE

Co-editor: J.A. Cooper

ISBN: 978-1-959071-30-3 (paperback)
ISBN: 978-1-959071-60-0 (hardcover)

Printed in the United States of America

PREFACE

Life's a wonderful thing once you are familiar with your surroundings. We get so comfortable in our routines and familiar faces that we lose track of who we are and where we want to go in our life.

I was diagnosed with post-traumatic stress disorder and rebooted back to the streets. Without any support from Uncle Sam, I began to realize that I just did not get PTSD from the service; it's been with me all my life.

Come walk with me and see my world from my eyes then you be the judge. R.I.P to all our lost Hood Heroes and countless others who left us so early.

This book is also dedicated to all the hood Hero's that are still here with us, for example Bust a Bust and Greg "the Brain" Smith. Thank you for taking a stand showing others like yourself that the streets are not always the right choice in life. It is not what you do in life but it's how you do it. Remember someone is always watching.

SUMMARY

Get Off the Bus was a wakeup call for me. I realized that no matter what you as a human may be facing you have to slow down. Re-evaluate where you are and where you want to go. Just as you seem to find yourself going in circles. Seeing all your dreams and friends passing you by then yes that is when you have come to the realization that in fact unbelievably, you're on the BUS!

A bus route you say. Yes, just like a bus that starts and ends at point a is a circle. In fact, the BUS I am speaking about are the things in which we indulge in that take away from the focus of what we are aiming for ourselves. It could be numerous things or just one. Either way it's in your way of conducting your goals.

A pastor once told me to receive my blessings I had to let go of my Demons. Well here they go, you can have them all. I thank God to be here to see the seven year anniversary of my first book. Now sit back and enjoy this journey as I walk you through my hometown in a little neighborhood called Park Place in the city of Norfolk, Va.

DEDICATION

I would like to thank God for being my beacon through life and my savior. My grandfather was in a coma and was told he would never walk again. Well once came out of his coma he walked again. He has been my inspiration ever since. To my mother for not having an air conditioner during those hot Virginia summers leaving me no choice but to hang in the library thank you.

To family members that were there for me I salute you and for those of you who did not answer my calls well let us just say expect the same smile. To my dear ex's I told you this day would come but you all laughed at me and left me dry. Well, I hope you have invested well because this my friend is the end. To my family and loved ones who were lost cousins Ray-Ray, Trisha, Diana, Lil Dave, and Mike.

Lastly my children who by now are all grown. I have paid my life for them to have what I didn't as a child. Now it's your turn to take this book to the next level. Never let them see you sweat and just remember the finish line is where you make it. And last but not the least I can not forget Quincy Gardner, one of the talented writers from the HBO special "THE WIRE." He showed me how to formulate my thoughts to compose this book. Thank you for seeing something inside of me that I couldn't see.

TABLE OF CONTENTS

CHAPTER 1

Norfolk's Bastard Son

As a young kid, Lil Tee knew life as one big question; why is the sky moving? What makes the wind blow? Who created the world? And things of that sort. However, the answers never came as easy as the questions. He was a seeker of knowledge and at an early age he would not rest until his questions were answered.

His mother Sharon was 15 years of age when she had him and at that time was living with my great grandmother. Her mother was in a nursing home. I was told it was from a lady who wanted my grandfather for herself and decided to put something in her food that would make her senseless for the rest of her life.

Because of that I only met her once or twice before her death. I had seen many pictures of her, and she was a beautiful light skinned woman with long brown hair. My mom looking back in time was exceptionally beautiful as well and I saw where she got her good looks from in the pictures of her mother.

Sharon was a petite woman with a nice warm smile. When you caught her during a good laugh you could see her deep dimples and the cute gap between her two front teeth. The early years were fun as I can remember. My mom worked for Burger World and all the toys that were featured there she would bring home to me, and I loved them.

A lot of the other kids picked on me because I did not have as much as they did, but I never allowed it to ruin my day. I knew my mom loved me and that is all that mattered. We used to take long walks together. These times I enjoyed with her the most. During these walks I would have her all to myself. One day as we were walking, I asked, "Mom, who is my father?" On these walks when we were all alone, I figured she would give me a straight answer. But as usual she will ignore me and that was fine too. If I had her nothing else mattered.

I can remember snap shots of my father and I as a kid. When I would see my cousins with their dads and my friends' dads visiting them on the weekends and holidays at times, I would ask who my dad was?

Did he know about me? Or if he knew I even existed? My mother would never downplay him or speak ill of him no matter how she truly felt about my father. She would simply say he was out to sea. If I really persisted, she would reply I am here. For a long time, I never knew what she meant by saying that I would just shrug it off and go play. Not knowing anything more about him then I did before I asked her huh.

(Life's 1st bullshit) Never letting her responses discourage or influence my feelings towards him. I just took what she said as a grain of salt. Now from about the age of five to the age of eleven I had lived a lie and as I was getting older, all the reality of life was becoming clearer as it got closer.

The earliest I can remember worrying about my shoe game was when I was 11 years old. I had an old pair of Pumas. They were so worn out that the top had detached from the soles. I told my mom that I needed a new pair of shoes. Her reply was if you want things in life, you must work hard for it. Now at eleven I was not aware of any job openings and living in the projects of Norfolk it was not any positive jobs that's for damn sure.

Currently the pressure of fitting in with my peers was just starting to form and by me being thirty-six husky people weren't breaking down doors to play with me. We lived in Lakeland apartments with her boyfriend or whatever you want to call him. I was only known as Sharon's son so his name will not appear in this book either lmao.

On the weekends we would stay with one of our relatives and they were mean to me when Sharon was not around. One of our relatives would always blame shit on me just to have a reason to spank me. Believe me it did not take much for her to have a reason. I was told if you cannot say anything nice well you get the picture. Anywho the world was so huge to me and not just in the since of my age.

Between the fifth and sixth grade a statewide announcement was advertised to all that qualified, Section 8 was now accepting applications for housing. Sharon woke me up at around three am and said, "we had to walk to get on the list for an apartment". I had to hurry up because they were only taking the first thousand applications on that day. You had to be a Norfolk resident to sign up.

If you missed the signing, it could be another ten years before the opportunity for section 8 came around again. We walked from Lakeland in Norview to the Southern Shopping Center on Tidewater Drive and Little Creek Rd. Damn I thought my legs would fall off, but we made it and I was glad.

There was a lady there that we both knew. Her name was Kitty. She was a nice young white lady with three little kids who lived in the next building beside us. My mom spoke to her but wondered why she did not offer us a ride. They both drank and got high together.

But, as always Sharon said, "I will pray for her". It was our turn next. At the desk, the lady asked a lot of questions and I think it kind of made my mother a little uncomfortable. Every now and again she would look down at me, smile and squeeze my tiny hand. Then say, "baby you are going to have your own room and get a lot of new friends". It did not matter to me. If she was happy, I was happy. After all, she had me so young. She was really like a sister more than a mother. Which made me love her that much more.

She was so young that we did everything together and people always asked if I was her brother instead of asking if I was her son. She had looked incredibly young for her age. A lot of women were jealous of her because she would turn heads wherever we went. You knew she had to look the part too. She did not have a whole lot of clothes to select from but when she did get dressed, she looked hot. She would alter a lot of her outdated clothes and they would look better than the original outfit in the store.

   After we made it through the interview for the Section 8 apartment sign up it was time to make that walk back to Lakeland. Damn I thought I was going to pass out. The sun was now up, and it was not playing even the trees were gasping for air. Luckily, they gave us drinks and snacks at the sign-up desk. Now if we could have found some shade this trip would not have been as horrible in that heat.

CHAPTER 2

The Root Is Planted

That summer, school ended, and two things happened to me that changed my life forever. My childhood crush had moved to California all the way to the other side of the world. Ok the country but I was a kid, which was far to me. So far I believed that at that time I would never see her again and if I did it would only be in my dreams. The second thing was that my mom's Section 8 was approved. Well at least I thought I was finally moving to a better and more stable community; boy was I in for a shock.

We arrived in Park Place to a tan brick four family apartment building. There in black numbers was 310 west 30th street. Seeing Apt. 2 on the door of the new apartment building made me extremely excited. A new school, friends, and places to explore (there were a lot of abandoned houses and cars throughout the neighborhood, and I planned on running through them all). I thought I was in heaven.

In the beginning all that we had were the clothes we packed a few pots and cleaning supplies she bought along the way. Once in the new apartment she told me I could have the second room and that it had bunk beds. I was in heaven for sure now and I could not wait to have my first sleepover.

My mom took no time settling in and she invited Coco, Crow, Janet, and Peanut, this man, a friend of Janet's and a few others to celebrate the fresh start.

She was a step closer to having her own place in life for her and her son. When we lived in Lakeland out Norview my mom worked at Jack in the Box. By the time we moved they had closed the chain of restaurants due to food poisoning. The hood was devastated. That place was to us as White Castle is to people up North.

So, in Park Place she did not work, at least not that summer. I was going into the sixth grade and if it was not for my grandfather, I would have been outback (no new gear for school). Since a lot of the talk back in the 80's was about African Americans being the majority on welfare, that the state made these stay-at-home hood moms get jobs at the local schools.

My school was James Monroe, the principal there was no joke. He had a log in his office and if you were ever sent there during school hours then you knew that log was not for sitting on, but it was for spankings. It was not called child abuse then it was called attitude adjusting. Of course, Sharon was given the job of lunch monitor. Lucky me. No really, lucky for me lunch was served in the basement. Coming from a normal school where we eat on the same level as our classes this was quite strange to me. We had three periods for lunch here and each shift was hell. a lot of running, pushing, and ducking low hanging pipes is one of the downsides of eating in the basement.

Also, people try to either gamble you for your lunch money or beat you up for it. Win or lose you must choose your battle wisely. There were two guys who adorned our depleting campus. Their names were Man Man and Mac. The two of them had a joint age of thirty. They shook everyone down and then ate lunch with the staff, confusing huh? Well thanks to affirmative action making Sharon have to work, let us just say it saved my little black ass on several occasions.

I had become the son of the crazy lady. Let me explain. I had gotten into a fight with a guy in the hood by the name big lip Donald. My mom found out about the fight. She may have (I did not see it however I was told this.) chased a couple of people with a machete. From that day on no one really messed with me. Or really played with me too much for that matter. That now explains a lot of other questions I had back then too.

Now the month before graduating to the seventh grade it was the last parent teacher conference of the year.

This was the last chance of the year to either pull up your grades or find out what summer school you will be attending. Since my mom worked at the school, she made our appointment last after her shift ended in the lunchroom.

They made me wait in the hallway as if I was unable to hear them discussing my strengths and weaknesses. Where I was standing from, I could hear them as well as see them. I moved back just a little bit because I did not want my mom to see me being sneaky.

So, I chilled and waited for the conference to end. At the sound of things even I was impressed with what Ms. Holbein had told her about my accomplishments. Just as I started to dance the dance of satisfaction, I heard a sigh of shock. It sounded as if my mom had dropped an expensive vase and she was embarrassed at the fact she would have to replace it. She sounded shocked knowing that she did not have enough change in her purse to pay for the damages. Then she rushed out of the classroom crying, pulling me by the arm rushing me down the hall. When we had arrived at the nearest exit.

I asked her what did I do? She turned around and said it is not you, it is what your teacher mentioned to me. When she kneeled and looked me in the eyes, she asked me if my clothes were uncomfortable to me? I am confused now (I am thinking to myself what does my clothes have to do with passing to the seventh grade? Life's second question?) I responded no momma then I replied a little tight, but I do not care. As a child you always told me to ignore the jokes.

To ignore the picking that came from the other students and to do my work. That helped when all the kids would make fun of me. Well, she said your teacher just told me what kind of mother would allow you to wear those types of garments to school. Well, I said mom if I'm graduating soon, she will not have to worry about seeing me anymore. "I'll work this summer to afford my own clothes. I'll be ok" I told my mother. She called me her big man for the first time, and it felt good.

Graduation was coming and she was going crazy trying to get money for a suit and shoes.

She received one hundred and ninety-one dollars a month in cash and two hundred dollars a month in food stamps. Yes, the paper bills of all colors. The kids today do not know how embarrassing it is to go to a store and must go through a line ten times to make change. So, your mom can buy beer and cigarettes lord have mercy. Well with her money all spent for whatever reason.

Like for instance she would give her boyfriend Moonie control of both her food stamps and the cash. Of course, he would buy food for us after he takes care of himself. For this and other reasons, I'm going to call it as I see it. He will not receive one ounce of accomplishment for my achievements as if he took any time out to reach a little brother. Or any credit for whom I became in life.

I cannot say I did not learn anything from him because he did show me how to be a good stepdad by him being a horrible one to me. The same way my biological father showed me how to be a better dad by giving me the example of being a bad father.

Even though it took a while for me to realize no matter what their shortcomings were, in my life soon I would have my own crosses to bear. My mom had to stay out the night before the graduation and I was nervous because I had not seen my new clothes for the big event yet.

However, that morning I woke up and on my way to the bathroom there was a light gray suit and dark gray shoes, white shirt, and a tie with light and dark gray stripes. It didn't matter if it was fresh. At the time of graduation my "best friend Saga" was two classes behind me and I looked up from tying my shoes and some act of God he was right beside me. Posing for my mom in my picture.

"Smile and say cheese' my mom yelled, snap and before I could say anything he was back with his class ooh next time I see him ... Sharon said he is your friend, don't be that way. "Ok mom" I replied and marched to the auditorium for the ceremony. I never told her, but he was a frenemy (another word for acting as a friend but smells of an enemy).

I did not want to ruin the day, so I shrugged it off and when I did, I realized out of all my friends my mother was the only parent who showed up. So, I shared her attention for now and I'll enjoy my mom's company by myself for the rest of the day. Afterwards a lot of people came up to me to meet my mom. Saga looked at me and said I was lucky. Until I got older, I could never understand what he meant. As a kid who had everything a kid could ever want. I mean he was like the Richie Rich of Park Place, but he envied me huh? (Question of life number three.) I had nothing, at least I thought to myself, but I must have had something. Because he said he was jealous of me.

That meant a lot to me only to be set up for a horrible downfall by my so-called best friend later in life. Professor Xavier could not have seen what was coming. Hell, I did not, and I knew the motherfucker. I am laughing now because it is funny. But when I look back on it all it was all at my own expense in the end.

CHAPTER 3

Eat or Be Eaten

Graduation passed and it is hot as hell outside. All my homeboys could afford the boys club. The only time I could go was when Moonie was around. He would give me the twenty-five cents which was the cost to get a day pass. Sometimes he would give it to me and other times only if his son was over for the weekend. He would give us enough to go because his son was there at our house, and he wanted to appear to be Cool huh! OK.

Half the time when his son was not visiting, I believe he gave up a quarter just to have the house to himself. That way he did not have to feel responsible for me. Little did he know half the time I said I had twenty-five cents just so I did not have to be around him while he was over. So, I guess we are even. This is the point of my life where things get a little hazy.

My mom allowed a man to use the bathroom and never thought anything was wrong until I asked for one of those coupons to go get a soda and some chips from the Corner store Pick up the Pieces. While I am waiting for her to give me a list. Whenever I wanted something, she would make a list not just for her but whoever else was outside at the time with her sitting out front drinking beer and smoking weed. She ran out the house screaming "Where the fuck Crow's ass at.......?" She ran to either end of our block only to return confused and upset. I at the time was going on twelve and the hood made me vengeful of mine. It was just her and I, Moonie rarely stayed overnight.

His job was on the Norview side of town. I never expected Moonie to do anything but bitch about the food stamps anyway and use that as a reason to distance himself from Sharon even more. This would allow him to have the freedom to do as he pleases without her knowing (In layman's terms so he could do him with no interruptions).

A couple of weeks had passed and still no Crow. It is an early Saturday morning, and all the money niggas will be out soon by thirty first street right across from Pick up the Pieces. There has been nothing to eat at home since that bullshit went down. I am just pacing the blocks waiting to see Mr. Crow. Damn I am starving. I had a few people I could go visit and get something to eat from, but I was very upset. I have not seen Crow's ass yet. After eating at big K's house his grandma gave him an allowance, so he treated me at times when he went to the store. On the way to Pick up the Pieces I saw Crow's ass.

Yo wait K there he is right there. K replied "who?" I said, "the asshole who stole our money." We ducked between two duplexes on thirty first & Debree Street and watched his every move. "Yo" I said to big K "he keeps going in and out of that milk carton under the tree between Black hulk's crib and the old white man's apartment building." I told big K to "go get Lil Gates and meet me back here." I will stay and keep an eye on Crow's ass.

When they got back, I told Gates about what happened a few weeks ago and Gates knew exactly how I felt because his Mom worked with my mother at James Monroe. She received aid as well and if the roles were reversed, he knew I would be down to ride with him. Now the plan was to get Crow away from whatever he had in that damn carton, so I said, "K give me ten bucks". He passed the bread only after I agreed to pay him back. then he coughed it over.

Lil Gates gave the ten spot to Crow and told him to buy us three beers and keep the change. He went for it. All these so-called hustlers could never turn down a damn dime low life motherfucker. I mean we are kids, why not buy us beer for free? We all are doing wrong, damn no honor amongst thieves I tell you. I told G to make sure he keeps his back to Debree as soon as he walked to Pick up the Pieces, I told K to "watch out" and I moved casually over to the stash.

I walked between the apartments where later the two kids who grew up across the street from me were killed (R.I.P. to them) and the huge apartment building where this scary old white guy lived. He rarely came out but when he did, we would bolt because we would hang in front of his building all the time and I do not think he enjoyed that too much.

Anyway, as G and Crow reached the front door and entered the store I ran as fast as I could and scooped up the carton. I ran down Thirty First Street then jumped Dickey D's fence because our backyards were diagonally behind each other I was just hoping him, or his gay ass brother was not home. Those boys were touchy feely a lot if you know what I mean. Back then people just knew not to undress around those two brothers. I jumped the damn fence, went up the backstairs to my backdoor and I was home free. K and G showed up about 10 minutes later with the cold beer. They had eager expectations of what was in the carton.

I did not want to spoil the surprise, so I waited for them to come to my house. My mom had finally got a job at BP gas station on Granby Street across from City Park, Below and Seven Eleven. I had the place to myself till about eleven or twelve o'clock (lucky for me she worked the third shift).

"Well, you'll be ready to see what's inside"? I asked K and he did not want anything to do with the beer or what was in the box he just wanted his ten dollars back. All he cared about was going to the downtown Granby Street mall to buy comics. We joke with him all the time but the truth of the matter is none of us could afford to buy comics. We would always tease him and pick on him about wasting his time and money on someone else's dreams. Boy were we wrong. However, when he got the latest comics, we all would crowd around him as he read each one aloud. Those were the good old days. Even the hardest guy in the bunch would stop to listen to what was happening with all the heroes like Iron man, Spidey, or the X-men.

Now afterwards he might receive a threat or two from one of the bullies, but it was fake. They did it to appear Kool again like we invited them over anyway. Oh, we had to listen to K read the comics to us because he did not allow anyone to physically manage his comics at all! And each one was stored in its own individual bag.

He was literally sick about his comics. Back to the milk carton. Once we got the box open a bunch of little corn colored envelopes fell to the floor like a miniature slot machine just this was not money. I did not know what the shit was, but little did I know this instant will change my life forever. Gates said damn we're rich. I could not see what he was talking about, but he lived out Park Place way longer than I had.

He always bragged about his mom dating a local drug dealer. This means he knew what they had put into those bags'... drugs. Nonetheless, he knew we hit gold. As K went to check in with his grandma. Me and G went to work.

We had counted all the bags we had, and it was like one-hundred and ten envelopes. Gates said, "let's split them up half and half". It sounded good but I still did not have a clue on what it was. Or what to do with it? Then I replied, "no, let's open them up and place it all in a pile and go from there". G hesitated for a second then he agreed.

Once we had opened all the bags only then I knew what it was chronic, M.J., smoke, mean green, some grass which all adds up to one thing: money. My first act of revenge felt good. No, great. I had a crew. We conducted a plan and walked away with the spoils of war. All done with no casualties furthermore I got his ass back without him or my mom finding out her small angel just burnt his wings. I'm twelve now. I am a general and not doing bad for myself. Gates said, "let's roll it all up into joints and sell them one joint for three dollars and two joints for five bucks."

I wondered for a second. My mom always told me that drugs were wrong and never to use them. As I was pondering what really to do with my half, he lit one of the joints up and it smelt so good. "Man, what are you doing"? I asked Gates. He said, "how we know if it's good or not until we try it." I could not back out. He was in my bedroom. What to do? "Yo pass that shit Gates" he did, and I said, "damn hurry up and let us smoke that shit up before my mom's punk ass boyfriend comes over here."

Moonie would show up whenever I was doing something wrong, and he could use it on me to rat me out to my mom. Lucky for me everyone in the four-apartment building smoked heavy, so the smell did not concern me. It was him finding our weed because if he did, he would take it from us. Then he would say he would not tell my mom. I know that would be a lie just like when he caught me jerking off in the bedroom after school.

I knew I was the only one home. I just sat on the toilet reading the mail looking for any notices from school to sign and return before it reached Sharon. I would sign and hide them from my mom before she came home from work and drop them off in the school office the next day. Ferris Bueller had nothing on me. I went to my room to look at this new black tail magazine.

I had waited forever to see this Issue. Big d and Lil Black had a copy but would not let anyone see it unless you paid them five dollars. They kept shit like that in their clubhouse under Big Boy's house across the street from the boy's club in his mom's basement.

Until they got high one day and tried to cook some bologna on a base heater and it caught fire lol. Anyway Moonie told me he would not tell Sharon if I gave up the magazine ok even exchange no robbery shit. He told as soon as he picked her ass up from work. And I never trusted him again after that shit not because of the magazine fuck the magazine I was a young man shit happened. He was supposed to use that as a bonding situation instead he snitched. I guess what you should've expected from a grown ass man who calls himself "Moonie" my point exactly.

Well once it was proven, he (Moonie) was not to be trusted, G hurried up and finished. When he was done, we had between the two of us something like a thousand joints if not more. We ran out of papers a couple times after the last pack we re-bagged the loose bud and split that up as well. That night I was out late allowing my mom to get home first so my clothes would have a chance to air out as well as my mind.

I know I have something now and it is time to put a new plan in motion. It's late summer, school is almost about to reopen. Gates moved to the other side of Park Place, lucky for me the money was on my side of town. I would see him from time-to-time walking to Red Ball, the other local corner store. The same family owned it just two blocks down the street from Pick up the Pieces on thirty second street and Debree across from the makeshift car repair shop.

That is a whole nother story. Here at Red Ball, they sold all the fresh meats and housing goods. The store had an upstairs that doubled as a rooming house. I had mad fun up there and made a ton of money. We will get to that later. I took my half of what we took from Crow and hid it under the duplex next door. The janitor only came out once a month. So, if I stayed on top of his schedule, I was Gucci (good to go bro).

I kept ten joints on me at all times in sets of twos now listen close all you want to be hustlers. You never roll with your shit on your person. this shit is not legal for one and second if a jack boy come for you (usually a Portsmouth nigga all they do is rob people) you will lose your whole stash.

(I mean how hard is it to stand on a corner and do what we were doing, really. They were just some lazy ass niggas that got high all day and robbed all night. We were all poor and we still had the poor robbing the poor.) You will have more product to fall back on later. It took a lot of failures, losses, and threats for me to figure that shit out. During the day, I would have two or three on me and if I hear kids my age were looking for some weed, they would hit me up (I serve them what they want).

A few weeks have passed, and I am halfway done. I have been stashing money all over the house and in the backyard. Out the kitchen window I could check my shit. I was never worried about no one coming back there because the people who live directly behind us had a bad ass dog and I do not mean bad as a good thing. This dog was a pain in the ass. You fed him, he barked at you, played with him, he barked at you, and if you came to the fence he went berserk. I loved that dam dog lmao.

One day I bump into G he had on fresh everything I mean he looked like he just stepped out of a RUN D.M.C or a L.L. Cool J video shoot ok my nigga. "Where have you been shopping at homeboy"? I asked. He said, "you haven't spent any of your money yet." "Null man I was too concerned with what my mom would say to me" I said to G. "Let alone what Sharon would do to me if she even had a clue, I sold weed." We had no food, the rent was late, and all the bills were due and to top it all off Sharon had no smokes or beer nor any weed. She didn't know I had any, so I did not offer any of it either. Let me backup a second, I did feel a little guilty one night before I even sold my first bag.

I went to her and tried to tell her if I ever found a bag of weed she would want it. I knew she was feigning (needed to smoke some chronic) and I wanted to help her with all the bills due because she had no help. If I did not know why people smoked weed, I now knew it was an easy escape route to say fuck it. Because when you take your first pull you forget what the fuck you were thinking about. Whatever it was now was on the oh well fuck it list.

Only till you come down I guess you will then remember what the fuck you were getting high for in the first place. I am no rocket scientist but the problem nine times out of ten is still there just now your fucked because you forgot the task at hand. G's mom on the other hand was a lot easier going, he simply told his mom he found it mmm no Sharon would have whipped my ass until I told anything but that I found it.

Really in Park Place where everybody is looking to find something so how I got to be so lucky I can hear her now. I did not want the others to hear what I was about to ask him. So, I held my question and I waited until we were at the back of the group. "G you sold all your joints" I asked him. "Yeah" he said, "I been finished". Then he looked at me and asked, "if I was done as well" I said, "no halfway but I did not want to sell all mine I wanted to wait for school to open and kill them at all the back-to-school jams." DJ P with DJ Super C have back to school dances at the boys and girls club every year. Everybody there is going to want some weed.

He said "DJ P knows we can buy a whole lot more from when we finished. I asked him "what did he mean we can get more"? (Do not laugh at that time I was as green as the bud we were selling). I had no idea that you could buy more than the ideas started to just pour in on all the money that I was going to make.

CHAPTER 4

Learning the Truth

The summer ended well and for the first time I looked the part of a kid that had loving parents at home. Even if I only had one and that one was the best one ever. I had re-upped with G's people a couple times now. So back to school was def. (Another word we used which meant fresh, sweet, or hot). I made money that summer from swapping Crow's shit. It was around twelve hundred dollars and I smoked lovely every day. I guess old habits do die hard.

(Excuse me for a second while I have a Lil Smoke break, a lot of choking and cuffing later.) Ok I'm back Yo I had to let my inner being have a break he's the one writing this story. Oh yes and at this moment in life I can afford being a kid man, life was good.

The seventh grade was wild. Different classes one here one there one way on the other side of campus. Damn I'm tired but since Sharon didn't at first take right away to Park Place until once I had reached Jr. high school (Norview Jr. high) she would move us backward and forward between the two-apartment complexes. Meaning when she wanted to party out Lakeland I had to walk to school and if she wanted to go out to the clubs, we stayed out Park place. I had gotten to ride the bus when we stayed out Park Place. Most of the time, it really all depended on how Moonie and she were getting along.

Good for them but it sucked to be me because I had no choice in the matter. He would piss her off or tell her to leave and you can figure out the rest. It was coming to the end of the year and one good thing came out of living in projects while walking you get to meet plenty of people. In return you can sell tons of weed. I have people out there pumping for me and with me. I had Park place, Norview and the Ville three power money spots but I'm only one hitting the tip of the Iceberg.

Well before the year had ended can you believe I had a chance to show off, stunt, do my own thing. We went on a class trip in Jr. High school to Washington Dc. Man, I was there buying up food like crazy. Hey it was only food but to me I could have whatever I wanted. The best part was no one was there to say no or stop me. Oh yes, I can't get enough... a monster was born. On our way back all my classmates noticed me doing my thing too. I said nothing to them. I had just functioned as if I didn't notice them admiring me.

I was having such a fun time. On the way back to school two blocks from pulling up to the bus port in the next seat in front of me there were two hot girls. Saga and I were sitting together when the girl in the seat directly in front of my seat turned around and asked, "if I would kiss her". She was cute but tall and I said "yeah" but when she leaned forward to kiss me, I moved. All the kids on the bus went crazy. All the kids were laughing so hard that they were shouting they had to use the restroom.

She was furious with me so much that she took both hands and before I knew it, she raked both sides of my face. I got suspended from school because she claims I hit her first. Well let's just say I thought we hit a bump. When I got home the bad news beat me there first. My mom was looking over my wounds. There was a new face in the kitchen. He looked like me, but I wasn't too sure until my mom said, "your dad is here". He asked me "who did that to you"? I replied, "no one did nothing to me"! He goes on saying "I hope whoever it was you had got the best of them". I shook my head and left to make my rounds and to see who needed more weed and to re-score more for myself.

On my way-out Sharon yelled to me "did you get suspended". I said I wouldn't know until Monday" and left. He stopped me on the way out and asked me again "who I had been in a fight with"? I told him "It wasn't a fight and I only swung to get her off me but not to hurt her". He said, "bullshit she hit you, did you defend yourself and hit her back"? I never really understood that, but I refused to listen because if a motherfucker hit my mom, I would have killed them.

Even if the man reflected me. Robert Williams was the name my mom told me to say whenever I was asked what my father's name was. As I got older, I learned it was not his real name after all. And to be a smart ass I called him Robert when he said something I didn't want to hear as a joke. As he was talking to me my mind was in outer space wondering if he knew I could give two fucks about how he felt. I don't know this fool. Once upon a time I did want to know him. But he stayed away, and I know for sure bonding with me didn't bring him here back to Norfolk.

To my understanding he was going through a divorce and now he wants to be a dad. Ok he can stay right here and playhouse with her. He was probably over here to get some money or some pussy or both. and since it wouldn't be the last time, he would pop up for something I knew he would be back again. You add it up either way they were my parents and it's gross. I wasn't mad at him, I just didn't have the time for his shit right now. Ok I know what you're saying, go easy on him. At least your dad came back even if it's for a piece of his old flame.

Well peep this (listen closely) he really came back to Norfolk, Virginia about a month or so ago. He pulled up on me and asked if I wanted to hang out with him for a while. I knew that was a lame ass excuse to get gas money from me. I didn't care at the time because I was fucking with this Lil slut out Norview by his place that he was sharing with a roommate. When we got to his apartment, he told me to wait for him and he would be right out. Well as soon as he went in the room, I jumped into the driver's seat and jetted. I drove past K mom's house. She lived down the street from the chick's house. I feel like Robert De Niro get your own fame trick. She stayed right across the street from the high school. It's funny how we met, me and big K were walking from his mother's house in

Tinners Creek. As we were coming from under the overpass, I saw a group of kids our age hanging out in front of one of the townhouses. They were playing loud music and drinking. I had a couple bags on me, and I wanted to see what was poppin' (who was making money or needed some weed) in that hood.

As we passed through the buildings, I saw the unit where the wild group of teens were. K and I walked up to the door, and it flung wide open. We looked at each other and K said, "he was waiting outside". I looked at him and said, "I didn't come all this way for nothing I'm going in". As I went in niggas were everywhere. I mean upstairs in the kitchen on the back patio everywhere. I couldn't help but notice there was only one girl there (now you see why I called her a slut). I walked up to her and asked her "who stayed here"? She said, "she did".

Then I asked, "Were all the people here good you know them"? She replied "yes they were all friends from the neighborhood" I thought to myself Kool. I had asked her "if anyone wanted to buy some weed". She said, "she didn't know everybody here might want some.

Everyone was drinking her mother's liquor". I thought to myself this can work. I cleared everyone out we kissed, and I played with her tits and smacked her on her phat ass. I promised to return to see her soon. But only on one condition their better not be a bunch of niggas in here when I do get back or I told her I wasn't fucking with her.

We exchanged numbers and that was dat. I bagged her. She wasn't the prettiest bunny in the bunch, but she was moldable and that's all that mattered. Damn I went to her house and back, dropped K off and my dad was still in the back room.

It's now been over an hour since I've been waiting for him. So, I got up and went in the room. I didn't see him in the other room because the door was locked. Then I went back in the room and looked again. I opened the closet door and there he was sitting on a cooler passed out. Now I always heard he would get so fucked up he'll pass out, but I never thought it was this bad.

I had just assumed it was from too much drinking that's what I get for assuming. He used that diesel, horse, and smack. Yes, he shot up and that explained a lot to me as to why I was so scared of needles and hospitals. And all that medical shit I told you before I learned from him how to be a real father.

At least the best I knew how, and not to shoot up any drugs because good or bad once the shit is released into your veins it was no turning back. You had to ride it to the end, but you come back to life (that's what they call an overdose) and a few to many of these and you are not checking back into the game you can ask Karen that!

I entered the closet not knowing what to think. I shook his arm damn blood was coming out the side of his arm. Where a tat was that read Sharon and had his name with the word forever in cursive. After he came too and got his head on straight, we left and went back to my mom's house out Park Place.

On the way it was awkward he had no excuses, and I wasn't looking for any either. I just didn't want any parts of him or that shit. Back at the house my mom was bitchin about how long we took returning home. He blamed me for having the car. I looked at him and walked out the crib disappointed as hell. Like that's really who I been looking for all my life, fuck.

He can go back to whatever rock he crawled from under. It made me no difference. So now you see why what he stands for don't mean shit to me at all. It was Kool we can talk but nothing else to me mattered at that time but money.

And if it didn't make dollars, it didn't make sense. It was nice outside and the whole hood was on their front porches. It wasn't too hot outside, but it still felt cooler than being inside those four walls. The winds were blowing gently from all directions. You could hear the children playing street ball and tag in between the parked cars. All the older residents would sit on their porches while the younger adults would walk back and forward from house to house spreading jokes and the latest gossip.

You always knew the latest song because everybody would play different versions of it loudly while enjoying their daily activities. See it be so hot in the hood with or without the police so while in the hood you just laid low and come out when night falls. It's easier to move without everyone in your business and the cops all up your ass.

Big K was my right hand as I was learning the game more. You know honing our skills and building up clients. While in our hood K did all the hand-to-hand combat. He received a two-dollar cut off each bag and the work I gave him for himself he used for the people who came with short money. He'll do about ten to twenty bags a day. We had a good spot. We played at the end of my block where the old white guy lived and no one would dare go on his property and me and K knew that place like the backs of our hands.

K was big but we did drill all the time. And only when no one else was paying us any attention did we oversee our business. We used to make it look as if we were racing whenever anyone asked us why we were running back and forward through the hood. Looking back now that used to be funny but it came in handy whenever the police or the jack boys was out.

The eighth grade flew by really fast. I couldn't wait either. This is the time when you said your goodbyes to all your old friends and got all the ones who got you by egging them. I was upset a little because I had a young crush on this teacher (I was tempted to mention her name to give acknowledgment of her beauty. Mmm she was hot with coffee brown skin and a shape like Diamond from the players club that's who Keisha Ray played as the star).

Everyday her nipples would be hard as hell me and this white kid named Terry we used to queue each other whenever she left her headlights on lmao. We were young but damn she could have raped me any day and I would've kept it all to myself.

But because of reasons beyond her control, she's not in a position to respond but I will hand deliver a copy of this book to her. As smart as she appeared to have been, she should've known Norfolk had a thing against principals selling cocaine from their school.

Then using their accounts to launder the ill-gotten profits. Oh, and having the janitors working for you. She could have beat the shit if she hadn't put the janitor on. I mean damn that's why you were hired as the boss, and he was hired to clean up the shit. Well as Forest Gump says stupid is what stupid does. But I soon got over it because I wanted Ms. Vain, he was a mean old bitch who taught home economics.

And the first part of course was cooking and in school I was a big dude she picked on me day one of class. My waist was size thirty-six husky my cuffs came up to my knees the kids used to call them soup bowls. Well one day in class we were all new to each other. She had asked for volunteers to help with the lesson.

I guess since I was a fat kid (me) I was marked by not standing up. "Smile," she said with "you're big, wonderful self" and pointed at me. And on top of that she said "as big as you are you should've been the first one up here" the class erupted into a loud laugh.

I hadn't felt so little and hurt since elementary school when my sixth-grade teacher told my mother about my horrible wardrobe. I was embarrassed and I wanted some pay back.

She looked over at me and smiled and she must have thought she was on a roll because after the laughter stopped, she added "It's not like you don't know your way around the kitchen".

I was now beyond embarrassed and from that point on she was on my egg target list. Every class of hers I counted down until the last day of school. And now that moment has come it was time for her to pay the piper. And I was going to be the one who's going to give it to her too.

Now the moment has come to pass the buses are lining up. Damn I had just made it back from be- low's getting my eggs. As the buses pulled off all the teachers were lined along the bus port waving goodbye to the loads of kids.

Boom. Splat. Boom. Boom. boom. Duck someone yelled from the back of the bus. I have Ms. Vain in my sights. I let go of two of the eggs. I didn't want a head shot and I really didn't want to hit her at all. I had just wanted to scare her but then I realized I'll never have to see her again. And all the embarrassment she caused me for the two years here oh no I'm going to let her have it.

The egg yolk splashed all over her hair, face, blouse and shoes. She was upset as hell. A job well done Lil Tee if I don't say so myself. Now somewhere between Norview Avenue and Tidewater Dr. a couple of fights broke out with the people in the front of the bus.

They lived in Layette Shores. It was the worst place in Norfolk next to Ocean View to live. There was trash everywhere: rats, possums, and mice. It was located right next to a local swamp. Let me tell you where we lived was fucked up but here was hell. rats as big as dogs hung in the front of the buildings. I didn't care though it was fun out there, anyway somehow in all the egg tossing the bus driver had gotten covered in yoke and she was heated.

She waited until she got to the first stop in the shores and threw everybody off the bus who didn't have eggs on them. People were crying and shit it was crazy! I had on a brand-new polo suit, and I was clean. She had stopped the bus and began to walk down the aisle. She was kicking everyone off the bus. I mean everybody.

Some people from my hood were scared. They picked on the kids who live out the shores hard and since the shore's bus stop was the first stop on the route, they never got any pay back. But now the roles were going to get reversed. We going to see who the Billy badass of Park Place really was.

Right before she got to my seat, I cracked the last of the eggs I had in my lap and as she came to my seat I stood up. She saw I had egg on me too. she looked at me and said "sit down baby" I had a sigh of relief my aunt lived out here I would have been Kool. I just didn't feel like fighting with the shores I had liked them; besides I was dating a chick out there on the low and she definitely would have been on my side.

However, I wanted the big mouths to get what was owed to them. And as soon as the Park place got off the bus the residents ran out the back doors to get some payback against all the bullshit they received all year round. It was funny as hell

CHAPTER 5

Cocaine made the front Page

It was the summer of 1986 and Norfolk was changing not too much for the best either. Having the biggest naval base on the east coast that made us a drug hub. Norfolk was Dubbed baby New York after having the highest number of drug busts and murder rate in the country.

Currently Norfolk's murder rate was highest in the United States even more then U. S capital where Ray was operating. Yes, Norfolk had reached the big times and I wanted ii on the parade. It just so happened I came home to grab some cash to go and re-up. Then I realized taking on the house bills and keeping up with the latest gear had started to take a toll on my little weed empire.

This is when I had started looking for the next new hustle. I needed to flip my doe faster but still stay under the radar. At the same time, I wanted to change my hustle game up. The hustle game in the hood had started to change over too from weed to powder cocaine and then to crack. and I wanted to be one of the first to have it.

A lot of out of towners began to move in fast. At first on the outskirts of twenty-six street and Debree, Thirty Fifth street and Newport. Then to Granby Street and Thirty Fourth Street, back up to Colley and twenty third street.

The money power started to shift in the hood as well meaning the old heads who used to hug the block no longer were there anymore. The shooters, wine O's and prostitute's that use to line the streets were now gone. At one time you literally had to step over them on your way to school.

I mean it was seriously fucked up, but it was home and I had learned to accept it. As I also had to accept the fact that weed just isn't going to cut it anymore. I need in on the coke game and fast before Sharon and these bills bleed me dry. A cousin of mine he knows who I'm talking about came to me and told me about a new spot near Villa Height's.

He and his man (we had the same first names only hint) was moving out there to set up shop. I was a loner and besides, I had my own thing going on and I didn't want to give up that location. I told him I'll think about it. In the meantime, I had asked him "did he know where to score some weed from?" he replied "yeah me". He went to the car and came back in the house with this strange looking shit.

Since G by now moved and came by every now and then I had needed a more dependable connect. Well, I wished I had waited for G my own fucking cousin got me.

That was ok I'll see him again he double me up its just catching up with him will be the trick. Lucky me that wasn't all my money or the only time I'll get fucked in the game. I went next door to the apartment building where my safe was and took out enough for a cutie (four ounces of weed). Later that night it was a breaking news report now normally I'll just turn the channel but something about this report had grabbed my internal attention.

I reached over and raised the volume. I at first didn't recognize the area but I could see what was going on. It was kids my age and younger getting money. I mean five, ten, twenty some even reported to have had up to a hundred thousand dollars on them at one time.

Damn I sat back in my chair and closed my eyes and pictured me in those cars I saw on the television. And me in those big ass houses and me with all that cash. It might sound strange, but I couldn't wait until I had a cocaine supplier.

After my little daydream my mind was made up, I'm sold. I needed to know one thing: where the coke is and how do I get my hands on it. At the same time, I wanted to get the coke to raise me and my mom out the hood. Sharon was young and I realized if she didn't want out the hood well, she could come visit me because I'm out.

All I really wanted was the normal things in life like food, water and shelter. As of now it's still just me and my mom and I want to turn up. Back in Lakeland Moonie must have seen the same news report because by him being older and way older he switched his green tag in a way before I could.

He was a low-level weed dealer as well, but he had way more contacts than I did at the time. Little did he know when I was younger, I had put two and two together. Once I kept seeing people coming over, going to his room and about a half an hour later, they'll come out laughing, smiling and shit. And he'll be like "a hundred dollars in ten minutes". If you asked me, he started me hustling.

Once I learned you didn't have to be a rocket scientist to do it, he wasn't. I played dumb though and just watched. I was getting older, and my mom allowed me to stay out Park Place by myself from time to time. Ok you got me, crack had found his way to her as well and wherever he was Moonie made sure she was. He used it as a control device for my mom. To the point that I couldn't understand who she was, and I think she had a feeling that I was starting to pick up on her cocaine usage.

"I'm getting it, you're a big boy now and you can start to stay at home by yourself if you want too" Sharon said to me one night while we were staying in Lakeland. What teenage boy would refuse that opportunity? I didn't admit it at first, I was a little scared of being new to the area all alone.

But the endless possibilities to grow my plucks (dope clientele) without her nosing around made the idea perfect. However, little did I know all the time Sharon herself made her habit become second nature. Seeing that my mom was not home usually gives people the idea that it's cool to come by the house and that's never an option.

Even though she wasn't home I told the plucks she was, and they had to meet me behind the house. or at the Corner store no exception. Today was Saturday and weed or not I never forgot our Saturday morning ritual at Big K's house. You know he received an allowance I didn't but by this time I had money.

But I had to show my money in bits and spend it here and there to hide it from Sharon. Sharon still didn't know I hustled, and I would do odd jobs in the summertime and on the weekends during the school year. Doing the odd jobs had helped me to cover up the dope money I made. Sometimes before we left for the side jobs, we would eat the left-over breakfast at K's house before we left for work.

Looking back now damn I used to eat beacon and eggs wrapped in paper towels that was stuffed in his pocket. Well sometimes his grandmother worked on Saturday, and he wasn't allowed to have company until someone returned home. It was good though my mom never got up and cooked breakfast anymore hell she stopped getting up in the morning all together.

That was if she was home. I was happy when she stayed home and slept. so, I would not have bothered her anyway she had looked so peaceful. I'd cover her up and kiss her forehead and leave forgetting the fact that I was mad at her just last night for not coming home or calling me. At least I knew where she was and that had made me happy. Sometimes I wondered who was the parent and who was the child.

My cousin would come by, let's call him Clue. He didn't have to do odd jobs like K. His mom's parents brought him everything he wanted. Clue had all the latest New York fashions and all the sport team gear. With all the trimmings in between. Lastly my boy Dip lives on the border of Park Place and Lambert's point. He once stayed behind K on Twenty Eighth Street, but they moved when his dad got sick.

He only came by on the weekends to do odd jobs and hang out. As you can see my house was the headquarters because Sharon used to say you be the leader and not the follower. I know seeing her little boy in charge tickled her pink. She said, "it made her feel warm inside". Now she must have thought if he listens around me, I know my boy is obeying me when he is in the streets.

Little did she know I was on my way to running the streets? We would discuss who would do what job? Who would hold the money? And who would do the talking? I mean you had to be organized when you talked to old white people. They scare too easily and that wouldn't be too good for business.

I started this up first before I was selling weed. I didn't have money to get into the boys and girls club so I'd walk to Ghent (a rich white subdivision adjacent to Park Place) once there I would knock door to door in search of odd jobs.

Once the occupants opened the door, I would give them the spiel about how I'm trying to raise money for a club membership and how deprived I was at home with no food. And of course, I wore the worst clothes I had in my wardrobe that at the time wasn't too hard to do either.

Nine times out of ten I'll make no less than one or two hundred dollars depending on how big the jobs were and how long it took to finish. Sometimes I'll get more than one customer because the people like my manners so much that they'll call friends and family in the same neighborhood and refer me to them with very high regards.

As I would leave their house others would be waiting outside on their porches waving for me to come and do chores for them as well. When that had started to happen more and more often, I knew then that I needed to recruit a crew but not just anybody.

I needed people who would just work and not fuck up the arrangement by breaking up the customer's equipment or by using foul language in front of the clients. Or for that matter just being themselves no I needed people who wanted to get paid and go get fucked up after work with no questions asked. So, I used my crew money. Why not? Me and Big K smoked together.

Dee nor Clue didn't start smoking yet so I would get them drunk and treat them to something to eat on the way to and from work. Not saying they didn't have their own money it was more as a thank you for coming type of thing. Because I needed them more than they needed me at the time, and they didn't even know it.

Once the jobs were done, I'd hide the bulk of the cash on me and the other half I would split between me and the rest of the crew. Ok say if it was a two-hundred-dollar day I would keep a yard and split the other hundred four ways.

I did the talking, I got the jobs and I collected the pay, so I took the biggest cut. On Sunday's we usually fall back at whoever's house. Their parents went to church and everyone knows K's grandmom was going to church. He often had to go with her but as we got older it was his choice and since I didn't go, he always had decided to stay home as well.

You might be saying how could shortchange your homeboys like that? Well, I started the side job game to get money. As I was getting older, I used it to hide my drug money from my mom. When they came for the ride they were happy. The more money I made doing odd jobs the more Sharon got for the bills. I was putting money in her mailbox way before 2 Pac was putting money in his mother's mailbox. I wonder if he knew what I was doing ...Naw I doubt it.

This was a different Sunday school. It was life you had to be in it to win it! While school was less than a month away the four of us were discussing what high school we would attend. What girl we wanted to date? No one was having sex at this time. We just wanted a girlfriend just to say we had one. While D, Clue and K were talking I started to daydream and pictured me flossing with all new gear and living in a house not a big one just a house with no roaches or mice.

My mom was drug free and she was home after school making dinner then someone said "the beer was gone" it was getting late now. We all still had curfews, so we all dapped each other up then split in separate ways heading home.

That night when I went home I had noticed the dude from across the street's van was parked in our driveway. Yo he was an asshole he wore a long ponytail and had his nails done all the time. but the weirdest thing, he got all the chicks though... I couldn't explain it. Pretty ass women loved this dude or he must be threatening those hoes or something.

Because he just didn't fit the bill. He now was fucking with the phat ass chick who lives in apartment number three. I would only see her when he wasn't around and even then, she was running to get in the house as if she wasn't allowed outside without him on her heels.

She was thick in all the right places. I always wondered if I caught her alone, what would I do to her or what would she allow me to do to her? Since he was always around that'll never happen. It was like Biggie Smalls said, "it was just a dream".

Man from across the street. Pretty boy would smell her ass when she'd pull up to the apartment complex before she even got out of her car, he was right on her ass. Well, I guess she felt the same way I did, but time wasn't on our side not yet. One night around two a.m. we heard a lot of screaming and bumping coming from upstairs.

My mom came in the room and told me to "stay put". I nodded my head and said "ok". I heard her run to the front door and it slammed shut. Everything was quiet then the door flung open I heard my mom saying, "hold on" and cussing under her breath saying, "that punk ass motherfucker I saw him leaving the building in a hurry".

She had to have been talking to the neighbor next door. "Grab some more towels from the hall closet" I heard Sharon say to the other lady, "ok" she replied. Sharon kept repeating herself "saying you're ok I got you, the ambulance is coming stay awake girl just stay awake. Lord I wish they hurry up" my mom said in a loud but firm voice. Now I see why she never came outside unless he was home or if she was with him. He was beating the shit out of her, and I guess when she was tired of his abuse, she attempted to call off the relationship.

But he wasn't trying to hear it and he tried to kill her. I felt sorry for her son because at the time Lil Bree was like seven or eight years old. He was young but he had heart. If he was older, I know he would have killed Pretty boy's ass. Yeah, I said his name because he was a low-down dirty bastard for doing that to her and had the nerve to try and make up with her when she was released from the hospital.

She let him in from time to time, but things were never the same between the two of them again. I couldn't wait to see Ike-Ike, her nephew. He was like me, he lived In South

Norfolk (that nigga was trained to go R.I.P Ike-Ike). A couple weeks after her discharge from the hospital they moved back to south Norfolk. I saw Ike-Ike and told him what happened to his aunt and if he wanted to get Pretty Boy for that shit, I told him I was down.

I didn't like that nigga ass any way. Unfortunately, Ike-Ike got killed before we could exact revenge, he offered me to go with him on the capper. It all happened so fast. The night he helped his auntie move he was telling me about a spot he wanted to hit in Young's Park right across from Ruffin Middle School.

You remember it's the same school where my science teacher became the principal, and she used the school staff and accounts to sell coke out of the school. I told you Norfolk go hard, well ok in that area. See let me let you in on a little something. I'm not a thief Sharon made sure of that for damn sure.

I didn't want my new Park Place friends to see me using food stamps, so I decided to steal what I wanted (wrong choice) that night from Be-low. I got caught and since I was too big to run, I had two options: go to juvenile lock up or call my mom.

Which one do you think I chose? Correct, I chose to go to juvenile lock up. Yes, jail.

My mom was crazy and he saw that I would have rather gone to jail. He immediately went to the front of the store and told the guys that I was with if they didn't tell him my mother's phone number, they were all going to jail.

My cousin Lil C thought it would be funny to give him my damn number. Let's just say this when Sharon got me home for the next two years I didn't care if I knew the kids or if I didn't know the kids but every time she heard of some kid getting caught stealing she would say "go in the room and take your clothes off".

"Huh?" I would reply, and she'll repeat herself and at first I would say "but mama I don't even know those dudes" she would always say "well if you were out there stealing you might have been with them. So go in your room and take your clothes off. I'll be in there to whip your ass. because I didn't raise no motherfucking thief".

And she would work herself up as if I was debating her over whether to beat me or not. I just wanted it to stop so since that one time of stealing I got two years of ass whippings. If you asked me if it was worth it my response would be hell no. The lesson she taught me however was priceless and it would aid down the road as you will later see.

So yes, that was the fastest career start and ending I think I ever made in my life. And being a thief was off the list. Pretty Boy now goes with the old candy lady from Lakeland who moved in the building.

Funny maybe a month after Diane was stabbed and he didn't waste no time jumping on Kimberly. She moved into the apartment where he stabbed his last girlfriend. Damn she is a pretty red thing too. She had two beautiful daughters, Ikea and Lexus.

They became like little sisters to me, and I made it clear no one was to fuck with them in any way. I couldn't get with her either. He played Kim even closer than he did the chick he stabbed. Oh well my turn with Kim will come but for now back to this money shit. School is about to start and I have only a few ounces of bud left, and I need to re-up.

But I don't trust a lot of people because people talk and that's how you go to jail. Next day I'm walking to Golden Gate to get some chicken wings and fried rice (Yo their food would make you smack your mama it was so good).

But then I noticed a car following not too close but close enough for me to notice them. Ok you are thinking how he sees this car following like he Escobar or something. No not like that but see if you even look like you unsure of your surroundings someone, somewhere would see that and before you know it, you're on the ground getting the shit knocked out of you.

Oh, and your pockets are going to get ran (meaning robbed). After I stopped to let the car pass me at the Corner, I noticed he parked and the driver had gotten out and asked me my name. I looked him up and down first and said why? He was like hold on youngblood we just moved in the house across from you on Debree. You are the kid that be standing on that block in front of that old ass apartment building?

To myself I'm like damn how does he know so much about me. I've seen him a couple times out and about the hood, but I never knew who he was or what he did? But little did I know he did his homework on me. Yes, that be me what's up? He broke it down to me and said I see you pumping that weed in shit and that you have a couple of runners working for you. I was like damn you the feds or something man? He smiled and said no but I can help you make a hundred times more than what you are making now.

It sounded lovely however my mom always said if it sounds too good then it just may not be good for you, and I told him I'll think about it. Then I walked away. The golden gate was packed and with no AC it was hot as balls outside and inside. I could have stayed home. The thought of eating in the AC was the whole reason for going up there to eat. Oh well, I headed to Park Food store, the next best place to eat. It's still early, so I'll get all the hot and fresh chicken wings and some potato logs.

Damn did you see that it was like ten mustangs all lined up in a row. Shit now six brand new jacked up Nissan four runners. Who was these guys man? Fuck that food I seen them turn in on Debree Avenue that's my block let me see where they went too. (I shared a blunt with my last client and I should have let him smoke his own, but he was just getting an edge up. so, I'm not wasting my shit....be right back).

I made it back to Debree. I'm cutting through Tony and Tracey's old house at the corner of my block to see where those cars were going. Damn these niggas are huge I said to myself they look like football players or something. it's about fifty or so of them.

They lined the block with the mustangs and had the four runners park three facing three right in the middle of the front yard. I'm glad for them Tony and Tracey grand ma don't live there anymore she'd cuss their ass out something bad boy let me tell you. Well, everyone in the hood took notice as I did to the new neighbors, I mean they had one of the car doors wide open brazening the beat another in the cross section of Debree.

Two of the mustangs were doing donuts at the intersection of Thirtieth street and Debree. One of the cars was a teal green with wide tires and deep rims. Black smoke poured from the back.

He wheeled his mustang around and around in circles people were cheering them on. Not knowing that this group of guys was going to change our neighborhood, our community, our city and even the fabric of our families forever. I was entertained for a minute, but they had theirs and I still had to get mine.

I still haven't eaten yet and it was around two or three o'clock now, so I went upstairs to Kim's house. She cooks all the time. My favorite was when she cooked Yok. It was a Chinese noodle she would boil, and she would add chopped up onions with a boiled egg, soy sauce and a little bit of ketchup. Damn I could go for some of that right now shit.

Yes, sir I lucked up. She cooked. It wasn't (Yok) the Chinese noodles but it will do. Her fried chicken wings were the bomb. Hell all her food was good and all of her was good too.

Pretty women I guess can make some good ass food lol. Got my food and I put it on the stove. Of course there was nothing to drink. I'll walk to the store, and this would give me a chance to see what the old heads in the hood was saying about the new people that I saw moving into Tony and 'em old house.

As I got in front of where all the people was, I notice all the fucking hood rats old and young were all in front of those new niggas shaking their asses in shit. Well, that's on them they couldn't give that funky ass shit away those niggas will find out for themselves. Shit I'm hungry I opened the door to the store and there everybody was inside talking about the new guys.

My cousins, they were like third cousins or something. Their grandma was my great grandmother's niece. However, all we knew we were cousins, they did them and I did me. We would joke each other all the time. I mean, I guess it was how we showed each other love.

And it also showed other people in the hood that we can fuck with one another like that, but they better not try that shit. Sometimes we would get personal but never to the point of fighting we're blood. Any way I was ear hustling and no one knew who these new niggas was. All types of shit you would hear like they from New York. They came to take over. At once you heard a lot of mumbling and grunts from the crowd.

The dude behind the counter he was my man Dickey D's uncle (gay boy who live on Thirty First Street) he was like they came in here today and said, "they were from Brambleton Avenue" and that "they had played for Norfolk State University's football team". Everyone got quiet and then reality hit they're out here to get money.

CHAPTER 6

Stepping my game Up

It's almost back to school and it's my first year of high school. I want to have the best of everything when I did my back-to-school shopping. Me and Big K did what we always did: play the corner where the old white man stayed. We hugged the block getting that paper. We had to be out there maybe about twenty or thirty minutes and I noticed one of the Brambleton boys (as they were dubbed) selling something to one of the girls that was over at the pep rally they had a few weeks back.

K didn't see he was shouting down the street at our peoples, he walked over to me and said, "let's go I need to tell you something". I looked around and retrieved my stash. It was easy to spot because I hid it in an old cigar box, and it was in the midst of more scattered trash that littered the avenue.

As we were walking back to my house, he started telling me what happened last night to one of my cousin's. Apparently, he had gotten in a fight and had gotten his house kicked in. They shot him to death. I was like "who" and he said "Lil Steve" (R.I.P Big Cuz) that was their first of many to come.

K went on to say, "they did it because he made a sale in front of their house". "What house"? I asked while I'm standing frozen in shock. Because I knew if my peoples really believed that they killed him he would've leveled Park Place. He went on to say "the house Tony used to stay in the duplex right in front of the old white guy's apartment building.

Damn if they are killing people for selling coke in front of their house then where they expect me to go. I'm not taking this shit lightly when we get to the courts, I'm bringing this matter up to the elders (the elders' old heads were the players who held all the weight and basically as a group controlled the flow of all things in the hood).

It really didn't matter what they said because I had no intentions on moving from my spot. That Sunday on the Basketball courts it was a nice day the sun was just hanging around one o'clock. The trees made shade on one side of the court and the breeze from the lake blew by and cooled off the families that littered the park.

City Park was the place on Sunday you could catch everybody you knew at any given time of the day. Be-lo's was across the street and beside that was 7-Eleven. So, if they were in the park, whether playing hoops, football, flying a kite, playing on the playground, cooking out, seeing a concert, or visiting the zoo, the park stayed crowded.

If you were at city Park, my hood Park Place was controlled by the house. We calmed Park Place from Granby Street all the way down to Colley Avenue. See if you looked down Thirty Fifth Street it was like fifty blocks by fifty blocks. Park Place was huge, and there was a lot of money that came through there all the time.

Well at the park everyone was honoring Lil Steve, so it wasn't a whole lot of laughing and joking things was really tight lipped around the court. And no one could confirm what had happened because it was so early in the morning when the incident had occurred.

As far as everyone knew, after he left the local club, he went home but somewhere between thorns and Colonial Avenue he stopped to make a sale. The Brambleton boys saw him, and they exchanged words. Lil Steve fought them off, went to get his gun and they beat him to death with bats and shot him.

For some reason they used bats. I guess it played as an intimidation tool because by looking at them they should be able to rip a person limb from limb. All of them played for Norfolk State University, the whole front line went rogue and it started in the Brambleton Neighborhood right across the street from Norfolk State University's women's dorm.

Now it all makes sense you would hear shit about brutal beatings and shootings in shit from the other side of town. It did not affect us, it was their problem. See no one person or group ever controlled the flow of drug sales in our hood until now. They didn't want no one selling in Park Place on their blocks and they would kill to keep it that way.

By now cocaine had Norfolk in a choke hold almost as if one day the biggest problems were drunks fighting in the street now people were getting shot and killed left and right like we were in the old west.

School started back up. I went to my main man Rail for a haircut. He was staying on Lafayette with his mom at the time. I was glad he now stays out Park place with his dad off of thirty-Fifth street. Which was good for me. He's the hottest barber in town and now I don't have to talk to his funky ass brother while I was getting my hair cut.

Rail man was nice with those clippers. Any haircut you wanted he could do. Any style and any design he was the man. The Reebok athletic high tops were in and the classic all white or the black one's either pair you could not go wrong with your outfit.

I could not go too big because I couldn't seem like I had money not when Sharon was broke. I now had a little job at the colonial boys club. It paid just enough to keep the home phone on and me with an outlet. The weed thing wasn't panning out too good and with the Brambleton boys laying claim from one end of the block to the other my lifeline had been severed.

Fall was coming soon Rail's Lil brother got transferred to Granby High School and I fucked with him on the strength of his brother being my personal barber. Plus, he had mad gear. He had the polo's, duck head pants, Izod shoes and his game made mine look tamed.

I couldn't have that shit not by my barber's brother. He stank too. No literally he played football and he would practice then afterwards he wouldn't shower put his same clothes on and want to hug you. I never understood why he never got the hint when he walked up people walked away, maybe because he was a good joker though I had to give him that too. He'll joke the shit out your ass he'll have a nigga crying laughing, but he stunk.

I never understood it. To change my financial situation, I needed to get a coke plug but who or where do I even start? On my way to the buses to go home I went out the front door to beat the other students.

They always lined up in the front of the school right beside my last class. I as usual was headed out the front and "damn watch out fool" I said. It was Cannon looking like fucking Will Smith jumping out a red BMW.

He was running up to the doors just as I was walking out. "Yo Cannon," I yelled. He said, "was good Lil Tee"? I said, "shit I asked him where the fuck he was working"? He was like "nigga you know me working for who?" He said, "he worked for himself". I said, "ok where and when I can start"?

(People, I'm in there now.) He told me to come out Hunters Village, not the area by Aunt Bee's house. He was talking about the Old Village damn that part of the hood was called the hole hmmm.

If I wanted it, I'd have to go across town to get it. "Ok" I said, "I'll be there tomorrow after school" he said, "ok Kool see you then". We dapped each other up and he went in the school. I boarded the bus heading for home thinking to myself I have my connect, time to make my dreams a reality.

In HuntersVille it was Kool with me I had mad family who did not know I hustled so I could visit everyone on the way. Stop to use the bathroom or get a bite to eat either way I was straight. I got home, changed my clothes, got a bite to eat and just rested. I fell asleep and there was that dream again but this time it's nighttime and this seems real.

The alarm clock going off the phone ringing ouch I stomped my toe hello. while trying to fight back my tears and pain. I must have slept here all night and it was time for school already. I knew it was my grandfather. He would call me every morning to wake me up for school.

He was the best grandfather I ever had. He is the sole reason I keep pushing today. I said, "Granddad, I'm up Tank." He would say, "Boy, get your ass up now and get ready for school." "Ok, Dad, I'm up. I'll call you when I'm walking out the door. I think he did that you know called me to wake me up to show me he cared. He knew my mom didn't come home as often as she should. So, he didn't want me to stop going to school in shit.

So, If he wakes me up he knows I'm not going to go back to sleep. I got up and I threw on my black and red M &M's Boots with my black and red two-tone lee's and my black and red lumber jacket way before Biggie wore his Black and red lumberjack jacket.

Norfolk gets cold at night and the way Cannon was dressing it looked like I was in for a long night. I ran out to the bus stop and just barely caught it. Shit the bus driver be at the damn corner on time and not a minute later. I really think she was scared of our neighborhood. She made her way up Debree making a right up Thirty Fourth Street doubling back up Debree weaving through the early morning streets.

It's so peaceful at this time of hour only if it could stay this way. Heading over the Granby Street Bridge to the left was a car wash man. You can find anything you want over there. When I get straight, I'm going over there. It's always money there.

You just had to watch yourself, the jack boys (police and robbers). They were always parked by Burger World using the parking lot as a disguise. K sat at the front of the bus because the older boys used to joke all the time. If you got mad, they would keep going until you cried and if you cried the whole bus jumped in on the picking.

Clowning you would become a team effort for everyone from the ugly ones to the fat ones, even the slow one's. If that's not bad enough once we got off the bus someone would always try you... it was like going in for the kill. A walk through the hall was like the red carpet. You got looked up and down in and around before you even made it to the front hall of the main building.

The cafeteria was around the corner from my home room class so I would get a soda now and again and stand by the front door's to watch all the girls walk in. I had to, it was the only way to see all of what the school offered without running around looking all geeky and shit.

I felt like why hunt for the chicks all of them had to eat and I'll just stand by the front door of the cafeteria. Then you could take your pick. I can't wait for the next bell to ring because I'm ditching the rest of the day. I have an appointment with Cannon out Hunters Village today.

That nigga be jetting all over, so I gotta jump on this while the offer is still on the table. While on the bus to the Ville I couldn't stop daydreaming about having a chance to make some real cash. Finally, I'm getting the chance to prove myself to my people out Park Place.

They should have kept me on the team. About the middle of the summer, you know when I told you I wanted to turn my weed hustle into the coke game. Well, I took a little money and went half on a package with my cousin out Park Place yeah, my fucking cousin anyway it worked out for around two weeks. Until one Saturday morning I went to his house on Thirty First Street he stayed across the street from the one out of two only white churches left in the hood.

They gave up their homes so the niggas can rent them for high ass prices, but they kept their churches. You knew it was Sunday because that's the only time the police would sit in the hood all day during church service. This is the only time you could hear a pin drop in the hood.

That shit used to always crack me up. Niggas would shoot kill and stab each other to death but as soon as they see the white cop in our own hood, they act like they were the most civilized people in the world.

I couldn't understand that until I had gotten older and later found out that to actually be a social project Jim Crow use to keep the newly freed black slaves in order. By turning us against one other so we'll keep each other from ever forming back together as a unit we once were before slavery. And to always fear the white face and by the look of my town it worked.

I eventually caught up with my cousin and told him I needed my stash, and he dropped the bomb on me. He said someone broke into his safe and he had it in his hand in two pieces. My stomach turned. It had that feeling as if I had just rode to the top of a roller coaster and without any warning it just fell endlessly without any notions of stopping.

He was family and that was my first major loss. That's why I said never leave all your shit in one place you will regret it. He gave me no time frame of when, where, or even how I was going to be reimbursed. I just left it alone. I figured he'd pay me back one day.

You know that mother still hasn't paid me back yet and he has the nerve to act like I owe him every time I'm in town... I'm lost. The next stop is mine damn that was a fast ride we're passing old Church Street now. At night you can find anything you want legal or not. It's as they say in Italy Italian sauce is all it's in there.

Damn Acie Dicey their food is baaannnnggging ok we are making the right turn to Princess Anne Rd. I'll get off by the nursing home and walk to Burger World and get a soda before I go and see him. It was a nice September day, sunny, warm and bright. The wind blew slightly just enough for me to wear my light blue and green polo jacket.

Leaves were everywhere and the pollen was thick. Traffic was light. I forgot to hurry across the street. My uncle works at the police city car pound. He tried to be a police officer in shit but for some reason something happened, and he was demoted.

He was now the janitor of the building where they impound cars. For whatever reason he would definitely tell my mom if he caught me hustling out the Ville. After getting my soda I went the long way back to the Ville to avoid my uncle in shit. Plus, this way I could see the back parking lot where Cannon's aunt lived.

Ok he is still there I can see his BMW from here. That whip was sweet. Cannon had purchased it as a gift for himself. He said he had it custom painted candy apple red. The interior was jet black with bright red trim with BMW in the back of all the seats. He was the first black person I knew that had a BMW fully kitted, it had a booming system gooseneck stereo and hammers.

He was the Niño Brown of Norfolk, and he was my homeboy. Yo Cannon was standing by the back storage bend that was connected to the unit. All the apartments had one.

He looked up "Lil Tee was up homeboy" I replied, "shit you my nigga".

Not to seem too eager but I was ready to get started making that doe. He looked at me up and down at the same time, talking to me with his eyes following my every move, checking to see I guess if my heart was up from the job. I'm never leaving mine. Yo if a motherfucker come at me with that dumb shit he gone get it quick.

Sometimes you don't have time to react. "Tee man this is no game" he said. I stayed quiet as a son would intensely listen to his father making sure to digest every word he's saying to me. He was where I wanted to be so what he was telling me was to keep me on point. I respected him for that to this day.

People will try you for this shit. I mean even try to kill you for real man. This game is the real deal. The fiends do not play by any rules. This is not by any means like the business world. If you are not careful you will lose your life.

They tell you if you get robbed you should give the robbers what they want "no!" he said, "you get my shit, or it comes out of your ass one way or another you will work it off". "Now we boys" he said, "so it's not like you would be out here by yourself"! I already knew he had just about seventy percent of the people working for him out here. So, I had stash spots and eyes everywhere. And please guns we had them tucked all around the projects.

Once he saw that I didn't back away I then confidently looked at him and said "man you know just how I do. I can hold my own. I told Cannon niggas are getting killed every fucking day. No matter where you're at in Norfolk you may think it's safe.

So, my motto was "why not get paid and live good until your day comes?". Looking back on what I said then now thinking about how my whole life has been seeing so much death amongst my family and friends I can't seem to wonder why or how I'm still here and they're gone.

He looked at me for a long time for a second, I thought to myself I may have fucked up and said something wrong and he not going to fuck with me now. Cannon said, "Yo Tee meet me back here in twenty minutes" I replied "bet" then walked off. I walked to the front of the complex. I liked the layout because the parking lots had surrounded the apartments' backside and the front of the apartments face each other.

So, if you were the customer or the cops you had to drive up first get out of your car then walk to the front of the apartment complex where everyone could see your every move. We had lookouts posted on all the corners so if someone did look strange the alarm would be sounded off and everyone scattered like mice to the nearest open door for cover.

Not returning to the circuit until the coast was clear again. But if you were not the police, I felt bad for you because you would get the beat down of a lifetime. The cops would never be able to run up on you unless you were walking up or if you just stood there and waited for them when they told you to freeze that was on you.

If you did that made you an asshole and you deserved to get caught. You better keep your mouth shut or you and your family got visited (dealt with). Remind me to tell you a little story about a certain sergeant on the Norfolk police Narco Unit.

You're really going to laugh at it and that little tidbit will also give even more credibility to my book lmao. Two times I told you motherfuckers I was going to get y'all you never listened to me now it's my turn to tell my side of things. I made it to the front of the complex where I could see everyone.

Everybody here was from school, that's the other reason I had chosen to hustle here. My mom wouldn't think to look for me out here and for the second reason was because I knew everybody that lived out the Ville. We went to the same high school and middle school. I was dating a girl whose grandma stayed in one of the unit's down from the money pit.

That's where all the fiends came when they wanted some soft (powder cocaine) and the Ville had the best in Norfolk. The special was the time Cannon started hustling eighty dollars for a sixteenth of coke.

They would buy a half dozen at a time. I was just watching kids my age and younger walking with cell phones, some had pagers, gold jewelry and cash lots and lots of cash. Niggas was shooting dice in the old laundry room, ordering food from expensive restaurants, drinking beer and smoking weed. People were even tricking in broad daylight dudes standing right in front of where I was pitching getting head.

You could not help but look at the lady. She was hot. I had never seen that shit in real life before, only in the movies. I mean I been flashed before but not up close and watching it in 3-D. He was fucking her brains out. The dude looked at me and was like "what you want to marry the bitch or something" before I could think of something quick and slick to say back, I realized it was Lee from the colonial boy's and girl's club.

We didn't get along too well back then because we were gunning for the same chick. She had lived directly across the street from the boy's and girl's club. She was brown skinned, very pretty and petite. She ran track so you know she was very flexible. She had mad stamina. Her name had fit her well; they had called her Missy.

That had been at least four or five years ago and we're much older now. Hell, I was fifteen years old. To us now that was child's play. We were now on some grown man shit. He zipped up his pants and tried to dap me up then I looked at him and we laughed realizing he was just having sex.

He thought I was going to touch his hands. He was crazy. He was like "what you doing out here"? I said, "I'm going to be working with Cannon and his crew now". He said "ok" (see his dad and mom had a divorce and his Lil brother went to stay with her. Lee had decided he wanted to live with his dad).

Then he added "I'm working with my dad so I can help you too". We flip a Lil four and a half ounces (that was called a cutie or quarter key). He said, "Follow me, I live right there". It just so happened to be in the next group of apartments where my ex-wife's grandmother lived but I didn't tell Lee.

It was a whole lot quieter and less foot traffic. Older people lived here so you had to keep it down. They watched your every move and would call the police officers at the drop of a dime. It was the perfect place to duck from the cops. When they decided to show up most important Lee could fill me in on the game you know the weights, terms, and prices.

Most important who to fuck with and who not to fuck out here in the Village. You must understand I had runners twice my age or older depending on what day of the week it was and sometimes up to five working for me at any time. So, it was good to have a guy your age to help you watch your runners.

If not, they will get you just as fast as one of the fiends you're selling too. We entered their upstairs unit, and his stepmom and dad were in the living room getting high and drinking beer. They were talking and laughing aloud with the O' jays playing softly in the background.

Lee said "dad" his dad turned around and said, "what you want?" And when his dad turned his head, you'll see why Lee was a junior he had looked just like his dad. Lee said, "this is my homeboy from the boy's club Lil Tee". I said "hello" to his dad then turned to his stepmom and said, "HI how are you doing ma'am"?

She plainly said "HI" and continued her drank. His dad however got up and reached out to shake my hand. We shook and then Lee said "da" he is going to be hustling out here now with Cannon and his crew. His dad said, "ok well if I can help you, I will. Like when we run out, I'll call you" I said "Kool". Lee looked and nodded his head in the direction of the back bedroom.

It was sort of nice except for the bunk beds were broken and it was clothes everywhere. Broken toys and bike parts, but I guess if they had it good, they wouldn't be selling drugs like everyone else was. So, drugs I guess at times are good and bad. It was all in how you used it and the money.

Lee was telling me like when the police officers come, whenever you need to dip off, lay low, or need a place to bag up just come here. See now my dad knows who you are, they will let you in. You'll just have to give him like forty or fifty bucks, but he'll let you in no problem.

That's all I was waiting to hear and what he just told me that was a deal. I told him "Since he wasn't down with no one out here to get with me and I'll get him in with Cannon" he said "bet he could use that extra bread. He wanted to move his dad out the hood too. So together we planned our next move. I left him in the house bagging up what he had left with his dad.

If you asked me, I think he wanted to start today. Everybody knew that Cannon's crew was eating lovely. His whole crew had big whips and pockets stayed on full. This partnership will work. Lee was a standup guy even though we almost came to blows as kids. All I know is that we had set the stage for a new change in the Ville. With this new found money making alliance I figured nothing could go wrong.

CHAPTER 7

Norfolk's First KingPin

I finally caught up with Cannon and he had changed clothes. This was the second time today. He was now flossing a lacrosse jogging suit with the lacrosse shoes and the fucking jacket. Topping it off with some fresh ass Gazelle's. He had the top and bottom rows of teeth gold flooded with diamonds with a thick ass solid gold herringbone necklace. His ears had big ass diamond studs hanging on for dear life; they were so big.

To make things sweeter his crew was decked out just like he was Tommy Hilfiger, Polo and Gucci it was like that! They all were clean as hell. Now it's my turn up to bat and all I can see is home runs. Cannon said, "where you go man, I was about to give someone else the key"?

"I was like what key to myself"? And before I could say it aloud, he passed me a key to his aunt's storage. Cannon said, "in the shed there are two bags you may or may not finish them tonight but either way keep the coke in here so if you have to throw the work it won't be a big loss".

You only take out five at a time, hold them or stash them on the ground somewhere you can keep an eye on it. Lastly, don't keep the money or the product together. stash the money in another place of your choice, not in the storage and not on you.

The last thing he said before he walked away was "the money better match the product or am done fucking with you".

He turned and began to walk away. I said, "wait how do I get paid"? He said, "my bad Tee you get two out of ten you

58

sell". I said "what"? Then I did the math in my head real fast and said "yo if I sell ten that's eight hundred dollars and I get only two hundred dollars.

He said, "the longer you hang out the more you make you came late so that's all I have left in less you want to come back in the morning"? "Naw, I'm here now. I got this" I told him. He replied, "I'll see you tomorrow after school" I said "Kool" and he left. I was acting as if I wasn't happy with the deal and if I was doing him a favor which really, he was doing the favor for me.

I went to the storage unit and opened the door. At first, I thought he was playing a joke on me because I didn't see anything in the shed. I looked around but it wasn't so big inside there. So, it had to be in here somewhere. Why would he go to all that trouble just to give me a key?

Wait, what's this? Under the lid of an old trash can there was a black trash bag. I untied the bag and inside it was well. I counted two separate bags and in them were one hundred and fifty bags. inside each bag held one sixteenth gram of coke. Ok once again I did the math in my head every ten bags I sold, I kept one hundred and sixty dollars. There are three hundred bags.

I'll make sixteen hundred dollars times three came out to Fifty-four hundred dollars for one night's work. Shit I almost fucked that up royally. I said to myself. I took ten bags from the stash out and re-tied the bag.

Then I thought I needed to be more careful. It felt as if someone else had heard me thinking. It felt like someone was spying on me to rob me of my drugs. I had become so nervous because that was a lot of cash for a teen back then. for one and in handling that much cash I'm going to need to enlist some extra eyes out here starting now.

I locked the door to the shed and started back to the front of the unit being careful to stay in the shadows. After getting back to the front of the building I noticed that it was jumping. People were everywhere. Most of the parking lots were packed with cars coming and going like a fast-food drive thru.

People were gambling and in other parts of the square you could see people just drinking and making money. I saw Lee shooting craps over by the laundry mat "Yo Lee" I yelled out to him he waved me over never allowing his eyes to leave the game. He was playing against other young niggas that were doing the something we were selling drugs.

They were side betting or just hanging out watching the madness. Lee must have been winning because as I got closer to the game, he had hundreds of dollars in his hand just as if they were dollar bills. He lit a blunt up with a hundred-dollar bill now I didn't condone shit like that, but I just think he did it to celebrate as a person would christen his yacht with a bottle of Champagne on its first lunch to sea.

I looked at him and blurted out "Yo you never changed, not one bit huh?" He passed the blunt and replied, "man Tee we going to make plenty more just you wait and see". Once the blunt was gone we walked over to the edge of the apartments and when I felt we couldn't be heard.

I told him I only had enough for me tonight but if he helps me get it off, I'll throw him five hundred dollars for his help. He was like see I already made a profit, and you were mad that I burnt a single hundred-dollar bill. Then he went on to say "if that's all you got you won't be out here long, I'm done" so let's start clocking your stash.

I gave him the ten I pulled out and he examined them, and he said, "damn Cannon bags are phat as hell they have no shake". At first, I didn't understand what he was saying until I held one of them up to the light. The cocaine was an off white with a rainbow hint of all different colors.

This was my first time learning the difference between good and bad coke. Cannon wasn't the only person out the Ville hustling heavy on that scale. He was just the youngest, but he was ten times ahead of the rest of those niggas because his connect kept him with the bomb product and he didn't beat the coke up (cut it so much that it would get high out and basically you have a bag of shit).

He serves it up the same way he got it and the fiends loved him for the way he sold his coke. They stayed loyal to him and his team. The first night went so well I not only finished before twelve, but I also caught Cannon. I paid him what he was due, and he was so shocked he had thrown me another package. I had started it but had to dip and I left the rest with Lee.

Later before I left to go in for the night, I had introduced Lee to Cannon. Doing that would only make me look good. Really because Lee's work helped me move the product fast. I mean I would have caught on but, being a new face in the crowd especially in this fast-paced dim lit environment it was easy to get stuck up or beat out of your package.

Then you'll be working off your debt for a profit you never received. So, he saved me a lot of money and my life by watching my back out there. Apparently, that's why I was brought into the crew, so I wanted to bring in Lee.

A lot of the younger kids if they weren't about making money, they were getting high. Then they would skim off the packages to hide their habits. The fiends would know and not come back to you so you'd either went down lower on the price or gave them a three for the price of two (buy two and get the third one for free) usually that worked because the person scoring would keep the extra one for himself.

Or sell it to the person they were running for, so everyone makes out. Once Cannon heard how slow your packages were moving, he knew you were either skimming from the top or you were hitting the bags. But he saw how fast Lee had helped me knock off my package and how he had my back he was Kool with us sharing the workload.

From that point on we were known as the young money crew. Some months have passed now and I'm punching the Ville like it's a time clock. To the point that I made my first five thousand out there, yes little old me.

Lee wasn't doing bad himself; we were shopping every day and eating good. Not fast-food restaurants either. No, we ate at shirt and tie restaurants renting limos for the weekends. As soon as the gold grills came to downtown Norfolk shopping center at the New York New York store we got ours made the same day.

It was extra but who cares if the money would be made back tomorrow. Lee had dropped out of school so he could clock all day and all night. And he didn't have to hide it from his parents like I did. Hell his dad became his runner. and as their money grew me and Lee became a little distance. Not in a bad way because his dad would help me too (even though it wasn't for free I paid him five dollars on every sale per bag, so he made a hundred or two, so it was a good look on both sides).

So, I didn't have to touch the work, just oversee and manage the re-ups and the opening and closing of the workday. They still supplied me with a safe haven whenever the Norco's would happen to pop up on the scene. Lee never told me he had caught a charge one night.

I had just left for the evening and he said that Lil Cat had gotten robbed. He ran up to the car with his gun and the driver shot him as soon as Cat pulled out his gun. That same night he had served an undercover officer and was arrested. Lil Cat had died later that night.

His death was the first time I had a friend that went to the same school and grinded with me in the Ville that died. He had died at an early age. That then made the game real to all of us young and old. Lil C was like thirteen years old, two years younger than I was. The whole Ville mourned his death.

No one sold anything the day of his funeral. We all had gone out and bought all black suits. Some had just got black shirts, pants, socks, and shoes. At the burial we all threw money into his casket. I tossed a grand but Cannon he threw in the most. It had to be at least ten grand or more and he paid for the whole funeral. He had brought all the food for the gathering afterwards as well.

Once the thought of the fact people do die from selling coke. It made me sick to my stomach, but not of the game. But to the fact that if you didn't play your cards right, you could end up like Lil Cat. That thought scared me not of leaving here but leaving here without my mom having anything.

That wasn't going to be me. Die here in Norfolk no, I thought to myself not me not here and definitely not like Lil C. However, if I played my cards right, I'll make enough money to cover my burial so my mom could keep the money in my casket to maybe buy a house and a car so she can get away from this bullshit.

You're probably wondering why or how he could think like that, ever since the Brambleton boys moved out the way (Park Place) the death toll had risen, and their name became a household word. I mean if you weren't talking about all the shooting every night or the fights then you weren't aware of your surroundings. That alone in my hood would get you killed.

No, every night you could set your watch by it. Violence was in the air and it didn't have any problem finding you. You simply better know what to do when it finds you or your time will be up as well. At first when I moved out to Park Place, I couldn't understand it until the people changed. But the shooting didn't happen, so I realized even though the power structure of the crime bosses had changed, each crew was telling the surrounding hoods that crime bosses are still in control of their turf.

Look we are here we have big guns still and we'll use them try us if you want too. and every night they enforced it by shooting off their arsenals one neighborhood at a time like clockwork. Any way as I was saying they were killing anybody that sold on their block the same block I opened back in my weed days.

I'm just glad I'm not over there anymore because they don't know Sharon used coke. She would never go anywhere outside the house. So, I did not worry about her knowing I hustled. However, when they would see me make a sale being the youngest one out of the group a lot of the older guys would hate on me. but couldn't touch me. I loved it.

Lil B would say "Yo what you are doing?" I would say "talking to my uncle or some bullshit like that" but I really think they had respected the fact that I didn't sneak around and sell to their clients in shit. In the hood sneaky people, you couldn't trust no matter what game you played.

Going to school trying to reach adulthood without getting shot was all you could do in the hood. It was a rare thing to achieve getting out of the hood successively. Only a few who had made it out of the hood and stayed out and I'm going to be one of them. A lot of people try but only to come back and have the jealous ones that you grew up with beat you up and rob you just because you wanted change in your life.

That's where I was from. It was hard, but you had to love it. The hood was your home. From the alcoholic fights and the drug abuse rages that leads to deaths in which on any given night either one of the two could pop off at the blink of an eye if not both. My motto became this: if "I'm going to lose my life by being an innocent by standard for free then I might as well hustle until I die and be surrounded by people with the same mind frame".

At least as a unit we'll have a better chance of making it. The money was flowing so hard I had made a name for myself, and I didn't even know it. Back at school around lunch time I would wait for the specialty line to fill up. I would laugh and joke with everybody all the way up to the lady working at the window.

Then I would excuse myself to the first person in the line. I'll order a pizza and a small slush. The cashier would tell me the amount and I always paid with a fifty or a hundred and tell her to take out what everybody I jumped in front of, and you keep the change. The girls in the line would start to mumble things about me.

Some would say who is he? Or did he just pay for lunch? And the most asked question was why he do that and not even wait for his change? I did that to let the girls know with me I got you, and to the fellows look at what I did, and I would say" you can do it too just get at me after school".

And "I'll put you down for a small fee". I didn't really want the change because whoever I brought food for in the line would say "thank you". It worked two ways I profited if they made doe and from them buying weight. However, if they fucked up money, I had to correct him our pay his debt nine times out of ten it paid out more than I had too.

So, I was happy of course and the niggas who fronted me was happy as well. They were happy because they were just like us poor, and they wanted to support their family as well as having a little extra in their pockets. With the Ville going good for me, Lee had moved.

A couple of guys from school wanted in on the action, so I invited them that day to come with me after school to the money pit. Al B, and Black came too after school. One of our homie's moms ran the office in the Ville.

So, he really did not have to hustle, he ran the girls. He reminded us of George Michaels, you know the singer that had all the hot chicks. He had the new car black Mustang GT. he was doing his thing for sure.

Al B was my twin in school, but he was a lot heavier. He played all the sports in school. He stayed working out all the time I had worked out only when chicks were involved.

We all planned to hang out after school in the Ville. Well Black for some reason wanted to start selling coke, he didn't have to sell drugs either. His parents were military and he had anything he wanted. I mean hustling mostly was for the poor and the people who couldn't feed their families and shit.

So, when he said he wanted to start hanging out with us I kind of shrugged it off as if he was just talking. Well, that night we were all standing around and chilling in the front court of the Ville and Al B and Black had showed up. They had their own coke and had started making sales.

We were all making sales and then all of a sudden police lights were flashing everywhere. Cops were running from every direction. We all dropped our forties of o' English and the drugs we had and ran to the nearest safe house. We had discussed earlier.

I went to a guy I knew from school's house. Well, he stayed with his mom and dad still, but they were Kool as hell. Even if he wasn't home, I could come over and hang out. However, if I was working or for that reason dirty at all I never went over there out of respect for him and his parents.

Al B ran to a girl he knew from school's house and George simply went in his house because he lived out the village, so it was a norm for him to just pop in and out without drawing any attention from his mom or the police officers.

But for the life of me out of everybody else that was out there that night why Black did not run. I could see him from the bottom floor apartment window. I mean he stood right there and didn't move not one inch. He was like a deer stuck in headlights.

And I said to myself well I guess he didn't have any dope on him, that's why he didn't run. So, he's ok not running he'll be alright. He'll just get a trespassing charge. They'll just write him a summons on the spot and let him go in a few minutes. An hour or so had passed and I went to see if the police had left the Ville yet and I couldn't see anyone outside.

The place was deserted, which was a good sign that meant the police had either left or they were hiding in one of the units. They think we don't know that's how they move. That's when you know when they're going to send the wagon down here. Plus, we saw a little red dot in one of the windows of the apartments that was supposed to be empty. If there is no one renting them why are there lights on in them hum?

Make you wonder if you're crazy, but we never cared because we had the inside scope. George's mom had worked in the office so if something like that went down, he would keep us in the loop. He would be the first to tell his crew. The next day in school the big talk was that Black had gotten arrested in the Ville.

Damn I didn't want to be here, the dogs came out and two undercover cops were here as well searching the lockers and questioning people from the Ville. This was new. Black apparently didn't just get a trespassing charge he must have gotten a possession charge too.

He must have had coke on him, and he did not tell us he was dirty. That was the reason he should have run. He must have had a front from someone, and he brought it out to the Ville the day we all had planned to hang out. He now owed that guy for his coke, and he is in some real shit he caught a charge too.

When he froze once the police ran up on him, he didn't throw the package that's the number one rule. Whenever you're in doubt, throw the shit? It's better for the coke to be on the ground then on you that could be the difference between probation and jail. We didn't see Black for a while after that and he never came back to the Ville either.

Once he did come back to school after about six months, he never was the same person again. After Black had made the news everyone that hung with him no longer felt safe. The Ville got even hotter one of my boys got killed and two others got locked up.

Even so I was still determined even more than ever to get mine's. After that, the plan now was to save as much as possible and get out the game for good. Since Lee was gone now, I had to find a new partner on the low without showing my interior motives with too many people. But it was hard trying to recruit without advertising to the wrong niggas knowing.

I had to do it without trying to let other cliques know I was down a person. Or they would try and move in on my spot. When people hear your defenses are down, that's a queue to offer you help then before you know it, they are running the show and you assed out.

Look, there was no loyalty in this game. But it was the best job or opportunity out there to survive in these streets' hands down. This time I wanted someone who drives and can pick me up for a change. Saga had told me about a person he knew that all he did was smoke weed.

Since Saga didn't smoke, he thought by hooking us up even though Saga had his own money. He was one of those people that didn't have to hustle; he had got an allowance and Leak did too. So, I never understood why they hustled.

But I guess they just did it cause all their peers were hustling not to feel left out was my guess. So, they were my boys, so I didn't argue with them over the matter. One day before I was heading out to the Ville this tan two tone two door mustang coup pulled up as I started down the block to Llewellyn Avenue.

I heard someone yell my name and as I started to turn my head to see who was calling me. It was Leak ok time to turn up. Just as me and Leak turned to go in my house, I saw these three pretty ass women. "Wait" I said to Leak look. A moving van pulled up and a long red thunderbird parked back-to-back. In it was three of the prettiest women I've ever seen who appeared to be exotic in nature.

The oldest of the three looked by far the prettiest of them all. She had a short, even jet black haircut. She had to be the tree the other two fell from... their mother. She was fit with her slim but firm features and her voice was warm as a summer's breeze. When she said "hi" to us her voice sounded of harps and bells.

It made you want to go and knock on the door and be like whatever happened I did it just so she can talk to me again. She had two gorgeous daughters. The oldest daughter Lacey was cute as hell with light brown skin covered with freckles and she knew who to use her Godly gifts as did she know how to wear her beauty.

But the one who caught my eye to me she was the finest one of them all and her name was Chelsi. She was shy and bashful. and like Sharon had a cute gap between her two front teeth. She really looked white in color and when she smiled, she had the cutest dimple that would appear all the time. I'm in love with all three of them.

Now the only thing is how to get past the dark skinned heavy knuckled guy. Wait, they have a little brother. I'll be-friend their little brother and I'll be able to get past their stepdad. Yo Leak, what the fuck Saga doing out here? I knew the only reason Saga was out here and it wasn't because he used to live out here either. It was because he must have been hunting for a new side bitch or he wanted me to ride along with him, to interfere while he was on recon to meet a new bitch.

Either way I wasn't interested. I started to wonder if he would ever change. He said he was the one who told Leak to come over here to meet me. "Tee damn why you always think I'm up to something"? Saga said and continued to say he be flipping weed like you do in shit and I wanted to hook yall two up. For a second, I had to thank Saga for helping me. I needed a driver.

I looked around and thought where the cameras no really when he helped you somehow you always still came out not solving your problem you had but you'll always manage to have five or six more problems when fucking with him. Then I said to myself this could really work out for me because Saga didn't know I switched from selling weed to coke.

So, he does not really know what kind of money I'm making. I got this yeah Kool good looking Saga. "Leak what you think I could use a nigga to pick me up and drop me off. I can pay you like a yard each time plus gas and perks"? Leak looked at Saga for a second and then me again and said, "what about the weed though"? I said, "you keep your people and I'll keep mine and if you come across a better deal than me, I'll get down with your people".

I was cool with that because I didn't sell weed anymore. That means more money for him and since no one out the Ville sells weed he won't have any competition and that's the less money I'll have to pay him. "Sounds like a plan let's get fucked up". Leak said OK but as usual Saga had to get something to eat first.

"Who want some chicken wings from Golden Gate my treat"? Saga asked. When Saga said, "he was treating which was often no matter how much money you had you let him treat or you'll never hear the end of it". The next day Leak came out with me to the Ville. He asked me, "Why I never asked Saga to come out the Ville with you?"

I said, I did one day and once we got out to the center TD had run up to Saga and punched him in the face. As Saga fell to the ground, I turned around to see who it was that ran by and hit him.

When I couldn't see who it was, I turned as quickly as I could to help Saga get up and that nigga was gone he was in the wind. I mean he hauled ass. No Tee let's go, I'm leaving, or I'll meet you later. Saga didn't even say he'll call me when he got home. He had just simply left me.

When they realized he had come out there with me niggas had begun to surround me. They were acting like I knew what all the beef was over between them and Saga. I was like what the fuck is yall doing? Lil K came up and said, "Why you bring him out here?"

I looked at him and said, "that's my cousin". He said, "well your cousin jumped me at the castle on Princess Anne Rd. a month ago". I said, "I wasn't there so how was I to fucking know yall two had beef not me. They saw I had nothing to do with either side so the commotion died down and the crowd broke up. They knew I wanted one thing and that was the paper.

I didn't care about all that fighting and shit because no one I knew got a check from a fight, only black eyes and jail. Now fuck with my paper now that was a no no. I'll fight anyone over those green guys. Leak said, "Saga told me you left him, and he had to fight his way out by himself". Leak knew Saga was lying and that's not how it went down.

Saga had told the story differently once he had said those few words right there. I knew Saga had gotten to him already and it was no telling how many other lies Saga told Leak. That's Saga for you, the master storyteller. That's why I call him Saga because he was all games and lies so you really never knew when he was telling the truth.

I should have known he wanted to tell his side because he thought I was going to tell people first. But I wasn't like him, so he really was the first person who told anyone. Leak said, "Tee I know Saga be lying all the damn time about dumb shit".

Well, I'm glad looking over to Leak I said, "you know now that he left me". "How could I have left him when he got home and paged me"? I called him from the phone booth in the Ville, so I never left Huntersville. He ran home all the way down Tidewater Drive lmao.

Leak, so just so you know I would never leave you hanging I told him. "We come out here together, we going to leave together". "Bet" Leak said and we shook on it. We never mention Saga or that dumb shit again. Leak had fit right in; he played the parking lot near the car's and on the playground.

He stashed his shit in the trees or on the playground inside the spring animal rides. He didn't have a storage shed like mine. Since I really had no control over it, he had to use the surroundings to hide his packages. I had refused to let him put our weed in there with the coke. Too much traffic was not a good look.

Not having the both of us being seen going in and out the same shed. He sold maybe three ounces of weed a day out here. I did my normal. I turned in like ten grand and got paid an even two grand plus the side change. Sometimes you'll get three people that want a dub (twenty dollars' worth of coke).

Well, the bag was eighty dollars once you served them a dub each. then you'll have enough to make four more bags. That's how you make double your asking price off one sixteenth of coke. Some of the other hustlers thought you should really turn in the extra doe.

But I didn't, it was an extra Incentive for being in the field. If you asked me as long as the money added up at the end of the day Cannon did not mind me breaking down the product. Things are going well with me and Leak. We started double dating and hanging out together before and after my shift.

And not just at the Ville we really enjoyed ourselves when we weren't out there hustling and grinding. That place was starting to really get hot, and I knew we would have to change it up to a new spot soon. Too much business I need to unwind Yo I said, to Leak "roll up some of that good shit you got" he said "ok".

We used to go to one of his dad's houses to bag up or have a place for the regular chicks. For our main chicks we got hotel rooms don't ask me how but at the time I had a light beard and a deep voice. I'll just go to the counter and say I need a room and place the money on the desktop.

Sign a fake name and wait for my change. I was fifteen when we started renting rooms though. I had my favorite hotel. It was the one on Granby Street right behind Burger World and Mc Drake's. They never give me any problems. I love this place. I had started coming here to count my money or if I had a lot of dope and I did not want to take it home.

I was never scared the police would find me or my stash oh no, I was scared Sharon would. She never asked me if I sold drugs, but she would rob the hell out of my safes. I could never figure out how though. I'll have four ounces bagged up. I'll make like eight balls. I could profit nine grand off it.

However lately I'll make like five to six grand so since she doesn't make me answer her questions about selling drugs. I don't ask her if she takes my shit, I think it was a fair trade at first but now it's costing me grand's. It was an early system of don't ask don't tell program I guess if that's what you want to call it.

I knew she was robbing me blind. I'm going to set a trap and find out one day but not today. I don't have time or the money to be wasting on Sharon and her habits. Me and Leak met these phat ass bitches over at the Burger World. Leak had the light skinned one with the plump ass and I had her dark skinned cousin with the thick thighs and big breast.

That night I had gotten so drunk my dick wouldn't get up to save my life. I was getting frustrated because all you heard was Leak tearing her guts up. That's why they had called him Leak I guess huh? His girl was looking over at us and I'm looking under the cover like man what do you have against her?

Then out of all things Leak said "maybe she should join us Tee" I was pissed. Note to self no more double beds next time we are getting separate rooms. The next day when we woke up the girls had left. Leak went to the bathroom and ran out screaming.

I told him to calm down before they send security up to our room. He sat down on the bed cussing up a storm looking for his phone. When the person he was calling picked up the phone he said, "you mother fucking bitch you gave me crabs". The phone went silent, and she said, "she didn't think he could get them".

He was mad as hell. After he showered, we went to the drug store for the shampoo treatments for the crabs. I am glad the girl I was with did not join them. I may have caught the crabs from that nasty bitch too LMAO. Looking at the day from the room window it was a sign of perfect hustling weather.

It was nice outside. The sun was shining brightly and the wind was blowing gently with the smell of fresh water since the hotel sat on the river. The smell of flowers filled the morning breeze. The hotel was located on the water by the bridge and the breeze was nice and fresh.

The sun light was peeking through the clouds every couple feet or so then the sun would shine hard and bright. Then hid in the clouds again and the day was perfect. Traffic was light so we walked right across the street and went inside the twenty-four hour dinner.

I went outside to have a smoke and I received a page. I had the pager that the message would come across the air, it said "Tee call me it's Cannon". I went inside to use the payphone. I went to the register, got some change, then called him right away. The phone rings six times then he finally picks up. "Wad up Tee" I said, "shit eating you wanted me to call you"

Yeah, Cannon said, "meet me at my aunt's house to move you up". "Ok" I said and hung up. Damn I was already making good money, but he wanted to move me up still. I wonder how much more I would make? The numbers started to dance in my head. I didn't want to tell Leak, so I just sat down and waited for my food.

I was so nervous about meeting Cannon because he'll kick you off the team in a heartbeat, especially if you get to the point where you can buy your own weight.

He'll cut you clean off, but I didn't have to worry if he did cut me off, I had enough doe put up to keep my little operation going so I didn't worry too much about the meeting. I still had hoped I was on the team. Leak dropped me off at the house and we agreed to meet up Friday. today was Tuesday so I'll get a four-day rest I was Kool with that plan.

I'll break these four ounces down and kill them out here real quick and re –up out the Ville Friday. Since I didn't go out to Cannon's aunt's house, he came by my house. He had asked for his coke back. I went to the bedroom knowing this was it he wanted his dope back. I knew it was coming.

He knew I was buying weight and holding his too so what can I do but to give him his back. We were still Kool though, but it will never be the same. When a runner moves up to a boss level you get no love from the crew or your old boss. You will be a shot caller, but you are also responsible for your own self no more security blankets.

I wanted to say something but, in a way, I had plenty to do my own thing. So really, I didn't need any more fronts. I was happy to be back doing my own shit. I went to my room, locked my bedroom door and removed the bottom part of the last draw. This would give you all excess to the whole base of the dresser without having to move the whole piece of furniture.

"WHAT THE FUCK? Mom this is it. Yo hold on Cannon. Mom, did you go in my shit again?" I never wanted to ask you this because I stayed under your roof. But if you going to keep taking from me, I got to go. She started crying saying it won't her, but she was sorry.

Cannon didn't care who had what he wanted his bread now. I was mad she went into my shit, so I didn't want her to see my money stash. I excused myself and used a stash outside. I only had to give him fourteen hundred dollars, but that was money I didn't want to touch in case of a rainy day. But with Sharon around it is always raining.

The whole thing embarrassed me and made me look weak in the hood. Because the New York dude who had stopped me last summer on my way to the golden gate was out on his porch watching everything that went down with me and Cannon. He had rented a house on the same corner of the Brambleton niggas.

I'm just glad everyone was inside because of the heat. Since it was so hot out today no one in their right mind had dared to come out until the sun set. In the hood no one had A/C except a few families like my next-door neighbors the Olton's. They were an older couple who had their son, his wife and little son Tay that stayed with them.

Damn the Brambleton boys just came outside too, shit. She really did it this time. After that Cannon later in fact did cut me off. Because someone had told him my mom was hitting my stash.

And I found out this nigga name was Mont that told Cannon about my mom stealing my product and he saw me shopping at the mall more than hugging the block.

He did see me. I had like thirty bags. I brought everything from five-hundred-dollar Polo sweaters to sixty-five-dollar Polo socks. See a lot of these niggas wore Adidas and other sneakers all the time not me. If I was going to risk my life when I was on the block then I looked my best when I was off the block. And when I was off the block that was just how it was man the best of everything nothing less.

I blamed her (Sharon) for everything that I didn't like or understand in my life. I figured she made me and since I was brought here without the basic necessities of life. She didn't properly prepare me for life. Nor did she have a life for me because she was chasing Moonie and her next high.

That's why it was her fault when she did not marry him. He always helped us out a lot with my school clothes and field trips. He loved me and her.

He later died sad and alone. I miss him dearly. His name was Mr. Welton. Even though he was older than she was he had taken to my mom before I was even born. When she had me, he was there for us. He was a Vietnam veteran from the Army and a retired steelworker.

He owned the two greenhouses behind Moton Park in Norfolk. His houses were right across the street from Booker T. Washington High school. Well apparently, he told my mom to marry him. He was dying, and he wanted us to be provided for after he was gone.

I never knew that he loved her so much until then. When Moonie used to act like an asshole, we'd go over to Mr. Welton's house. He treated my mom like a queen, and I wanted that for her very much and when she turned his proposal down it hurt me so badly that I wanted to leave her and stay with him.

I asked her "why didn't she marry him?" I knew she loved him a lot. He gave her whatever she wanted. All she would really ask for was things for me like food for us to eat and maybe a bill or two to be paid. She didn't take advantage of him though I wouldn't let her because I had loved him too. He was the closest thing I had to having a father. I'm in tears now just sitting here thinking of him.

I really felt as if I could have been something if I had remained under his wings, but she had even taken that away from me. I hated her for that. Choosing Moonie over our happiness and our future, and I really hated her for that looking back on it now. I still feel the same way I did almost thirty years ago.

I now believe that's what pushed me to do what I did in the streets. She chased Moonie and I was chasing a dream. A dream that included a family, a mom, a dad and a happy son but the man that I considered my dad was dead and I cried every time I saw those two houses' when I visited my aunts in Roberts Park.

The daydream had ended, and the present had re-entered my thoughts as if a gun was pointed at my head and the shooter's hand has the trigger half squeezed jabbing it at my temples. I had Leak on the team, and I need to find a new outlet. We were heading to the Ville and all that day I had a bad feeling and it felt as if I had to throw up.

I had eaten already so I knew it was a whole lot deeper than food. When we got out to the center court where all the action was, people were standing around talking. Even though I didn't work for Canon anymore I made enough to get my own cutie.

Back then what ever you brought as long as you didn't fuck with the product motherfuckers would front you the same thing. So now I got nine ounces to flip. I would work their product off first then I'll work mine. I'll make good money depending on how I sold it. I would see around eleven to fifteen hundred sailing to other hustlers wholesale. But if I sold the coke broke down, I'd make around fifteen hundred to two thousand dollars an ounce.

We went to Lee's old man's house to bag up. I gave him a hundred. It was only half of that, but his son was gone, and he was barely holding on. I knew every bit helps. His stepmom was passed out in the bedroom laying half on half off the bed with her head on the floor. She looked bad, his dad did too. I'm just saying all of our parents were getting high. Some parents you couldn't tell that they were getting high and some you could see it all over their face.

I guess like I was hiding the fact I hustled from my mom. After we bagged up, he asked if I'll sell him something. I said to myself I just gave that to him for food and shit. Well yes shit if I didn't sell it to him someone else would be getting my money. So, I gave him double still now he had two hundred in work he smiled, and we dipped outside to start the day. Since I didn't have Cannon's storage anymore, I rented Lee's dads for a hundred a day.

It was worth it but most importantly I trusted his dad. Leak went ahead of me to get us good spots just like any other large gathering you had to pick the best spot. Coke moved so fast fiends jumped out from everywhere then the rush was over. It's like a burger joint lunch rush hour.

But a hundred times busier and a million more times as deadly. And the only difference here other than the burger joint is that you get their orders wrong, bullets will fly and people will get hurt. Out here over wrong orders will get you killed.

People were all grouped up close. Let me make my way to Leak and see what all the fuss is about... yes without pointing one of the older guys was saying that the apartment over there, the one right in front of the sea sawhorses with the red light on, has been there for a while now. That light has been there for a week or two and we know for sure that that place is not rented.

It would be nice if yall find out what the deal is young soldiers. One of the older hustlers mentioned as he was puffing a cigar filled with cooked up coke and weed. When they came to us it was usually important. We would stop and listen. It was their way of holding street class.

They let us do whatever we wanted to do unless it caused the cops to come. Everything else was Kool. But this time the Ville will never be the same again after this day. We packed up and went back to one of Leak's dad's houses to regroup. Now I see why I wanted to find a new location.

For some reason it had to be the cops. It was just curiosity eating at me more than ever, nothing else had mattered. Leak said "he was going to hustle in his hood" he made enough to fall back but for me I took care of my mom I did not have it easy like him and Saga.

And I was responsible for my own shit, so I had to rough it out. I had met a chick through Saga. She had dated a goon from Booker T Washington high school. I was only a freshman in high school, and she was a freshman at Norfolk State university. That was a big deal around the hood.

She was very pretty and smart, which means she wasn't cheap. I was like that about her. Plus being in college she had her own credit card that helped. That was how I cleaned my money, and she knew that so in a way she had me by the balls.

When she saw something, she wanted I had to get it or lose my little money washer. Back then girls in the hood did not have credit cards. She became a big asset to me and my enterprise.

I needed her on the team until I could replace her ass. I had to say that the pudding was good too. I decided to stay out the Ville until the eviction notice was placed on my forehead. I didn't care fuck it I was in it to win it. This was the only place I could make ten grand in an hour. But if you were not on point you could receive ten years in prison or worse a bullet to the head.

The old spot I had was being shared by the Brambleton boys and the New York boys. They trapped one on either side of the block. I didn't have a choice but to play the middle. Plus, they sold hard cocaine. I sold soft so that's two whole different markets. Leak picked me up the following day. We were standing in front of my house. Everything seemed quiet and the flow of money was off and on.

I told Leak "I'm going to go get something to eat and go check my Norfolk State hoe". Leak said, "ok he'll go check out one of the OG's. stop by his girl's house and we'll hook up later" I said "bet".

When we caught up with George whose mom managed the office in the Ville. he said, "no one was renting the unit. So, one of the og's said the police must have placed a camera in the unit and set it on record". The old heads that night instructed us to go in the apartment where the small red light came from. It seemed as if no one was inside the apartment when we first entered.

Then as we turned the corner we ran into them. There they were three undercover cops filming everything we did in the money pit. I guess they were surprised that kids had enough balls to run in on their little operation.

But to be honest I don't think no one thought anyone was in there for real. I mean they had us locked on film for the whole city to see. How we took their poison and made lemonade out of drugs, poverty, and violence. That they planted to kill us off.

And now they wanted to watch us like we are some fucking animals. I really thought that was fucked up. That night the commissioner of the Norfolk police department came down to the Ville. No one had ever seen him on any crime scenes before now and he was pissed.

I happened to run to an apartment that was right where he was standing. I can remember the whole thing as if it was yesterday, he was furious and said in a strong loud voice "I want this place shut down no more coke is to be sold out here ever again"

He didn't care who heard him no literally. It was an embarrassment to the department because the niggas out witted them we didn't just roll over and die like they intended us to do. We played dead and always got back up when they retreated, but that wasn't going to be the case this time. He sounded like he meant business this time because right after that the commissioner madness hit the nightly news.

I never paid attention to the news, so it went over my head. I didn't go to Tyesha's house (my Norfolk state boo) last night because of the raid. The police didn't leave the Ville till like four in the morning. And they were still parked at all four corners of the projects.

As the dealers were driving away from the Ville, they would tail them hoping to find drugs or something to detain them to get a search warrant. While I'm waiting for Tyesha to finish cooking breakfast, a Good Morning America commercial came on that said something about video coverage of a city in Virginia under siege. An interview with the commissioner coming up at nine.

I hurried up and turned the channel. I did not want her to hear the announcement. Tyesha kind of knew what I did but I never gave her any details. I didn't trust people. If my mom would rob me anyone would get at me, I figured. So, you can say I always had trust issues with people. No matter who you were.

After we ate, we started to do us. She came in her bedroom where I was eating fully nude. I was a big young dude so I was still a little shy. I thought my money (private) was small in size, but she was my first real female partner that it felt like she obviously enjoyed my company (me as a sex partner). We had sex regularly every morning after her mom left for work and before I went to the Ville.

But for some reason this morning I felt different. While we were having one of our fuck sessions my cell phone rang. I didn't tell her I had a cell phone because I did not want her calling me every hour on the hour. Plus, she would have wanted me to get her one too. Hell, no they were too expensive as it was for me.

Having one was new to me too. I did not know how to work it that well, but I stopped talking to her because my granddad was the only one that had my number. He only called me on this phone. So, I knew it had to be something serious.

Shit you think cellphones are expensive now hell they charged a flat rate then it was like a dollar a minute or something like that it wasn't cheap. "Hello" I said, "Tee," that's what he called me, "yes granddad, what's the matter, you ok"? I asked him as soon as he said hello.

He said, "boy what the fuck you doing on Good Morning America"? I said "what I'm not on no damn TV" he allowed me to cuss when we talked, I was his first grandson he let me get away with murder if he was the judge. I got off the bed and turned to Wavy 10 news and sure, as shit stink I'm on TV in full color.

Come to find out that's what they were doing in the apartment just videotaping our daily routines. When the house got ran in it interrupted their investigation. Damn I thought to myself I'm fucked my granddad knows my secret now everybody's going know now. My teacher's, my doctor's, my family, and my mom oh shit granddad "that's not me" I said. That's you and that's Leak standing right next to you.

"Boy what the hell you doing out there"? I didn't like talking on phones then and I still don't know. I said, "dad I'm down the street I'll be right over". I went into the kitchen and told T "I'll see you later baby something had come up". She was like "when did you get a cell phone"? "Is that" I had cut her off and said to her "no you not getting one, not if I have to pay for the bill".

Then I was like mind your business man. I'll call you later. On your pager... I'm not getting you no damn cell phone. I repeated it and drove away. I didn't go straight to my granddad's house. I didn't want to see my aunt's negative ass. All she would say if I caught you selling drugs, I'm going to call the police on you.

So, I don't mess with her. I feed her sister and pay her sister's bills so if she doesn't like it, she can pay it herself. She's not going to because she is too busy drinking and chasing her baby daddy's all over Norfolk. So, I got stuck taking care of Sharon. And she be burning up my pockets and my stash.

The spot was gone and now my picture was all over the news. I went back to school to regroup myself and to just try and be a kid, but it was hard. Especially when I'm dating women my age and some even older than my teachers. I'll just play the lunchroom all day and find one of these chicks to cut school and go home with them too chill.

Just as I was walking up to the express line as I always did, the security guards came and grabbed me by the arm and took me to the assistant principal's office. The football coach was sitting in there with him when I came in and they shut the door. The assistant principal looked at me bluntly and said, "I saw your little ass TV show the other morning and I wasn't impressed".

He went on to say, "now every time you step on this campus and I even think you have drugs on you I will personally strip search you and call the cops". I looked at the coach and he looked back like he was disappointed but was down with the assistant principal.

I looked back at the assistant principal and said, "that wasn't me and I don't do shit like that" he said "ok" the coach grabbed me and the assistant stuck his hands in my pocket and said, "well look at here". See school was also a place of exchange. I'll front people but the next day they had to pay me at school. I had like twelve hundred on me at the time and he simply took it

And said "no I'm not calling the cops on you" I was relieved but however I wasn't out the fire quite yet. He went on to say, "whenever I catch you with more than a hundred dollars on you at a time, I'm taking it till after the school year and you can have your mother pick it up for you.

At the end of the school year". He knew my mom and he knew as well as I did that, I wasn't telling her shit so basically, he's saying in a nice way fuck you and have a nice day. That damn news clip made me hot and will slow my money up. I knew that wasn't going to be a good look for me.

I had to chill out and leave the Ville alone for good.

CHAPTER 8

Cutting Jokers Loose

School is almost out, and the summer of 1987 is almost here. I can't wait since the Ville had closed, me and Leak's picture was plastered all over the whole country. I decided to chill for a minute and hang in the hood. You know, reconnect with plucks out there. I had to move under the table though. Just enough sales to flip an ounce or two without drawing a lot of attention to either of the Brambleton boys or the New York crew noticing me.

I'm going to have to choose one of them but until then I'm playing it Kool. Just lay low and eat until somewhere new to hustle comes up. Leak called me up and asked, "what I was doing for the last week of school?" I replied, "I really didn't have any plans bro just laying back and stacking my bread".

Ever since the last time me, Leak and Saga all had hooked up, I had rented three rooms in that hotel by the Burger World off Granby Street. Well, this bad ass white chick from Maury High school where Leak and Saga attended school wanted to hook up with me. She bumped into Saga in the stairway. Mr. Saga told her she had to give him the pussy before she could meet me. She must have fell for it. She and her family were rich and she spoiled all her lovers.

Her dad was a doctor, and her mom was a lawyer. They stayed in a million-dollar house, and she had it all. She wasn't interested in Saga, and he knew he couldn't be with her any other way other than to use me once again.

Long story after she had sex with him then he called to my room. I wondered who would be calling me. I picked up the phone hello. Saga was excited to tell me Tabby was here. My mind started to scroll all the chicks I was fucking at the time then it hit me. I remembered her. Now I started wondering why she wanted to see me.

Damn, was I getting that popular that all the who's who chicks know of me. Wow I thought to myself. That night she became my first white chick I ever had sex with and burn me at the same damn time. I could see why the whole Maury High school basketball team loved her too.

We hung out all night long then right before ten o'clock I got another phone call. It was Saga who said, "Tyesha was coming up to the hotel". How did she know what hotel I was staying inn? I never brought her here before. How did she know about this place? I said to myself while I was rushing to get dressed. Tabby asked me "if she did anything wrong?"

This place was my refuge and now that too is gone. Yo Tabby we can finish the conversation another day. Now I did not tell her I was seeing someone and now my girlfriend is on her way up here to the room as we speak. She looked at me and turned whiter than before. She looked at me seductively then said "well ok if you still want us to see each other you know how to find me" we kissed, and she went through the back stairway.

Tyesha found out she was pregnant that day. She had been looking for me to tell me the good news. But as you can see, I've been busy all day smoking weed going to the basketball games in shit.

I called down to the front desk and asked for another room and sent Leak down to pay for it. I told him to "take Tyesha up there and have her wait for me". Then I told Leak to "tell her I went to the Burger joint, and I'll be right back". Tabby and Tyesha didn't know that they knew each other. I saw when the white girl was leaving, she saw Tyesha and they spoke to each other for a while.

I was sweating bullets wondering if she was going to tell Tyesha who she was up here to see. Or worst tell her she was fucking me. I know if she knows my soon to be baby mama then she had planned to get with me all along. That's when I knew how dirty girls could be to each other.

Tabby was relieved she saw Saga. She looked back up to the room window and smiled. Then she placed her arm inside of his and they walked towards the back parking garage where she had parked her BMW. I on the other hand was glad their seeing each didn't get ugly.

One night was all she wanted so I know she was not telling who she had just been with. That is when I knew I could fuck with her again she was Kool. After seeing them walk off I thought to myself I really wasn't worried if she would have told Tyesha that me and her was together. Ty came up to the new room. She tried to talk to me, but I did not want to answer any of her questions about who she bumped into. So as soon as she got into the room, I told her to undress. I at once took control and beat her cheeks up until we both passed out from exhaustion.

I thought maybe if she did tell her then Ty would appreciate me more for what I do for her. A few days had passed, and my man was on fire (my penis). I wanted to know what it was. I went to the bathroom and the head was stuck to my drawers. I started to get scared as hell. I did not want to wake my mom up and I did not want to hear the speech about having different chicks around all the time again.

I jumped in the shower and at once no homo one person came to mind, Saga. For some reason I knew he had something to do with this. At this moment I can't prove it yet, but I know he was behind this in some way. I'm going to call him as soon as I get out the shower. Just as I thought he sounded hyper on the other end of the phone. Like he was just yelling words out, but he was not making any sense.

I'll look into it further when I get over his house. I mean I'm not going to inspect him or anything but when I talk to people, I learned a long time ago to look them in their eyes. Then you'll be able to see their reaction to the subject at hand. You couldn't see that over the phone. I said, "yes ok I'll be over in a minute" he said "Kool" and we hung up.

As I was getting ready to leave for Saga's house, Tyesha came over to my house. She came in my room screaming and cussing at me. I was like what the fuck you want bitch coming in here yelling in shit. "What do you want?"

I asked her she said, "you hurt me you fucker and I'll never forgive you for that! fuck you we done". She turned around and left. Later I saw some papers on the dresser. and the baby was mine. It had her and my name on it. Before I could run out to catch her, she and her cousin had pulled away. I looked down at the papers and they were from her doctor's office. She was pregnant with twins.

The other papers were termination of pregnancy notification paperwork. She was pregnant and had had an abortion. Hold on! as I started reading further into the content of the letter it said that the termination was due to virginal complications.

I apparently was to blame but she broke off the relationship with me without allowing me to say a word. Funny because I never saw Tabby anymore after that night either. Tabby may have thought I gave her the wrong number or something. Or She told Ty about us so we could be together.

Ty may have put two & two together from that night they met at the hotel. Maybe Ty was too embarrassed to show her face around me knowing she burnt me and her best friend in the same night. Who knows I was hurt but what could you do after the fact?

On the way to Saga's house, I saw Jay Jay from the New York crew again. He was at an apartment down the street from where I lived on 30th street. Just on the opposite side by Man Man house (R.I.P). He lived in front of the Dillard house.

He said, "I see you're not in the Ville anymore". I said, "yeah I am letting the Ville cool off a little bit before I go back out there". He knew why I wasn't out there anymore. That place was on fire. No coke could be sold out there anymore. I wasn't fooling around.

No one believes me when I tell that story about me letting it cool off. The Ville would never be cool again ever and he knows I need a strong connect more than ever now. Especially if I was to keep supporting myself and my mom.

He said "Yo tonight we are meeting here just come by and meet everyone and hang out for a few" he said. "Okay" I told him, and I continued to Saga's house. Saga lived off Lafayette Ave out Ballantine. It wasn't that far. I had a moped and when I didn't ride it, I used a friend's car to get around town.

I didn't have a license, so I rode my bike or got a ride uptown the majority of the time. I went to the door and his sister Nessie was home. All she did was smoke crack and take care of her dad.

Their mom worked really hard. God bless the dead. Nessie, Saga and two other brothers ran the house. Saga was in the bathroom I tiptoed to the door. Before I could reach the door, I heard him scream. I said, "I knew it nigga" to him through the door. You fucked Tabby before you sent her to my room.

You must have burnt that bitch and she burnt everyone else. That bitch burnt me you fucking asshole. See he knew he did it because he didn't care about no one's feelings but his own.

Therefore, no matter how pretty or phat or freaky a chick was I wouldn't fuck them on the first night. And made a promise that I would never have sex with a chick if he touched them. If I even thought he had used to date them. He looked at me and said, "oh there's nothing wrong with me I was just joking with you".

I said, "yeah right I'm going to the clinic you stay here and pretend". "Wait" he yelled "how are we going to get there?" And what are they going to do to us? I don't know this is my first time you fuck face and besides Clark Client I thought you said, "you were fine". I lied and he said he didn't want me to be mad at him.

Then he told me he told Tabby that if she had wanted to meet me, she had to fuck him first. She went to his school with him, so you knew he wasn't going to let her come to see me before he got a piece. He always felt entitled to whatever is offered to me first. I could never understand that shit when he already had everything just handed to him.

I should be jealous of him but that was not the case with Saga selfish ass. I was so mad at him but when he admitted it,

I was just like call Eater up and he'll know where we need to go. I guessed the reason I still dealt with Saga was because I did not have any brothers and we had been friends since the sixth grade. Our birthdays were two days apart, so we had our parties at the same time when we got older.

So, when people saw either one of us, they knew the other one wasn't too far away. We got to the health clinic and we was joking the whole way down there. At the time the health clinic was located on the side of Norfolk general hospital. Ironically, that's where I was born man.

Hurry up Saga, Eater said evidently the effects are really kicking in and the pain is only going to get worse. While we were parking the car Saga jumped out and ran to the clinic doors. Damn they weren't open, yet Eater said the shift was about to start after lunch.

We started to wonder how Eater knew so much about the health clinic. Then I remembered his aunt worked in the school cafe and here at the health department. So, that's why Eater was the one to call. While we were waiting in the lobby to sign in to be seen. The waiting area became packed with people. There were cute ass chicks all over.

In the staircase as well. Most of them look like college girls hold on! Excuse me sweetheart. If you don't mind, may I ask you "who did this to you?" I'm going to kick his ass. I sat by her, and someone had grabbed my arm. and right as I was about to pull away and finish my wrap to that little hottie Eater's aunt said little boy don't yank your arm from me.

She let my arm go and said she came out to announce that the clinic was now "open for service" she then turned to walk back towards the counter, and she whipped her neck around as if she had seen a ghost and said, "Eater what are you doing here?"

I'm calling your grandma. He pleaded with her not to. He tried to explain that he was here only to bring me and Saga for a checkup. When she saw Saga running away then he noticed E's aunt, he got really nervous because she knew his mother really well. I did not tell Saga that one was for him to find out for himself.

After Saga realized me and Eater had told her the story he came from behind the cars and faced the music. "Yes, ma'am" "Boy get your little narrow behind in here and stop all that childish mess. Your time for being a kid is over now. at least it will be once you get that long tail needle in your backside."

Now you will have to come inside and fill out these forms. so, you can be seen by the doctor. I see the girl that was in front of the clinic when I first came in the door. I went up to the counter and got my forms. I sat beside her and then said, "Look you and me, we have the same thing so let's say in two weeks I'll give you a call".

Before I could say the word hook up E's aunt looked at me. As if looks could kill well I would not be telling this story now. She said little boy that's what got you in here in trouble now. And if you don't sit down, turn around and fill your forms out.

And stop trying to pick up one of these young ladies in here. or during lunch tomorrow, I'll tell every girl in my lunch line to watch out for you because you were in the clinic for the cooties. I looked at her as if she was bluffing, I know she can't disclose anything that happens here.

But when I thought about it, how or when would I know if she did spill the beans and to whom? I was so confused about what she would do with this valuable information. It would ruin me. I looked in her eyes and sat down. And I acted like I had a zipper on my lips then threw away the key.

The process was painful as hell so much I wanted to whip the doctor's ass, but I was already in too much pain. Eater dropped me off first. I got into bed and fell into a deep sleep. All I could dream about was peace and comfort. Sharon had just had my little brother, so I guess it was better I was back on this side.

Just in case she needed my help with my little brother. Shit was all over once she had him. Ricky was small and black as hell, but he was my mom's son so that made him my brother. My mom hung around the house a lot more since she had Ricky. She even stopped getting high and had started going to nursing school.

He really made her try to attempt a fresh start in life and I was proud of her. Later that night I showered and remembered that Jay from New York wanted me to come and check them at their new spot. Let me see my black and red Jordan's and my black and red Jordan jumpsuit with my gold lion head necklace and the lion head ring check.

Ok now I'm ready for this meeting. I didn't wear my Gucci link I just got. I had brought the dope necklace when I brought my set of gold grillz. I only wore them to the club or special occasions. Other than that, they stayed home in my safe. That safe so far has been Sharon proof. I thank God for that small wonder.

As I started up the street Saga came from around the corner. "Yo Tee" he stopped me and asked "where you going?" I told him to shut up and follow me. We walked down the street and saw Ms. Jackie on the porch with her husband. He was in his wheelchair. He didn't walk or talk much, just waved, so I waved and kept walking. I crossed Llewellyn Avenue and headed to the apartment where they were located.

It was right by the lady who sold dime bags, beer and shots. You know the neighborhood bootlegger. I went to the door and knocked twice then someone I had never seen before opened the door slowly and said come in.

I looked around for a second to make sure no one was going to jump out the shadows and stick me up. When I stepped in, there was Jay sitting in the corner between the front room and the hallway. They had only a sofa bed in there with a table and a few chairs. They had seemed to be in a big discussion, and I had just interrupted them.

Jay asked, "who was that with me"? I told him "Saga was my cousin". he motioned for us to enter, then I said, once the door had closed behind us "that Saga had hustled for me uptown near Ballentine Blvd.

He pointed to the chairs by the window that had a seat. I sat directly in front of the window. It gave me a quick getaway route just in case shit went to the left.

Good thinking I'm jumping right out the window if I needed to leave in a hurry. He introduced us to everyone in the room. He told everyone that I was the one he was telling them about who had opened the corner up they now shared with the Brambleton boys.

And from left to right he said "that's Jeff Brown (he was the dust head enforcer). He was known for doing whatever needed to be done to get that money... _anything_. Fred he was the smooth one he had all the girls you know quick draw with the thots... like face man from the A-team. Then there was Rod. He was the hot-headed fast talker. Whether who was right or wrong if Jay gave the word you were done.

You pushed him, you were getting shot, that was just how he rolled. Then lastly Porky the oldest brother he got high and a lot of the operations he wasn't included on for input. Everyone got up to leave. Jay said, "we'll be right back. Just stay here". I rewound what he said in my head we'll be right back"

Who leaves a person in their trap house with work and guns everywhere? This did not feel right to me but whatever I was down, but I'm keeping my guards way up. They were all leaving hell. I wanted to leave too shit. I did not own shit in here nor was a house sitter.

An hour had passed and Saga was getting inpatient. He wanted to take some of their coke and guns. I had thought to myself after Sharon had beat my ass for two years over stealing a damn sucker from Be-lo shiiidd. Man, he was crazy as hell for even suggesting that dumb shit.

Hell, she had only beat the skin off my black ass. They would kill us. No question asked hands down. I told Saga "You better not touch a damn thing. Sit where I can keep an eye on you". He gave me a look as if he wanted to try me but decided to take my advice.

He was hesitant at first then did as I asked of him. See he knew he did not know these guys and he did not want any beef with them or having trouble falling back on me. At least that is what I wanted to believe. However, if I would have slept on him for one second, he would have made off and left me to hold the bill.

He decided to wait with me. I said to myself I was leaving as soon as they got back. We had gotten bored fast. The guns were over on the table and we started playing like we were shooting each other. They had tec nines, Uzi's, nine millimeter handguns, ar fifteens, Ak's, sawed off military style shotguns and a few more I never seen before wow.

Out of nowhere one of the gun's Saga was holding mis fired. He had almost shot me for a second, the thought of dying kicked in on me. Looking back, I do not know if it was on purpose or accidental. As the near fatal accident had passed, we started to calm down. At that moment we both realized playing with guns was not the thing to do unless you were going to use it for protection.

We heard a key entering in the door keyhole. We put the guns back in their places and acted as if nothing ever happened. Just as they started to enter. Yo Jay, I yelled and asked him what the deal was for leaving us in here like that"? he replied, "I'm right here nigga". I continued to ask why you leave us in here?

He seemed to drag his answer. so, "I'm out Yo" I said as I was reaching for the doorknob. He said, "hold on, you not going nowhere". I had that funny feeling in my stomach. It felt like some bullshit was coming fast and hard. "What do you mean I'm not going nowhere?" I said back in a surprising way like who was going to stop us from existing.

I thought he was going to say we stole something to get me to work for him to keep me on the team without pay. That happened to a few guys I knew. That got their coke fronted to them. Only later having their connect rob them or set them up.

This would put them in debt and they in return must work for free until their debt was paid in full. I turned around and said, "what Jay?" in a stern voice. He said, it was a test to show them you were not a thief.

I said "what?" then he said, "I left you in here to show the rest of them that you can be trusted". This is why I chose you to be my right-hand man. Jay said, "I want to just supply and front the work to you. You will have full control of everything. I'll give you whatever you can move. You must buy all your cocaine from me.

But your cousin can never get shit. Me and Saga looked at each other at the same damn time. Then I turned back to Jay and asked him "why did he feel that way about Saga"?

That is when he reminded us that he heard everything. He must have meant when Saga wanted to steal his shit. He had to show the crew which one of us would be loyal to the team and who was the snake. He started telling us again, this time less angry as the first time. That all of them were standing right outside the window.

That is when I looked at Saga without saying one word. Deep down inside he knew what I was saying loud and clear. I am glad he had listened to me and didn't steal shit. Saga had failed the test and he chose me. This deal was better than what the Brambleton boys had offered me. They expected you to work in shifts.

You got paid two hundred a day. At least with Jay I have room to grow my empire while working for him. He turned back to me and asked me "how many ounces can I move in a week?" I told him "Like a quarter key to a half brick (kilo).

But that was in the Ville out here I really didn't know". Rod walked over and looked at me like he wanted to shoot me, but he put the coke up on the table (crack) in front of me. Jay weighed out four and a half ounces of hard cooked up cocaine and passed it to me. Jay then said "just call me whenever you get done. There's plenty more where that came from."

I was in heaven, but the smell of the coke had brought me right the fuck back. Ahhh the smell of sweet success I could not wait to hit the block and set the streets on fire. That shit stunk, it was like looking at a big white nugget. All I could see was dollar signs. I accepted the work only on one condition.

He had to give me a second to get used to the crack game. Up to this point I only had dealt with powder, and this was a whole new ball game. Jay said "yo I got you" the others were upset but I didn't care I was back in the saddle again. I did not care what them niggas thought I was now on top. He gave me a little white Honda sports car to drive and a Tech nine. I also had unlimited access to all the hideouts and ammo I needed. If someone got out of line, I now had killers to handle my light work. All I had to do was place a phone call and they would get dealt with. It was on. Our crew was everywhere now, not just in Park Place. We expanded all over Norfolk. We were in all the seven cities and growing.

On the other hand, so were the Brambleton boys. Everyday all you would hear was this person got shot in the head over ten dollars or did you hear this guy was beat to death with bats. Or being a witness to someone getting beat to death on the avenue. Those boys were relentless if you got in their way police or not, they didn't give a fuck.

You got dealt with and whoever you thought would come to your rescue. Just as we were shaking hands and growing our crew, they were breaking necks and planting flags marking their territories. We were bound to cross paths sooner or later either way I was preparing every day for the battle.

I worked from the house and kept my coke under Lacey's building next door right across from my bedroom window. That way I could keep an eye on it. If someone messed around with my work, I could be right outside on them before they came out from under the house.

A few days later Saga came by, and I told him about Jay. Well not everything, just the part that I can get whatever coke I wanted. And if he knew anybody looking for any weight throw them at me. He knows plenty of hustlers as well, he said, "ok". And walked off.

I played the front porch hard because you can spot the plucks that wanted weight better and whenever I spotted one, I'd send Big K to intercept the mark. Then he would find out what they wanted and signal me. I would then prepare and weigh the coke.

Then shoot out the back door come thru Gay boy backyard (Dickey D) and I'd come out on the back end of Llewellyn Avenue. Signal K and they both would walk over to me. K would take the coke and in return would discreetly take the money. When I left safely K would pass off the coke to the pluck. Then he would return to my house ready for the next sale.

Look K what do you know it's Saga's girlfriend. What are you doing on this bad side of town? I had asked her. We were like brothers and sister every time Saga fucked up, he would threaten her by saying he was going to jump off the Granby Street Bridge or some dumb shit like that.

No one would ever know the creative shit he would come up with to try and keep her from dumping him. She said "she was out here with T Mac and she had needed to talk to me" ok I told K to keep an eye out for da plucks and I'll be right back. We went into the house and then into my bedroom.

She was like damn "your room is nice". I vision different pictures in frames out of the GQ magazines on my bedroom walls. That was the same way my personal barber had his walls when I went to get a haircut. And expensive shirts and ties stacked on shelves attached to another wall. On the other side I had a fifty-inch screen television with a sweet Kenwood stereo that had a vhs player that was voice controlled.

She was amazed but I said, "what is on your mind?" She was saying how Saga has been cheating on her and how she was tired of him." I was listening but this shit happened every weekend. It was getting old. Yes, I thought so too, wondering inside how long was either one of them going to last?

I really was not listening to anything she was saying. She went on to say I heard he went with Leak, and they took your peoples (my girlfriend at that time) with them Cindy or something like that. I knew exactly who she was talking about and that night someone else told me they saw all of them together at the beach too.

No matter how mad I was, I did not want Shea to see my anger. I played it off. then said "Yo that's small shit Yo" even if it had happened. I was not a snitch so she knows she can't pump me for info. Saga was my boy, and I wasn't going to let her come between that. I'll confront him later about it and if he's lying, I'll fix him. Starting now I said "Yo Shea why don't you do me a favor?" Yeah, she replied" what is it?"

Can you go in the box on the top shelf of the closet? She came into the kitchen with the box and placed it on the table. I know what I was going to show her. I had like twenty bands in there. Saga was going to run over my house mad for showing her my stash. Before the day is over, I will bet a band on it.

See I never showed him the shoe box and he'll swear I was trying to fuck Shea. She opened the box and was amazed. She said, "who all this money belongs to?" I asked her "where did you find it?" She said "in your closet" ok just take some money out and go have a good time. She asked how much could she have? I looked at her puzzled and she said Well, how much you giving me? I said however much you need to cheer you up and stop you from crying all the time over that fool.

You love him, he loves you if that's all that matters, forget the bullshit. Go have a good time. See I was not like Saga because if the roles were reversed, he would have fucked my girl quick and fast. I did think about it on the low of fuckin Shea, but my heart would not let me.

She was a good girl, and I wanted to be a good friend. She was looking for a steady boyfriend to hold hands in shit that wasn't me. Their relationship was too much in each other's faces. She gave me a really big hug and left but before she did, she turned back and was like "thank you". "Girl, get out of here and remember to have a fun time."

I hope she can have some time without worrying about Saga. At least now she got the money too. She took like two or three hundred out the box. I only had about twenty-five or thirty grand in it. She would not have hurt me even if she had taken a band out.

Money was flowing like that nowadays they refer to it as Reaganomics (when the president allowed cocaine to be sold in America by the CIA to the real Ricky Ross in Compton California.) If it was sold and contained in the hood you were good.

But once you crossed the line and entered into the suburbs that was your ass. A week later I was over at my aunt's house, she lived by Shea. When I saw her outside she yelled to me and said to "come over". Damn this is what I didn't want to ever happen... me and her alone. All the shit Saga had done to me, messing with all the girls I dated.

He went behind my back and threw dirt on me to all of them. And some he just planned to tell them I had a girlfriend, and I was no good. Yes, it all came to me as I entered her house. Pictures of them were all over the place in every room too. I was laughing inside because just thinking of being here with him not knowing is making me feel like revenge is best served cold.

I was looking to do some serving of my own. "Yo Shea" I called to her and she was like "I'm in the bedroom". I had never been in her house before, so I kept talking to her while trying to get my bearings. Then I said, "what did you treat yourself too"? She said, "huh oh that day"?

"Yes, the day you came by and got doe from me". She turned to the closet, and I noticed she had changed clothes. She was now wearing this low-cut cheerleading polo skirt. I think that's all we wear, people's polo, tommy, or Izod anything else was garbage. She held up this cute little skirt set and some shoes. Now I don't know if she used the money for that particular one or she just wanted my opinion on that outfit.

But I said, "it was very nice "thank you she replied". "I was like damn that's hot ma" she smiled as if she was waiting for an approval to keep it or not. All the clothes still had the tags on them. She placed the clothes back inside the closet then grabbed my hand. I was shocked and froze in place. Right now, I felt like a bitch, and she was the dude. We fell onto the bed, she was on the bottom and I was on the top.

I looked into her eyes, and I put my lips on hers. She pushed back and before you know it, we were locked in an unbreakable French kiss. My heart was beating so hard that I thought I was having a heart attack. After twenty minutes or so passed, I reached down and began to rub in her panties she bucked back. While letting out a soft moan and grabbing the back of my neck.

She then shoved her tongue deeper into my mouth. I moved her panties to the side. They were so wet with her excitement. I couldn't help but notice slowly she started to go crazy, and she smiled even more. Then I inserted my fingers deeper inside her pussy. She moved back and forward as if we were making enthusiastic love.

I'd ease up and she would relax then I'll shove them in and out faster and faster. She bucked back harder. I was finally going to be even closer to Shea now once I made her bust all over her bed. While I was sucking on her lip, she was loving it but not more than I was enjoying this moment.

My money (dick) started to grow. It was hard as nails, and it felt good to me too. We both wanted revenge. She was getting hers because she was wet from all the excitement and deep tissue massages. By the way she was carrying on the sky could have fell and she would have never known the difference. She was in another world, and I was the pilot taking her to ecstasy.

I was doing to her mind and body everything that Saga did to everyone I dated. Now it's my turn for a massage right as she began to rub my head with her soft nicely manicured nails. The phone rang. I was like "don't stop". It was her mom, she knew me and Saga were super close.

She would not have been happy to catch me over here without Saga. Damn I was blown back now her mom was Kool as hell. But this will have to wait till another day. I didn't want to get caught in here half naked on top of her daughter getting a massage. That was probably the reason Saga told her I was his cousin.

I think he told girls and their parents that so if I come over without him, they'll tell him. Not directly but like your cousin came by here and shit like that. He was good at setting people up and juicing them for info. I replaced her blanket that I pulled to the side and kissed her one last time. I put on my shirt and zipped my pants up and she was like "what's wrong?"

I replied "not a damn thing but I didn't feel any better like I thought I would have felt." I didn't want to tell her that knowing her mom was on the way took all the excitement away. I thought to myself that if I did something with Shea, I would lose a good friend. She was like my Lil sister, and I know we would never be a couple because Saga would have never let us be happy.

So, if we ever had a thing for each other or not I didn't want to lose our friendship that we already shared. I was like "your phone keeps blowing up go answer it and see who it is Shea"? Whoever it was they just would have to call back later.

She let the phone ring three times and hung up then did it all over again. "Shit" she said it was Saga he was on his way over to her house. I knew it was something. I told her I had a bad feeling. I headed for the front door. I made it to the street and right as I was turning the corner to my aunt's house, I heard my name Yo "Tee" Yo "what's up?"

I turned and acted surprised and said, "what's good Saga"? He was like "I just came to see Shea". I said, "oh ok". He said, "what you up to?" Oh, I said, "I'm just walking to my aunt's house. Her and my uncle just bought a house around the corner from Shea". They were the first ones in the family to buy a home.

My uncle Keith knew my aunt was fucking around on him, but he was an OG. He didn't let the trivial things bother him. He had worked for the post office after he came back from the Vietnam War. So, a lot of shit didn't bother him like it would most people.

Saga looked at me then at Shea's house. He figured that I'll have an excuse to be over here now and I didn't have to be with him. Now I'm up one on him and it was his chess piece the "queen." I wondered what he was thinking of next. I made it back to my side of town and just as I entered the house. Then Saga called me and he said, "he wanted to talk to me". He was on his way to my house now. Before I could say I'm about to leave he hung up the phone.

Since he told me he was coming over I had to wait for him. He was lucky I had no plans to leave the house. I just re-upped so I had to bag this shit up before Sharon came home with Moonie and my little brother. Saga got there before they did, and I was glad he had a habit of bringing my mom in on our discussions and she'll feed into that shit every time. "Man, what you want Saga?" I had asked him as soon as he came through the front door. Shea told me (here it goes I thought to myself) that you had like twenty or thirty thousand dollars in a shoe box.

I breathed easy not that I was scared of him. It was not like that kind or fear. He just loved her and even though he fucked many of my girls I didn't want to be the dude she cheated with on him because he couldn't handle her messing around on him with me. I did care about Shea, and I didn't handcuff my girls like he did. But when he had fucked one of my chicks and I found out I just cut them loose. I figured that if they were truly mine, they wouldn't have fucked him. So, he did me a favor by playing on their loyalty to me.

I told myself to hold in my anger. Now if you looked at it, he did me a favor because I could have married one of them. Only to later find out my best friend fucked my wife. I would be hurt like hell. So, if that made him a man fucking his best friend's girls so let him do him.

I'm not fucking behind him no more I had learned my lesson with the white girl Tabby. I said, "Yes she was over here" and that was all I said to Saga. Besides, "she heard you was with some chick at the castle. Then you took her to the beach with her and you had sex". So, he replied "why are you buying my girl stuff?" He totally ignored the fact that he was busted for fucking one of my chicks. He was only concerned about the fact that I gave her money. He said "he been out Lakeland and he won't making money like me"

He had like five hundred on him. I told him I wanted four thousand five hundred for a cutie. I gave it to him and told him "As soon as he gets the balance to bring it to me. I'll hit him up again with another pack".

Saga was happy as hell. He was about to leave. I warned him not to go down his old block. See on Twenty Eighth Street the police have been running undercover stings.

And if you did not look like you from this neighborhood you were the next target. He said, "I know, I know". It was funny because I had just found out so he couldn't have known.

I just nodded my head and said, "ok Saga". Now I told you that he always does the opposite of what you told him to do. Why may you ask? Because he thought he knew everything. Ok I told him to call me when he got home. Not even five minutes later I felt something was wrong in my guts.

As soon as I started to feel better about the Shea and Saga being out of my hair for the day. That's when the drama began. A kid came knocking at the door Yo I said, "what the fuck?" "Who kicking my door?" the fiend said, "Tee my bad but the cops got your cousin in the back of the police car".

Damn I knew it, Saga and his dumb ass. Ok I'll be out there give me a minute. I put all the coke up out the house in case that nigga got loose lips. I went to the corner to see what the fuck was really going on. No shit he is sitting right there in front of the chick house who be tricking that old white man by the bus stop.

I told him not to go that way. I should leave his ass right in the back of the car too. But he was lucky he was my home boy. What would you have done? Man shit I know I can't leave him like that shit! I'm almost by the police car. I lifted the handle on the police car door. Lucky for him they didn't handcuff him. We ran down Debree Avenue and we made a right on Thirty First St.

I saw two plucks but once again fucking with Saga I can't even stop and get that money, damn Saga. We jumped over Dickey D's fence... he wasn't home. Nobody was hardly there at his house. That shit seemed spooky as hell. Hurry up I told Saga we landed in my backyard.

We ran up my back stairs to my apartment and went straight into my bedroom. We changed clothes and went back out on the front porch. The cops were flying all over the place two went up Debree towards pick up the pieces. One went to red ball and another one came up my street.

The car stopped right in front of us and my heart dropped. From the car the young white cops said to us "did you guys see two black kids run by here" we looked at each other and laughed. I told him "Yeah all the time". He looked at us and turned red as hell. All of them always say we all look alike so I played him on that fact.

However, they were mad they couldn't arrest the whole hood. We had won that round. But I was still out of four grand. He promised to pay it back, but it didn't matter. I would have lost more than that on a lawyer and even more if his punk ass decided to talk. He had four and a half ounces of crack cocaine on him too.

Shit he'll still be in jail today and me too. Because I knew he would have broken under the pressure then told me too. I could hear him now singing to the cops come out Lil Tee they got us he lives right over their type of shit. I didn't have time to give Norfolk nothing, especially no time out of my life. Especially over another niggas fuck up.

You would think he would have been grateful for what I did by opening up a police car door to let him out. But not that black mother fucker and from that day on I wouldn't give him a rock off the ground. He was too careless and reckless. He had all the wrong reasons for being in the game. That is why I did not like hustling with guys who had everything, all of them were the same as Saga.

And later, looking back it was wise that I stopped fucking with him like that. A few months right before graduation he sold coke to an undercover police officer. In his own neighborhood. How does one do some dumb ass shit like that.

I mean in your own hood that just means you're careless. It shows he did not care who he served. That shit like that will bring a crew down or worse killed. After that shit I was like fuck a crew. I sling now solo all over the seven cities fuck with me. And I will show you around my seven cities. Let's go!

CHAPTER 9

Going Solo

I roll by myself now, and I don't grind out the Ville anymore. I went back to school. I wanted to get out of my mom's house with or without her blessings. I had stayed with her for now at least till school was finished. Then I'll move back to that chick back in the beginning of the book who lived in front of Norview high school. Well, she had gotten pregnant come to find out the same time Tyesha was pregnant.

And like Ty she had gotten an abortion as well. Tyesha was pregnant with twins. We could tell from the ultrasound but we did know if they were two boys or two girls. We just knew they were twins. We had still talked from time to time but that was it.

Now the chick from out Norview would have had a little girl, I was seeing her. She had become my ride or die bitch. No matter who I fucked with or whether she found out she'll be there no matter what at the drop of a dime. I could be with another chick having sex. I call her my bitch because she was with me before I had the money.

For example This happens all the time. I would be at another chick's house fucking around before I can bust a nut, she would be right outside of wherever I was at. Yes, outside and this was way before gps and smartphone apps.

It was like as if she was like okay, he's washing his balls

Right abbbooouuutttttt nnnnoooowwww. And he should be done.

Next my phone would ring. Yes, she was the only female who had my cell phone number. Every girl I would be with would be like "how did your girl know you was here? I would look at them and say "she must have a crystal ball or something" I don't know.

She had her car before me, so I tricked her car out. For her I threw in a booming system and put rims on it the whole nine. She had worked for her uncle Horse. He owned a couple of record stores somewhere out the View and another one out Park Place in Kingston. I'd keep the car when she worked and pick her up when she got off.

She gets on my fucking nerves. The only time she is happy is when I'm going inside of her pussy dropping off deposits lmao. She made sure my nuts were drained before I hit the streets. She'll pee all over the sheets every time we fucked.

In the beginning that was Kool because it shows me how good my Dick game was as a young man. I was on my game hard when it came to getting these hoes. Ok I dropped her off in the View today. So, let's head to Roberts Park. I grew up here as a kid. The hustlers out here hated me when we were younger.

My cousins couldn't fight too good, and I had to fight for them. Everytime I stayed the weekend out here in Roberts Park it was strange. I hated it because I'll be fighting for them and get jumped, they would run and leave me. That made me even madder. That's when I went crazy, and I would tear up the park. That was my younger days though now we look back on those days and laugh.

Not at me fighting the whole park every weekend. But because my cousins were some punk ass motherfuckers. Except Olivia and Tom Tom, they took after me when it came to fighting. They made me proud. I went to visit my granddad. He stayed there with my aunt Lillian. I hung with him every now and again whenever he was there alone.

I didn't get along with my other family too well. "Hi granddad, how are you doing today"? I said to him as I approached the back porch. He said, "I'm ok. I got up at five thirty this morning and went for a walk".

Then by six o'clock I sat down and had my coffee and watched the news". I said, "OK whose home"? I would go in but if she (Aunt Lillian) was there I would just stay outside. Ever since she heard I was on the news she was acting funny towards me. You would think I was Charles Manson or somebody bad like that, so I paid her no attention.

He said, "your aunt's home" and that was my queue to vacate the park. "o alright granddad call me and wake me up in the morning please". "Ok" he shouted back. Just now I saw one of my Lil dudes that be hitting me up for coke. "Yo what it do I asked him" he replied "shit you got an ounce on you"? If so, what you want for it?"

I looked around because even though I was from out here as a kid I still wasn't welcome to sell drugs out the park because they couldn't come out my way and hustle. That's just the way it was in Norfolk. If you weren't from that area, you could not get money.

You'd better have family somewhere close cause as soon as you can't be identified by just one of their runners you were fucked. And sometimes people from their own hood got rolled on, if they brought outsiders in to hustle. Only until you have the og's blessings could you hustle. Outside of that you could only visit, that's it. Even then you were suspect.

You would get jumped or shot. "Yeah, I got one but not on me. Is you crazy, meet me here in twenty minutes? I told him to give me the bread now". He asked me if I still got his number. I said yes fool you gave it to me the last time I saw you oh yeah, I forgot.

I peeled off to retrieve the shit he wanted. As I was turning onto Princess Anne rd. I saw this all-white Mercedes ride by. It had curtains in the windows that were Moet. He was from New York. Him and Cannon had the seven cities on lock. He was fronting Q from the park and the weight he would move for Moet was enough to keep everyone high for ten years.

They had Roberts Park on lock for the most part. Back out at the stash spot this other chick held it down for me. Now her name was Tracey and she was from Chicago. She moved here last year with her mom, three brothers and two sisters.

She goes to Maury high school with Leak and Saga. When I go there, I try to be in and out.

She hounds me about getting her a crib in shit. Man, I don't have time to keep discussing this every time I come hit the stash. I pulled up with the system blasting "Dumb Girl" by RUN D.M.C. and the woofers were hitting hard especially on the drop oh hold on boom boom boom dumb dumb with a capital D you just dumb girl dam. They go hard. That's my favorite rap group.

Now W.R.A.P. The local record station always has the top jams on. Knock knock who is someone screamed from the top of their voice from inside the house. They lived up the street from me in a duplex. Her sister is hot but she's an asshole.

She fucks with those niggas out the point in shit. This nigga named Malcom is stalking her hard too man. "Yo, Tracey you up there?" Yeah hold on for a minute, the voice said. Five minutes later Tracey came downstairs. She was thick and cute as hell. She had on some red jeans and a tight red sleeveless top.

She had half her head shaved and the other half was dyed blood red. She was wild but I loved that about her, and she knew it. She came up to me and was asking me when I was coming back? What did I do last night and who was I with?" Damn one question at a time" I said I need to come in and get something.

"Hold on" she said I'll be back when you see me open the window come in ok. While I waited for her signal I sat on the hood of the car and enjoyed the late spring breeze. I wonder what them niggas out here was doing. Since the Brambleton boys came here they then pushed everyone from thirty First Street to thirty Fourth Street.

But they do have streets out here all sewed up. My female cousin was on one side of the street and big Todd was on the other side of her. Sophia was a bad ass trick. And she would send me mad plucks. Let me tell you baby boy she was off the chain. All my family was ok because they had an inside man who was a probation officer. He grew up with them out the hood.

He was a Deja named Super Cat. He gave them tips about upcoming raids, indictments and shit like that. So whenever I was on the block with them niggas and they dipped off I left too. I wasn't stupid I know Cat was helping them and in return he do their parties. It was a nice little hook up until Todd went to jail. Cat fell back from what I heard. He was even promoted. Isn't that a bitch. She just sent me the signal to come in.

I motioned back. She grabbed my hand and said, "come with me." She led me to her bedroom. Her mom was home but she didn't pay me any attention. Her man was back from overseas. She was a cougar and a damn good looking one too.

She was mixed with Indigenous people, Irish, and African American. All three of them were fine as hell and there were two more up and coming. Roxy and Tracey, I know they are going to be stars when they hit the scene. I need to get one whole one and you need to put this away I told Tracey and she hurried up and came back out.

How much is it? She asked me "twelve hundred dollars you can keep the two". I did that from time to time to make her sister mad. Her sister's boyfriend Lil K was always getting locked up and he didn't give Roxy doe at all. He would beat the shit out her ass too.

She would see me and make faces at me. First, I didn't know how to take it. Until one day I asked her why she made them faces every time she saw me. She said you don't remember you had asked me if I wanted to fuck with you. And I had said "yeah but we were just bullshitting" I thought but apparently, she had been serious and hurt that I ended up with her younger sister.

Well, I wasn't into skinny chicks anymore. Tyesha's pelvis used to tear my stomach up. So, my chicks now had to have an ass and Tracey fit the bill. When she took the money, I asked how much was in there and she said "twenty-five hundred plus this it's thirty-five now" "Ok." I kissed her and patted her ass and left.

Just as I was leaving this fake ass wannabe New York fucker that lived next door spotted me. His name was Slim, and he drove an older model jag. It was burgundy. He looked over at me. We exchanged glances and he went into his house without saying anything. I went to my car and jetted to get that bag. I did not have time to deal with these petty ass people.

I headed up Thirtieth Street. I was going to go by my house because when you ride dirty you don't just run errands. You must go to do the drop off then you run around doing the other shit afterwards.

As I started to turn right onto Debree Avenue there, they were all of the Brambleton boys standing on the porch. It was about fifteen of them. Whenever they were all together someone was about to die. They just had a standoff with the Norfolk police. They didn't come out the house till the police had left but they had enough guns to hold them off for a good half an hour.

But I have no time for hood politics. I got this oz. and a half to deliver. I hit Princess Anne from Colonial Avenue. I kept Princess Ann all the way to Roberts's rd and there he is right by the dumpsters. Yo get in and check it out. What you think I'll be done by Friday then I'm going to want two ok Lil Trigger. Him and his crew were no joke.

It was about six of them and they all played with guns. As a matter of fact they're my stepbrother's cousins. They were off a little bit all their uncles were in jail for murder. That's why no one fucked with them at all.

Since I been clocking with Jay from New York I've been in the hood a lot more than I used to. I see why I didn't like it out here. The girls out here were not as cute as the ones from the Ville and all they did was fight each other over the same niggas.

They passed them hoes around like old shoes. Besides K, the only other person I messed with out Park Place was a girl named Tikka. Yo that was my boo no matter who she fucked with she always had time for me. She was happy that I hustled on this side of town again.

I loved it the most when she took me in the back room after we had a couple drinks. If her mom was home, she would sneak into her bedroom. She'll have me a face cloth and towel waiting. I'd shower, and she'll be in her room rolling up a blunt. I'll pick up like two packs of Philly's, the grape ones and a twelve pack of beer. She sold weed so we didn't need that, and we would just lock ourselves in her room all night long. Her mom loved me because I stayed on my grown man shit and I always came to her house by myself.

Plus, she never had to stop us from fighting in shit like her old boyfriend. While I was there, she would make sure I didn't lose any sales too. She had her oldest cousin stay in front of the house to catch all the sales for me. If someone wanted something he had to call her. She didn't want anything for helping me. That's what made him leave her something whenever I came to see her.

Whatever I left she really didn't need it. She had a booming weed game. You know everything helped when you stayed in the hood. "Here" I said to her. "What?" she answered. I said, "take this and get four more of them". She said, "I'm good, I have plenty of weed". "Well throw this in the hole for a rainy day. I told her".

"Ok" she replied, and she turned and reached for a box under her bed and threw the doe inside. I gave it to you Tikka because you never turned me down for anything I ever asked from you. Do not worry I know if I need it, you have it for me.

She kissed me and said Tee, why can't we go together? "I said, "you be with me everywhere I go". She smiled and replied "you're right", laid her head on my chest and went to sleep. She sounds so peaceful I didn't know if it was because I was there with her or because I had just fucked her for the last two hours.

I had to leave when she was asleep or she would keep me there forever lol. I waited until she was in a deep sleep. Then I'll get up and leave before everyone else notices me leaving. Everybody was knocked out.

Usually, I'll wake up the person nearest the door and they'll let me out, but they had a new lock since her ex had tried to kick the door in or something. I just let It go in one ear and out the other ear. I was good at it too. When I got home, I went to the kitchen. I looked in the fringe damn nothing to eat. How come Sharon doesn't tell me she needs grocery money. there's never nothing in here to eat but baby food shit. I'll just get breakfast in the morning.

I went into my room and at first everything looked normal. But that didn't mean anything Sharon was good. But she hasn't hit me in a while. Well really since she had my little brother. But something tells me things were about to change. School is almost over. I can't believe I'm going to be a junior next year. I'm almost out of Sharon' house for good.

I really didn't have a clue what I was going to do after school, but whatever it was it wasn't going to be at Sharon's house that's for damn sure. I got up and I didn't feel right. I went to check the work I had. Last I counted it was supposed to be fourteen ounces left. Tracey, she had thirty five hundred dollars in the safe that's eighteen hundred total missing.

Sharon struck again damn, I'm moving. I ran away before Saga had got in trouble for fucking with this white girl at his school. Her parents kept finding his black ass in their daughter's closet. He was brave because if this had happened nowadays, he'd be dead.

It would be nothing for her parents to be like oh shit a niggas in my daughters closet shoot him POW. Yes, officer. I saw him on top of my daughter. She was screaming for him to stop. I asked him to freeze, then he passed gas. It reeked of something bad, and I shot him. Well, it was a good thing he didn't get shot but her parents moved her far away. Saga's mom gave him hell too. His grades had dropped so he called himself-trying to convince me to run away with him. At the time other than my mom's light fingers. I was ok at home. But it did sound fun so after he begged me to come with him, I said "what the hell even if I get the room for the weekend, he'll change his mind and want to go home ".

Let me get some clothes and we can get a room at the hotel behind seven eleven. He went home to do something and we agreed to meet back up at the hotel. Meanwhile after I packed, I went through the hood to collect some money that was overdue. I hit the avenue heading to Thirty Fourth street that's where my cousins trapped.

And they had blown up once they met this dude from Philly his name was Ron. I think that's why the Brambleton boys didn't apply too much pressure on them for hustling. Like they did everyone else. Once a nigga knows where you are from the bullies tend to fall back because if you have to run back home, you'll have your enemy right there waiting to crush you.

To prevent a home front retaliation the Brambleton boys stayed back. The fact is my people weren't weak either; they were strapped and willing to use them too. Don't get it twisted Ron became heartless and cold when you saw them. Each time his body chemistry felt deep and dark. The game was taking a toll on him, and he was showing it in his body language.

You could see it every time he hit the block. Damn there they go Tikka she stayed across the street from Todd's sister. Todd's sister was named Stacey she fucked with this New York nigga. So, she stays with the good coke.

She is a big girl but she stays clean and Gucci down. She kept her hair in an uptown style and smelled good all the time. She was a girl that any hustler would want as a partner. She held it down. She was so hard in nature then soft in appearance, a deadly combination.

She gets her own money too. She's going to run this city one day. She took what life gave her and made her own juice. you go Lil Cuz.

HI baby even though Tikka and I did not go together in public we kissed, held hands. We displayed feelings for each other openly in the hood. She was my hood wife (a girl that you fucked with in your neighborhood that understood no matter the other girl was second).

And if we called each other no matter what that person was doing or who they were with they left that person to see if things were ok. That's why I love Tikka so much, preoccupied with company of the other sex didn't mean anything to her. The person must hold their heart and the next time we are alone you could display how you felt to whatever level your heart felt.

At that time, we kissed. She asked "If I was coming by tonight?" I thought to myself if I'm going to run away with this fool ass Saga I might as well stay here with Tikka and leave in the morning. Yeah, mama I'm going to stay here with you tonight.

Just let me go home and wrap up something. I'll be back after dark. Tikka smiled. She had a cute little figure, not too small, not too big. She had a Ceria shape, but she had had a walk that made my dick hard when she walked by every time.

She was pigeon-toed and kept her hair up in a ponytail so it would be wrapped twice. It looked more like a rabbit tail than a ponytail. Saga called "Yo, you coming out tonight" Yo he tried to con me again but no matter what he wasn't changing my mind. Recently, me and Tikka had broken it off. It was my first feelings about a chick, and she calls it off.

That wasn't the norm for a handsome nigga like me. I really was in my feelings. She had asked me for a full commitment I refused because I did not want to hurt her. See look my game with the hoes was this I targeted an area that wasn't crowed with young niggas trying to get money.

Once that was established, I'll then see what bitch that was down for her man. It can be the hottest chick out the group or not it didn't matter. And then I moved in (I know you're saying to yourself of course he's going to get the hottest, but it really didn't matter, it was about getting that money at the time).

Not the hottest chick. I would rather her best friend, the ugly bitch. Lmao see your mind is bad. Anyway, the friend wasn't ugly but just needed a dude to spice her up. Take her out shopping and make her feel good about herself that she would become loyal to him. Now she would have the ass and features.

You just dress her up and work on her confidence. And I'm the one to build a bitch up because I'm always up on the latest so, my bitch game has to be up in the heavens too. If I'm Gucci'd up, she'll be Gucci'd up too. That's just how I rolled and now the prettiest bitch in the hood would get jealous and I fucked with her on the low.

And the cycle continues every hood I move in on. But one thing people in her hood knew for damn sure is that Tee came and picked that bitch up and now she's straight.

Now I have two bad bitches in the hood and all the other niggas be on my dick sweating me.

Then it's a ball game. I took over the hood by turning an ugly duckling into a swan. Now here's where the money-making part comes while we fucking, partying, shopping and so on. I'm picking though their family members not to fuck them but to put in charge of the business.

I explain to them what I am doing in their hood. And the same way I chose my girl I chose my predecessor. The dude everybody ignores or takes advantage of. That person I'd focus on. The one who was cold but had compassion.

Why would you want a person with a cold compassionate heart? Well, you don't want a fucker that walks in on a family of four and kills them over five dollars. In all actuality you lose more after the shooting then you did fucking with that dude that owed you the money.

So sometimes compassion can save you more in the long run than the money you lost in the first place. Now that I found my right hand, I'm going to appoint him ambassador to his hood.

I let him know in private who I am. Ask if they're tired of being pushed around and did they want in on the money flow? After that they'll kill for me. Putting money in people's pockets and still lining mine at the same damn time. This was my life and I'm loving it. Now I'm fucking the hell out of his sister or cousin even their moms sometimes. They might not have liked me in the beginning, but they liked the bread that was coming into the house now.

So once again with a fair exchange there's no robbery. And now I don't have to travel with guns. My dude will have the hood on lock. And I'll be his connect. That's why all the out of towners wanted me on their team. They saw me as a money maker.

But I was loyal to Jay, and I stayed with my crew. I kept the empire growing daily. I ran this game with every chick I met and if I went home with you, I was moving in their hood. Before going to Tikka's house.

I had planned to get the regular supplies for our romantic evening. So, I walked down Thirty Fourth Street and spoke to everyone on the block. At night it was like a swap meet. The streets were littered with fiends, hustlers, women and guys.

Todd and his brother Skeeter had that end of Park Place on lock; they had people on shifts, and they got paid per bag sold on their shifts.

Others that didn't work for them were able to catch the plucks before they got to their house. The only difference of buying from Todd than a regular dude hanging around the trap house was that you just didn't know what that dude had but you could count on Todd to not only have the amount you were looking for but it was guaranteed to be the best in town.

That says a lot when you're taking a chance already. Instead of going through all of those risks only to find out you just brought some cero or homemade crack. So now if you were a hustler, you just lost rent and if you were a user your monkey has now become a full grown gorilla.

Thorns was the only place to buy beer after hours. As I began to cross the street, I heard someone call out to me yo Tee I couldn't recognize the voice but I knew one thing was for sure if they had called me by Tee, they knew me from like the second grade.

Because from the first grade on up I hated my name. Think what kind of fear that puts in you if someone was to say oh, I heard Tank was looking for you. Exactly no fear whatsoever so from the time I realized that I fought everyone who called by my real name in class, on the playground even in church.

So, when I heard that name, I knew that person had to know me because after the last fight I fought the person for calling me that aloud. Every punch I threw landed on his dome. I would tell them my name isn't Tank it's Tee! And that's what you call me, so it stuck.

Good thing I could fight too. When I turned to see who called me, I couldn't see that far because it was dark and late around eleven or twelve o'clock. As I focused on the voice, I noticed it came from a black Volvo and the driver was my nigga Bear from Lakeland. "Yo man what it do people? It's been a minute" I said he was like "I know". I looked at him and said "Yo what the fuck you are doing out here on this side of town" because people just didn't visit Park Place let alone neighbor's from hood to hood.

It just wasn't wise too and this was a good reason why. As me and Bear was talking a guy came up to us and said "Yo move your fucking car. It's hot out here and by you being double parked you gone, make the police come". he was right and I knew that, but Bear didn't know that and at the time I really didn't think he cared either.

Bear shrugged it off and kept talking to me. Ok in my head I'm thinking Mac didn't know who that was in the car. Had just told us to leave or park. The dude's voice had sounded like it was Mac from six grade the guy that bullied the whole fucking school.

Damn I don't have time for this shit right now. I was dirty and I had Tikka waiting for me at her house. She just got out the shower and everything too. But as I said, there was a lesson in all this to be learned while Mac was just doing what he did every night making sure the block stayed traffic free.

He was running and keeping the block clear of the loitering. He hustled on the side too, but he made the most money keeping the block clear from dumb shit because a lot of people respected him as an O.G. (original gangster of the hood) but he didn't hear what Bear just told me before he had walked up on us talking.

He must have taken Bear for soft and had expected him to just leave. However, Bear had told me he just killed two niggas that tried to rob his trap house. And before they could get him, he opened up on them niggas and he dumped the bodies out Norview by the high school near the under pass. I froze and was like why did I ask him how he was doing?

Note to self never ask another person how they are doing for now on it's only Hi or bye. He had gone on to say "he was leaving town, and did I know anyone who wanted to buy any guns?" but before I could answer him Mac had interrupted us again and the rest was a blur.

Bear said Tank (my homies could call me that because we went back to first grade) I see you later and he peeled off. Mac yelled out to him as he left "yeah nigga I thought so leave with your punk ass". I was like Yo Mac you didn't just hear what he was telling me man he wasn't listening to me at all. He was high, drunk still beating his chest over a sweet short lived victory.

I said fuck it and started back to Tikkas house. When all you heard was pop pop pop pop pop pop then the sound of tires tearing through the concrete. The night was quiet before that happened. The streaking sounded as if you were at a slot car race.

But instead of stopping at the finish line Bear was fleeing the murder scene and Norfolk. The moral of this story is that no matter how tough you may be, it's all somebody with a gun that will gladly add you to their body count. This city had placed anger in us already.

All you have to do is push them then their reply is with bullets. At Tikka's house she had looked at me and asked if I was all right. I said, "yeah I'm fine". She then said that "she had gotten out of the shower and I didn't see me". My mom told me "You left". Yeah, I got to the porch and forgot the beer. So, I went to Thorns. Why didn't you tell me I would have walked too she said in a funny but concerned voice.

I'm glad I didn't tell her I was going to get beer. Her nosy ass would still be out there. For the police to find out I'm underage drinking and just brought beer. On top of that I can hear someone telling one of her people that I was the one talking to the guy who shot Mac.

I shook my head and looked, smiled and said, "if you would have come with me, we wouldn't have made it to Thorns because I would have fucked you behind the school". She laughed and I grabbed her ass, and we went into the house. I ignored the family member because I did not want to be a witness to shit.

She turned back and said, "it's a good thing your back here I heard them niggas shooting again". I said, "yeah I heard it too. I thought it was a car backfiring while pulling off". Shit I dodged that one. I can't wait to smoke a blunt and drink that beer I earned it. That morning I left and headed out to the hotel to meet Saga. he claims he didn't have any money but I see he was able to pay for the first night. He brought this dude named J here too. His car was in the parking garage. That red escort you can spot that shit from anywhere. He was like Saga's personal driver.

It's just Saga didn't pay him. Instead, he would take him along on dates as a copilot. It's just sometimes when you went along with Saga you never knew the bullshit you had to go through as his wing man. He would always get the dime. Ok he found the girls he gets first pick. I can go with that but if whoever he is hooking you up with was prettier than his girl the next trip you will not be going.

And the next time you see the girl he hooked you up with he'll be sporting her as if she was his girl. You'll be like that was fucked up, or the bad part was he would always lie on me to fuck the hoe he told their friend or family member. Say something like I told him I had fucked one of them before. He would lie to her and have them hate me for something I had no idea about.

I would get a call from the girl questioning me. And I would be clueless to what was going on. I stopped going on those suicide missions with Saga because whatever you tell the girl he'll switch it up and you crash and burn.

He was just a friend no matter how fucked up he was I still stood by him. I was just wondering when he would display the same loyalty or would he ever try too was the real question? I went back and forth between Park Place and Roberts Park hustling and all between since all I had to do was keep gas in the car. He'll take me wherever I had a pluck.

We did this all day while Saga had given up on hustling. After the second undercover sale, he did to that cop, he was shook and I did not blame him. I continued to hustle; it was all I had. I was in it to get the bag.

Now the money game he learned from his funny ass brother Cal. Saga was good at it made me laugh every time they did the switch on the cashier. I mean every time. I couldn't understand how dumb some cashiers had to be in these stores. They count your change to you right in front of them.

And then in a blink of an eye they replace the largest bill with a dollar bill. They had it before she closed the cash drawer. The switch would happen so fast that if you turned away for a second you missed the transfer of the money as well.

Just like clockwork every time the cashier would apologize and ring for the managers. Then they would apologize and refund the money. Saga and Cal used to kill that shit.

But after that ass whipping Sharon put on me plus, the extra ass whippings for knowing when to walk away from people stealing. So, as they performed their magic I always walked away and watched them from afar. It was a game to them. So, everywhere they went a quick exchange of cash they got them.

Until Saga and Cal went to Hamilton and tried that shit with those white country hicks. and their asses got caught stealing steaks and doing the money switch game. That was the end of Saga's career too. However, Cal ass from what I heard continued to do the game and in fact he went up and down the east coast chasing his baby mama.

He finally caught up to her, but she didn't return back to Norfolk with him. She said" his attitude was too fucked up for her to deal with at that time in her life." Cal was an asshole, and he did handcuff his chicks, crazy. When he went with you, he would spoil the shit out of you and if you did anything that he told you not to do he whipped that ass too.

All up and down the Blvd. in front of everybody, even their own kids. He was a beast for that shit. And for that he couldn't keep a girl once they found out how fucked up in the head, he was but that was Cal for you. Me and Saga held up in the hotel for almost two weeks. Until Saga's homeboy got trapped off by Saga's mom.

He did the right thing and took Saga home. I didn't get in trouble because I told my mom the next time she hit up my stash I was leaving. So, When Saga went home, I went to Bared Park. I stayed in this crack house. I slept on the sofa. I was on it, clocked all day and all night. My man Teflon was out there locked up. So, I always had access to coke. Everybody knew me from school or from the bitches I fucked with that lived out here.

Teflon knew I dated this girl named Cindy that visited her grandmother out there every weekend.

She was just like her name Cindy. I was her first and I can remember that first time right now as if it was yesterday. She finally was going to let me fuck her and her parents had just left for the day. I was at Saga's house (this was the first girl he fucked behind my back). he had introduced us, so I'd go pass his house before I went to her house.

Well, her two sisters were home that day and I thought she wasn't going to go through with it. The littlest sister had gone to sleep, and Saga was talking to her adopted sister Tiffany downstairs. They were in the television room. She was kind of slow but knowing Saga he was trying to get her attention away from me and Cindy.

I know he was because I heard her say if I kiss you like you want me too, you will tell people that you like me. I thought to myself that he was going to hell for that shit. I could not believe he was trying to hit. Once Cindy knew her sister was occupied with Saga.

She had invited me upstairs in her room. At last, we were all alone. We started to kiss and as she closed her eyes she asked, "if I had loved her". I said "yes I had just wanted to be alone with her without Saga or her sisters in our faces. She asked, "if she didn't start to kiss me would I have liked her or be there with her at all". I said "yes" (knowing what I know now I would never kiss or have sex with a virgin again after her). She was like ok, and she lifted her head and pulled down her hair and she moved in closer to me.

And as she did, she turned her head then slowly stuck out her tongue. She had let me do that often but that was the farthest she would allow me until we were older. She got wet fast and her body jerked hard every time she got excited. She was probably embarrassed but I told her that was natural. Next thing I knew she wanted more. She laid back pulling me down on top of her.

Not even breaking our lip lock. She had on my mouth. I held her by the back of her neck, kissing her slowly. My lips and tongue moved slowly up and down her neck occasionally I would nibble on her ear lobes. She was sticking her tongue in and out of my ear too it was turning me on. With my right hand I unzipped my jacket, and she held my dick slowly rubbing the head.

And she sighed at the size. I thought to myself she wasn't scared anymore, and I told her to "take it out so she could see the full size". She was hesitant so I said, "it's all me baby take him out it won't bite you." Mmm she did and I got a rush seeing her get aroused at the sight of her playing with my cock.

I could feel my head throbbing and I wanted to take her to penetrate her right then. With the head on the game my heart was set at the entrance between her thighs. I noticed she wanted it too but with the responsibility of her sisters she knew time was really tight.

And they weren't trying to cooperate with her at all today. I'm clearly getting nervous now. I think she was about to call our session off. She was all together because she was upset that I was going to go shopping with or without her... Think fast, think "hold on" I said, and I slowly slid my tongue inside her mouth, not too deep but deep enough to make her forget the mall.

Once I felt she was comfortable again I put my hand on hers and just like driving a stick shift I slowly let off the clutch while applying the gas. She fell asleep and I just laid beside her waiting for her to get up. Baby I want us to both wait until we are older so our first time will be together. Aww she replied and kissed me on the lips. We went back downstairs where Saga and her sister were, they both knew what we wanted to do and they both were eager to hear what happened.

I didn't say nothing nor did Cindy because she for one didn't know what happened herself. I told her she was still a virgin so that's what we told them absolutely nothing damn it felt good. We weren't together anymore after Saga told people he had fucked her. We still spoke to each other, but I forgave him but her I couldn't you might say that's fucked up I shouldn't talk to him or her your right.

But I didn't learn that until years later. Being out Bared Park was different then all the other places I hustled. First of all, the neighborhood was made up of all houses. We hustled in the front of the hood. Once you passed the park the apartments on the left is where all the coke sales went down. You had to use lookouts because running really was not an option.

The best weapon you had out there was keeping your eyes wide open and always staying alert. No drinking or smoking while on the block. From time to time, we'll get lucky and the bootlegger in the hood. For a small fee you was allowed to pitch from the house. Only if we spent enough money that night on drinks and food.

Those nights she let us stay. I was happy to be inside at least you were off the corner. The school bus used to pass me all the time. I was sometimes ashamed to look at the people on the bus because I've become that kid you used to talk about at school... the dropout. But despite the negative looks they didn't know what I went through at home.

My mom's habit had reached a point that even though Cannon was a friend the situation could've gotten serious. He could have sent dudes to shoot us up or something. she didn't seem to get that fact.

What if he wasn't a friend and I didn't know him we could have been killed over her addiction. People die every day for less out here in Norfolk. This place was like early Iraq. Just with a hundred Arabs running around with money and don't know what to do with it but dumb shit. A month or so passed and fall was setting in. The leaves were turning a bright red and the days were getting shorter. The cops use different cars now so it's hard to get a track on what they were driving these days.

So, you must be sharper than ever now. I was out of school when Man Man died. The world had stopped for one long minute. Everybody that knew him paused that day to remember him; he was deeply missed. He was the second fastest sprinter in Norfolk, and he was a friend.

We all went to Teflon's house. He had a nice townhome not too far from the hustle spot. He made some jello shots and we all just sat back, some laughed, some cried, a lot of us that really knew him just sat there and did both.

I've now missed a third of my junior year of high school and things aren't getting any better. Just as I was about to head in for the night, I saw someone who looked like no wait it was my cousin Hank. "Yo Hank what's up man?" He was my first cousin and he said, "everyone has been looking for me". Then he asked, "if I was ok?" I'm not sure why he asked me that he couldn't change shit and all he really cared about was himself.

Yeah, I'm ok (inside I was screaming no I'm not ok you asshole). I knew if he saw my mom, he'd tell her I wasn't ok, and she would come looking for me for sure then. Hank went to say the social services told your mom if she didn't sign papers to turn you in as a runaway, they were going to take your brother away from her.

Then lock her up for child neglect. No matter how mad I was at her I can't let them take him from her. Nor have my mom be put in jail. She'll end up worse than ever. I wouldn't be able to live with myself if that went down. Tell my mom if she signs my papers to go into the military I will come home. He agreed to pass the message to her for me. He was about to leave and turned to me and asked, "if all the money I made was worth it"?

I said "the freedom yes but its life anyway you look at it you going to have to deal with it sooner or later. No one stayed a kid forever". He nodded his head and left. If I had agreed to come back or not, he was going to tell on me.

That's how my family was quick to tell on you, but slow to help you. And even slower to tell on themselves. It was two days after I saw Hank and he had called me on my cell phone. Hello, he said my mom said she'll do it. On one condition, I came back today and finished high school.

I agreed to do my best. She then said to me baby come home I really miss you. I paid Teflon what I owed him then I left Bared Park. Hoping for a better tomorrow.

CHAPTER 10

Becoming a Man

Back home boy did I miss my room. Nothing changed. My mom kept my brother in her room. So, I still had my own space to entertain my female company. I started to hang with Big K again and he still was the same. A virgin and a little weird at times, but he was my homie. He asked me where I had been? I told him everywhere not really wanting to talk about it.

Then I'd change the subject by asking "if he is still going to church on Sundays with his grand mom?" He said, "Yes, as a matter of fact we have family day this Sunday. You know my grandma would be happy if you came too". Let me see I thought to myself then I looked at him. Then I asked him "Do a lot of chicks go to his church?".

He laughed and started to give me the virgin speech for half an hour. Later he smiled and said "just don't let momma see you because you know what you're doing she will be mad at yo ass. Then put you on front street in church." I told him "I'll see him at school in the morning". Then I headed home. I couldn't wait to have a decent bath or shower.

I hadn't had a good shower since the hotel. That was two weeks ago. I had the house all to myself. This is going to take a while. I cut through the back of Twenty Ninth Street. I hated coming this way now those damn Brambleton boys put a dog cage back here. Every time you pass them, they sound off. I knew it wasn't going to be long before they were going to put dogs out of here.

Their regular plucks all but stopped coming to fuck with them. Brock and Pappy were alternating with Boo and Big Bob so whenever they started to move different faces around it was to start the burn process (melt down, sell everything and anything and take no shorts).

They all started to smoke crack inside laced blunts and to drink all the time. With that and the fights people were getting more and more afraid to fuck with them each passing day. They would beat up their runners claiming that they stole from them, so they didn't have to pay them for working.

I went into the house undressed as soon as I hit the door. I gathered my clothes and went in my bedroom. I grab a clean pair of boxers and a white tee shirt. I went in the bathroom and adjusted the water. Mmm that feels good as hell, the water ran down my face. I was picturing all the events up until now. I thought to myself after all that I was still alive.

It felt good and with the thought of going to church on Sunday. I was going to get a chance to thank God for keeping me safe. He had watched over me while I was out in the wilderness of Norfolk's ill streets and survived. As I started to wash my face, I was thinking where do I go from here.

Myself answered and I said with God nowhere but up. I got out of the shower and dried off. I then wiped off the mirror and looked myself in the eyes and said out loud Lil Tee this was just the beginning. The weekend came fast as hell but at least I was able to get reinstated in Granby High School.

It really felt good being back in school. I didn't regret running away at all. I felt like it had made me into a man. I was looking forward to graduating and going into the service. I had looked at running away and it had really shown me what the real world was made of and what to expect out there. I know my mom may not go through with me going into the service, so I went to the reciters office on Monday.

(a friend of mine Dip who hung with me and K from time to time). He was a little older and he had gone to Maury High School. We were graduating at the same time.

He only came over on the weekends. We would get drunk, and he'll smoke weed every now and again with me. I was the only true weed smoker in the group. I didn't mind that it just meant more for me. Well Dip had mentioned before that if he had known someone that wanted to join the service, he'd go in with them on the buddy plan.

I'm going to take him up on that offer. I will ask him to come with me Monday to the recruiters office. Sunday in church I sat with K. Apparently you had Sunday school first and then they held the main service at eleven o'clock. While we were in Sunday school, I indirectly scouted out the chicks and the pickings were good. One stood out to me; she was short and slim with a nice round butt.

I asked K who was that girl over there sitting by herself. He said her name was Tasha. I thought I could mold her to be what I wanted in a girlfriend. She was cute as hell light skinned with long pretty hair.

In service I sat with Ms. Baker and K who in return had always sat by Tasha and their family. I thought to myself this church thing is going to work out just well. The service was very moving and it made me realize I wasn't lucky when all those times of trouble passed me while I was in the streets. Why the police had always missed me. Like when I'd pack up for the night and leave the block five minutes later the Norfolk police department would show up.

Next day niggas would get locked up yes, I was blessed. They said God looked out for the babies and fools. Well, I was far from a baby, so I guess I was a fool. I'd rather be a fool for God than those assholes in the streets. "Amen" I said after the preacher said the morning's prayer, for a strange reason I always felt warm all over when I prayed.

So, I did it as often as I could. I just never told anyone. The service was about how kids grow up in the church and as they get older, they fade away from God and when and only when they are defeated, they return to the church.

Only to be buried without giving God back any of their time. They don't think to come as adults to further their life in Christ. As the road of a child was free of life's pitfalls. For us, the world would be given to us. As a younger person in this ever-changing world, we do need him in our life.

Then he went on to say this ever-changing world the pew repeated what the pastor had just said "the world once again he said is full of all types of pitfalls. We were his children. He will allow you to be tested, don't get me wrong". the pew repeated him again then said, "preach it pastor preach it" and he had resumed to preach.

He went on to say but the tests are set forth to see if you're worthy for the blessing that he has in store for you. Then he continued the lord our God will pick you up if you fall but I'm not here to speak of physical protection.

I'm referring to the protection of the spirit, yes spirit protection. Amen the audience shouted and another lady jumped up and began to dance. I wasn't shocked. I'm used to seeing the older ladies dance for joy in the spirit of the lord. I saw that all the time when I was younger at my mom's old church in Linden Wood, so it didn't bother me none.

The soul needed protection and so did the spirit. You can't get it when you're dead in a coffin. You need it as a guide, a map and as a comforter so please little ones as you grow the message today is to remember where your protection comes from and that's in Christ. I looked around yes in here he said but most important remember who your protector is outside of the church as well.

If there's anyone who needs that protection today let him or her stand up and come down here to receive that protection today.

Right now, and you can take it wherever you go if it's yours for life. I looked around and a few people stood up. A little kid ran down to the altar and the pastor smiled and said, "before we close out today's session. Is there anyone who needs a father? Who needs a loyal friend? Anyone who just wants someone to listen to you? You can still take this opportunity to have that and so much more". It's here waiting for you right now. I said "excuse me" to Ms. Baker and she smiled and allowed me to pass her, and she gave me a look of pride even though she didn't say anything.

That's what it felt like to me. I accepted it and made my way to the altar where the pastor placed his hand on my shoulder. Then prayed silently over me and the other people.

In a deep voice (I don't know if it was to scare the devil out of me but I know I'm not going to type it now in respect of the lord, but I know what he almost scared out of me and it wasn't sugar let me tell you). He said, "I say unto you dear heavenly father to protect these young men and women who on their own came and kneeled down before you and your followers". Amen someone yelled from the audience. He further went on to say, "You're such a grateful God, caring and merciful in all things, lord, please watch over them and comfort them, bring them peace and prosperity throughout their life dear father".

"In your name all things are possible. In your name I pray dear father amen and amen." He returned to his chair behind the altar and sat down. I stood up and the little boy had returned to his seat.

The next person on the microphone started talking about the congregation bake sale. In the back and for everyone to visit the table before leaving church services.

Then they asked two of the young men who just came up to report to the church office. I'm thinking like how I got in trouble in church. I must have had a puzzled look on my face because Ms. Baker turned to me and said, "you're not in trouble" a sigh of relief came over me she said, "you'll be baptized next Sunday" and it's a few things you have to do before you can be reborn.

I was now confused, reborn she said "yes once you're reborn Christ will forgive you of your sins. When you get baptized the father washes all your sins off. So, the next time you slip and you commit a sin, God will see you've been washed of your previous sins. Then you repent and he'll forgive you and wash you off again.

I was thinking kool because I'm going to need a lot of washing. This weekend I got baptized so I have been running with Jay from New York a lot now. I'm not making as much money as before with Cannon from the Ville, but this job comes with a car, guns, and an unlimited supply of work.

So small bites were better than not eating at all. With all the things I've been getting myself into I'm going to need to be baptized. Even though it was against my better judgment I introduced Saga to Jay. They didn't hit it off too well in the beginning. Saga and Jay had wrestled in my front yard, and they were slamming the hell out of one another.

That shit was funny as hell. But when Saga found out Jay was my connect his whole attitude changed real fast. He was all but trying to suck Jay's dick to get on the team. They became friends but Jay still didn't trust Saga.

He limited Sagas work so he had to come back more than Jay's other runners. Since I was Jay's right hand, I always knew what Jay fronted Saga. I had to collect from him since I was the one who introduced him to Jay. Jay was like that he made you responsible for whoever you brought into the circle.

I didn't blame him. Because niggas get a front, and you wouldn't see them for a month. Then act like they forgot to pay you. Jay did not have to deal with that bull Jay made niggas oversee who they brought to the crew. I'm getting baptized in the morning. I invited my mom and she said she was coming. I'll believe that when I see it.

When I was younger, she made me go to church for lunch every Sunday. A bus came through the hood, and they would take whoever was at the bus stop to church and feed us lunch. We would play games and activities they had us. After all the games we would receive a snack and say a prayer and then they would take us home.

I had always wanted her to go with me, but she would say I already know Jesus. Now you need to meet him. I know what she meant it was her time to unwind and have the apartment to herself. If she decides to come to my baptism It would make me happy to see that she cared about me still.

With her habit and my brother now, she had no time for me it seemed. Or for anything else these days. My mom shocked me when I saw she got up to get ready for church. Sharon was in the bathroom fighting with her hair as usual. She always made a fuss over her hair. She had a great texture of hair.

It was thick and deep brown with a hue of honey. She hated TT damn she said my curls won't hold Tee you up yes. I been up and I said ready to eat. K and I stayed out all night. I got drunk as hell celebrating my baptism.

Hold on I hope I don't go to hell for that really, I had hoped not because that would have defeated the purpose for going through with the baptism today. I'm just thinking too much. I did that a lot and thought about a subject to the point I'd be obsessed with finding out how shit works. Where did It come from? In shit like that pointless, huh?

Yes, damn it's only one bathroom in the place and she wants me to get ready while she is there how? Boy I know what you got! That was her famous line. Then she would say I had you so get your ass in the shower right now. We must go to Ms. Kimberly's house. She is going to keep your brother today while we are gone. So, we can go out for a mother-son lunch when we get done with the ceremony. Mom that's nice but I'm not getting in the shower with you in here for one.

And secondly, they will have food there for after the baptism. Some people cooked and volunteered to bring food. Ok she said "that's even better" in a crackling voice. "Tank I'm very proud of you for walking up there without me having to force you."

"Mom, you were with me when I was up there. All the things you taught me were repeating itself in my head. What the pastor was saying just reinforced the fact that you were telling me the truth about God." He is everywhere I need him over me now in my life.

AAAAAHHHHH mmmmm stretching neck popping, I feel good. It was Monday and I had brought an outfit after we left the church. It was some duck head pants with a two-toned polo golf shirt. The colors were the same as our school colors. I be killing them.

With my yellow and blue crested polo socks? I paid thirty-five dollars for them. I picked up all the colors of course. My feet were too fat for the canvas polo shoes. so, when I wore my polo outfits, I wore my Sperry top siders

You know the ones with the thick ass soles, or I'll wear either my all white or all black Reebok Classics. No, today I'm wearing the all-white classics. They just came out and mine were fresh out the box baby.

It is nice outside today. I went to K's to get him in the morning, and we were off to the bus stop. At the stop we weren't like other kids. We would drink and cuss but what I liked to do was shoot dice. Just as it was my damn turn the bus pulled up, K was tapping me laughing in shit. "What man?" I said then I put my foot on my money on the ground niggas was slick.

If you weren't careful and looked away for a second and all your money would disappear. I scooped up my twenty-dollar bill and went over to K. He said, "isn't that your dad?" "What?" I said, "man it's too early for joking in shit K". Damn you want to fight. I just got baptized yesterday fool. No look I turned and looked up and sure as a bear shit in the woods Robert was driving the bus.

I smiled and walked up to the bus and asked, "who did he steal this bus from?" He was a mechanic but I never saw him chuffer anyone. He said it was a job and majority of the drivers were women so I couldn't believe he was a bus driver now.

"Get on the damn bus boy!" He yelled as I got on, he motioned for me to sit behind him. He shut the doors and headed to the last two bus stops on the route while he was driving, he was telling me how he heard I ran away. And how I shouldn't have put my mom through that I didn't want to hear that shit especially from his ass. He was out of my life from zero till just a year ago. There was a fifteen-year gap since I last saw him.

For real I really did not know him. He ran away so he was no better than me I thought to myself. My mom use to tell me he'd come to town, or she'd come across a picture with him and me in it sitting on his lap or holding his hand. I couldn't remember it so to me it didn't count.

"Yeah" I answered him. I didn't even give him a reason to finish. I said" Yo what you are sipping on?" I could smell it. That's the only time he cared about anyone other than himself when he was drunk or high. He looked at me in the rearview mirror of the bus and said, "it's in my bag".

I looked down and there it was his favorite drink. That was really the only drink that was always on sale in the supermarket this time. It was some wild Irish rose wine that shit got you pissy, shity drunk. I was on my way to school but I'll take it and trade one of the football players, they drank anything. I slid the bottle in my bag without him or the other kids noticing any difference.

Once he dropped us off, I was like Yo K look what I got. K wanted some. I didn't know he had been hanging with one of our home boys Big Wood (rip) and they got it in son. I asked him if he wanted some of this shit. He said, "hell yeah".

I gave the bottle to him, and he turned up. Ok man damn. I thought he was going to drain the bottle. When we went to my locker on the loudspeaker my government name was announced and said for me to report to the office.

What now I thought to myself. On my way to the office, I see why I've been called here. He was standing behind the principal making faces at me as I was approaching the office door. The principal was like the bus driver said "you picked up his cooler by mistake" I underestimated Robert... he was good. He had the school principal call me to the office to retrieve his wine that he shouldn't have had on the school bus anyway.

He was laughing at me. I wondered to myself if he thought it would have been funny. If I had said "yeah and once I realized it was liquor and I threw it away". I wanted to say that so bad just to see the look on his face. No matter how little respect I had for him I would never turn him in to the man. He walked with me to my locker, plucking me in the back of the head whenever the hallway would be free of people.

The late bell had already rung so I received a lot of them. Ok man stop with the plucking me already. My locker was located on the electives hall. Here you go I don't drink that cheap shit anyway and I laughed. He said, "but your momma does" and turned away laughing out loud.

I had given it to him. He had balls. Since I attend day and night school now the days go by so damn fast. I'm caught back up and I'm passing to the twelfth grade, damn I made it. The summer was here and I didn't have to go to summer school. I'm happy as hell. I wish my cousin was here for the summer. She got sent away to London after she told my Aunt Pam that her son Mat had raped her.

I was mad as hell when I heard that, and they protected that asshole. He had stopped coming around after Deanne left but I promised myself the day I found out where he was, his ass was mine.

The closest side of my dad's family that I saw everyday was my grandma, my Aunt Baby and my Aunt Rachel. She was an asshole mean as hell. She was an editor of the local newspaper. Then it was my Aunt Ester and both of his brothers (rip Pete and Lil boy).

Out of all my cousins at that time the only one I could relate to was Deanne. Our family thought it was for other reasons. My reasons were clear as rain. When my dad introduced us, he never told me he'll hit, beat, or harm me in any way. We would talk tall shit to each other. I knew he could joke well too.

However, this day he had looked me in the eyes and said "don't you let nothing happen to her or I'm going to hold you responsible". Ever since then I looked out for her. I did as much as I could whatever it was, or I had to do if you fucked with her, I was on the way. But not just because he told me she was my family, but because she was an outcast just as much as I was.

I was an outcast because Robert didn't bring me and Sharon around to the family gatherings. So, as I had gotten older they would accept me coming around. However, I didn't feel the same as the other kids did in the family. Until Deanne came to stay with our grandma.

We hit it off good and we both were not outsiders anymore because we had each other. She was white and black mixed. In Norfolk that type of shit wasn't normal. Her mom was from New Orleans and my uncle was Native American and black, so she was very pretty and little in size.

She always got picked on by all the girls in the hood and family seriously. It used to hurt her a lot. So, I would make her stay at my house when she came back and forth to Norfolk.

That would make her happy. And we did whatever she wanted to do for her while she was here on vacation. It was my way of saying I wish I could change things that hurt you but since I couldn't we would do whatever she wanted me to do to make her happy. For the whole time she was home.

CHAPTER 11

Earned my Wings

I'm a junior now all summer. I perfected my swag, walk, and stacked my gear up. I'm going to kill them this year. With Jay I'm keeping a nice piece of change on me, but I haven't been out there too heavy. I did what I had to do for two reasons: Sharon said she would sign me up for the military and I wanted to give her my diploma.

I had this one girl in my sights. The one out the view was acting up. The new girl's name was Kesha and I had remembered her from the Ville. Her grandma had a crib out there by the hustle spot. She was cute as hell. I dated the two of them at the same time, her and the girl from Norview.

"What can I say?" I need a lot of attention. Since I was known to have doe, I chose to take care of her. She was sweet and her mom just didn't have a whole lot like most of our parents back then. Kesha and I would spend a lot of time together in and out of school especially at my house.

She would watch my brother for me while I was on the block. In return I bought her dinner whenever I got home. We ate dinner and I sent her home in a cab or had her dropped off by a friend. She was my world. I mean it was two sides of me: a hustler and a family man.

I had a wife for both of my personalities. Junior prom coming up. I want to take my girl, but we've been off and on for a while now. I didn't want to be the first to break the silence that had fallen between us. And I had been seeing this chick at school on the side. She was a white girl named Wanda.

She had dated one of my boys so I really couldn't talk to her like I wanted to. Even if he didn't hit it. She was hot too. She brings to my mind looking like Khloe or Courtney Kardashian. She was a dream girl and if things were different, I probably would have asked her to marry me.

She'd let me drive her around all the time. Her car was a convertible baby blue mustang. I fucked that up though, but it could have never been she was from a whole different world then me. All the dope money in Norfolk would not have made me feel comfortable around her family.

She was a true white girl, none of that white yo girl shit either. And I don't think her father took too kindly that his little girl is dating a black person. Now that school was out, and the summer was here, my time was spent watching my little brother and having fun. Too many of my friends had died and I was lucky that it wasn't me in those coffin's laying there all dead and shit.

Yes, I was thankful, but I still lived my life on the edge of death. With Jay I did a lot of wholesale. It kept me under the radar, and it was less foot traffic to the house. I gave up the cell phone. It was too costly, and it drew the wrong kind of attention. In the hood I was above the runners and shooters (a person that's known to make moves) but because I had Todd as a cousin that helped too.

Hank started to come by from time to time but I blew him off saying I had to watch my little brother. I had no time for his jokes. After a while he'd leave. Good, I didn't want to hustle with him. He had a good life with his mother, and he knew who his father was. They did for him, so I didn't want to be blamed for the shit he was doing in his hood.

Between Tikka, the chick in the view and Tammy I had all the company I wanted and needed. I would break an ounce or two down and give it to big K. I did that often. It kept me with extra spending money, and it gave K a means to be like the rest of the fellas in the hood by having slinging dope. He didn't need to, but he kept his allowance for his comics and the new money he got from working the block was used now to support his weed habit.

It was Kool with me. Jay came by on Mondays or Tuesdays to make sure I was ok, and that the product was moving. Plus, to catch up on the week's events. He was more like a big brother than the average drug dealer. He went to college the same one that the Brambleton boys attended.

That's why they respected him so much. Hell, me and Juice were at 7-eleven as we pulled up to the store Ted Riley was at the register.

As he was leaving Jay said "Yo watch this" as Ted reached for the door, he came eye to eye contact with Juice and Ted choked "yeah that's what I thought," said Jay. Jay knew him from a hundred and twenty third and St. Nick Street in Harlem.

That's where Jay was from and when Ted spoke to Jay and Jay looked at me and said "Yo, you hear something" and walked into the store. Ted looked back to see if Jay was behind him. Once he realized we entered the store he was relieved.

He got in his truck and left. While at the register I asked "what was that all about?"

Jay looked at me and said, "that Ted had crossed one of his homies up top and he knows that I'm aware of that fact". He was shocked that he saw me down here. I said "why you didn't cash in the marker" he said it wasn't time.

In the park the dude Moet from New York had got shot. Man, that was the big news of the hood. The dude he had working for him got robbed and Mo gave him a deadline to pay up or else. That to me was one of the biggest problems of the game.

At first everything would go well and next thing you know you get robbed. Then the deadline becomes a do or die situation. Then you get that I'll see you at sundown. If you didn't satisfy your debt or you better have a gun and homeboy did and he blew Mo face off his body.

And that was that. The dude that shot him had gotten like five years. There were a couple attempts on his life too. Someone had planted a bomb at his house.

They were gunning for him. And after all that all he had received was something like probation. It was getting to the point that you could kill a nigga in Norfolk and they'll give you the gun back and say good boy do it again.

Well, I didn't have to worry about shit like that because with Jay I only took what I needed, and the money was always correct from my end. And that helped me keep an eye on it too. We used to all hang at the local club a little bit past Thorns. It was called the Nine and it was the place to be if you were a local baller.

After the police did the midnight run only fools and stick-up boys were out there hustling. Any and everybody else would be here at the Nine. Cindy's aunt worked the front door, so I never got frisked and I always had my gun on me. It was an all-black nine mm and it was ready for war.

Todd always grabs the back booth and sits so he can see the door. I normally stand and walk the floor scooping out the women that may be free from their man for the night. Oh, shit somebody said something to Black Hulk, he's about to go the fuck off. Before I knew it, he threw two dudes over the bar too late. It's on now until I see a gun being pulled. I'm holding this area down.

And just as I said that a dude rushed me, I side stepped him and just hit the dude in the head with the bottle of beer from the table beside me. "Todd" I yelled damn someone is trying to hit my cousin. "Park Place outside" someone yelled as I'm trying to make my way to the door. I get stopped by security. "Yo you wait right here" he said and just before I could say anything Hulk slid the dude into the bar with one hit.

I looked at Hulk and I left the club. He followed me only after turning around to kick a couple more people back into the front door. We all loaded back into the parked cars and went our separate ways. The days are starting to get shorter, and school will be back in soon. I'm actually looking forward to not going to school. Since my birthday passed over the summer I can now get my l's (driver's license).

And I'll be old enough to sign up for the military. I was going to the Marine Corps. If I wanted to change my career branch, I wouldn have to do the boot camp over.

At least that's what my mom's best friend tells me. She never went into the service herself, but she worked on the base, and she dated a lot of servicemen. And what did you expect? Norfolk had the biggest naval base on the east coast.

The male to female percent was maybe back then fifteen to one. The women outnumbered the men. So, when the naval ships would come in, those navy boys got first dibs on all the women in town.

If Aunt Dolly was in the crowd, they were lucky because she was the catch of the year. She had a body like Jacko with a thin waist with a big round ass. She was about five foot four and she had long wavy jet-black hair. Her eyes were a deep hazel brown with a coco toffee skin complication.

When she walked past you couldn't help but to notice the very sexy walk that made traffic stand still. I was young and she was priming me for man hood. She'd come and visit my mom then on her way out to her car she'd pull me to the side, and you know give me like fifty dollars here and there with a nice hug.

Every time I wanted to get up the nerve to grab her ass, but I was too afraid she would think I was disrespecting her. I will wait until I have a place to take her to of my own. So for now I will have to just settle for hugs. Before she left, she used to always ask me "did I know how to mow grass?"

I responded sure. I did it plenty of times before. It was easy, she said, "OK. I'm going to take you up on that before the summer ends. I'm moving and I'm going to need some yard work done before the fall sets. I agreed to help but then thought It must be a lot of grass because she's been giving me money for more than a few years now.

Deep inside I fantasized about her wanting me to do more than her lawn. Because I was a young man now and I heard that's the way she liked them. I had always pictured the day we would have sex. I hoped it would be like one of those cheap porn flicks.

Hi, I'm here to mow your lawn and Dolly comes to the front door in a tu-tu smiling from ear to ear. As I began to ready the equipment, she offers me to come and cool off before I get to work. Then it skips straight to when I start to finger her pussy. She comes and sucks my finger then well you've seen the way it ends.

I don't know how to explain it to you based on how much I pictured the encounter or the vision of me being the lost little boy who needed help finding his mommy. No, I'm just playing. But it could've happened, and I would have gone with it and the whole nine yards.

When the chance came for me to keep good on my promise I made her on cutting her grass, I'm going to try my hand and see if she's all talk. Daphnia (I called her Aunt Dolly for short) had called my mom in advance to make sure it was ok for me to leave with her for the weekend.

I was happy to see that she didn't forget about our deal. I would have done anything for her to get out the hood for the weekend. She had lived way off the grid meaning I didn't have to worry about the Saga or Leak coming by to see who I was with, and possible cock block the whole weekend.

It was going down. I wanted no interruptions. We stopped at a couple places on the way. She really made me feel like this stay was about me, boy was I in for a surprise? We arrived at her house. It was an exceptionally large townhome and it had a huge front yard, but it was manicured perfectly huh?

I was puzzled to see that it was already done. Whatever I was already paid to do the job so she must want me to just do the backyard. She went up the stone stairs to these two huge wooden double doors and unlocked them. Wow this place is nice as hell!

She said, "thank you like It" Huh? "Yes" I said back to her as I dropped the bags in the front hallway and I began to explore the castle. She called home. She yelled "I'll get the groceries and you look around". The last part sounded as if she wasn't too pleased to have to put away the groceries alone, but she'll get over it. I kept walking towards the backyard.

I had a blunt I rolled up and I was looking for a place to smoke. Until now I've stayed in hotels that were this beautiful, not a home that someone I knew actually owned. I was really impressed. And the fact she was single gave me a whole fresh look at Daphnia like maybe I could be more than her little helper.

More like her young lover. I snapped out my daydream or should I say fantasy. I met her out by the patio doors and she said, "come here" and she reached out her hand. I placed my hand in hers and she led me out to the gazebo where the patio set was set up.

Just when I thought, we were going to sit down right here in the chairs I had paused. She continued to the fence and the yard went down maybe twenty more feet. The steps wound down three more levels; each level would have to be mowed. It too was already done. I mean it was perfectly cut and edged.

I was about to ask her "what work she wanted done and as I turned to look at her?" She kissed me long and hard. I was stuck. I didn't know what to do. All my feelings that I felt for her had now become true. Then all the blood had rushed to my rod and all surfaced at once I was in heaven.

When she stopped, I was still in the pucker position. Frozen by the moment of reaching puberty and I couldn't wait for lesson one. I said "wow your lips were soft as I suspected. Then I leaned over to her and asked, "if she had any cognac"?

I knew she had some. She brought me every Friday she got paid. She said "yes she had some, but it was back in the house on the kitchen counter. On the way back to the house I couldn't help but notice there were speakers outside. Not seeing any wires or stereo system I was puzzled.

Because where I was from you didn't leave your speakers outside. and I was wondering if she had wanted me to bring them inside with us. You didn't leave anything outside you wanted to keep? I asked Dolly. She said, "they were remote and if it did rain, they were waterproof.

Furthermore, she said "no one will come back here. Everything you see behind us is private land" and I own it. Inside the house as she approached a hidden bar it was under the counter. I pushed a button under the counter. The mirrored glass door slid open. I grabbed a new fifth of Remy Martin and two cognac glasses. She had to have ten more inside the bar.

GET OFF THE BUS

She said "I'll have your drink ready and waiting after you shower Daddy." I wasn't planning on showering till after work but since I did not have to sweat, I was going to shower after we fucked or before bed I laughed to myself jokingly it must be time for bed. Which meant I was about to get my grown man on.

I showered in the guest bedroom. The bathroom was laid out. She has gold and silver assent marble tiles everywhere. The shower was encased in smoked glass. Inside there were two rainfall shower heads. The most impressive thing was that the shower doubled as a sauna.

I got out the shower wiped off the mirror. I wanted to look in my eyes as if to see if this was really going down. I started drying myself. I heard the other shower going in the master bedroom. I hurried up so I could be under the sheets before she dried off. I wanted to present my youthful body as a token for all she had done for me along the years.

I entered the master bedroom with caution not knowing what to expect. "Daphnia" I called out? I felt funny calling her Dolly, so I called out her real grown and sexy name. "I'm in here, Tank". she could still call me by my nickname. She had done that from when I was a kid. I said, "here I come". Damn she was hot, and her body was shaped like an hourglass.

I couldn't wait for her to let me eat her pussy. I didn't think I was the best. Eater said "women love when you kiss and lick their clit". He went on to say "if you want to keep them you have to eat them" that was his motto. I never met a female that I wanted more than the one I was with now.

She was beautiful, smart and she had her own everything. If oral is what she wants, I was going to give her that and much, much more. Looking around at the room she had it decorated nicely with ceiling trim and oak wood furniture. Damn she also had a queen size bed mmm nice and soft. "You comfortable over there?" "Not yet" I replied.

She said "why?" And I sat up just enough laid on my side to see her as she dried off. Wow, she was a lot of woman and I was ready to be all the man she had hoped for. I've been with other girls before, but this was my first real woman. She

141

started to put lotion on her arms and was telling me to go lay back on the pillows.

I did and then she bent over and there It was peeking at me. As if it was saying daddy do what you want to me. I can take it. She glided to the bed and pulled back the covers. As she pulled the covers back, she slowly started to reveal my well-built body. She was amazed and turned on at the same time.

"Wow" she said. Then it popped out and she said there it is. You are built just like your father.

I started to wonder if my dad had fuck Dolly back in the day. She could not have him, so she groomed me until I bloomed into a man. Wow I felt really special and not because of that, hell no!

She had grabbed my dick and started sucking and stroking it at the same time. I thought I was going to lose my damn mind. Then she slowed down. She must have felt it too. She looked me in my eyes and said no I want you to hold that nut for me daddy.

She motioned for me to get off the bed and she laid down. She was on her back then I thought it was my turn to give her oral pleasure. I started at her lips then gave her neck a little attention. While gently rubbing her nipples one at a time.

She began gasping for air whispering in my ear "I've been waiting for this moment ever since your mother said, "she was having a boy". I thought that was a disgusting thing to say but, then again you could probably say. I was fully erected then she said that bullshit.

I guess I was just as bad. I mean I grew up calling her auntie and she would babysit me for Sharon. As I got older, I started getting a hard on every time she was over my house visiting my mom. I used to eavesdrop on them when I thought she was getting ready to leave just to get a smell of her perfume and a hug.

I had to focus back on now. I continued slowly moving down her neck, licking and kissing every inch of her beautiful body. She was soft and smelled of flowers and honey. I reached her clit then I placed both of my lips on top of hers and gently started to lick and kiss them slowly.

At the same time, I inserted two fingers inside of her pussy smoothly gliding them in an in and out motion. I guess I was being rough and not as smooth as I thought I was being. After a few pointers she moved her body back and forth until she squirted all over my arm.

She told me I had done a damn good job. She asked me "if I had cum yet"? She knew I did not cum yet because she had told me to hold it. She reached down and pulled me up to where we were eye to eye. She started kissing me and licking her nut from my face.

I have never seen anything like this before in real life. My dick had gotten even harder. She motioned me to lay down and she rode me until I came. I was turned out and was looking forward to the next time she needed her lawn mowed. I'll be more than ready to help.

In my head I knew that I just had a three-day crash course on how to please a lady.

CHAPTER 12

Laying from Norfolk to Ptown

I was old enough to sign up for the Marine Corps but my mom still had to sign the consent form. My homeboy Dip was going to go in the buddy program with me. After school he came over to my house, I smoked a blunt and after I was done, I said to Dip "let's go and sign up today". We caught the bus to Janaf Shopping Center. I was extremely nervous, and I really didn't know what to expect. Dip was like he knew what was going to happen. His sister was in the Army and she schooled him on what to do when we went to the recruiting office.

We both agreed on one thing and that was, we were going to sign up today in the buddy program. We had to go together and that was ok with me because I trusted him like a brother. Once in the recruiter's office they separated us as if we were just in a murder case or something. One of the marines took Dip to the back office and my recruiter directed me to the office across the hall.

Inside the office I was given a booklet with all the rules and regulations. I was nervous but I knew I had to get from Norfolk, and this was my only out. The recruiter saw my facial expression and said, "that's what Parris Island looked like".

Then he said to me "hold on" and handed me a test.

Before he walked off, he said, This will give us a range of what job you would qualify for in the United States Marine Corps. He looked at the clock and said, "Now you may start.

You will have forty five minutes to complete the first part of the exam".

At a first glance it seemed easy and boy was I In for a surprise. The marine came back in a few moments after I finished. He looked over the papers to make sure it was filled out properly. Once he checked over my test results, he was like ok let's go outside. Now! I was like "what for?" He replied, "Well what was pt. times?" It was your physical training portion of the exam. He said, "I had to run a mile under fifteen minutes, do at least twenty-five pull ups in two minutes and as many pushups as I could do in two minutes." Ok well I'm ready whenever you are ready sir. I was not prepared for this part of the test.

I smoked a blunt before I got here. I was not worried because I had told them I had smoked weed. I received a waiver for smoking bud. But I didn't know I had to do any physical training until we went to boot camp. Well here goes nothing. Yo Dip, I saw him after I ended my run twenty-one minutes "not bad" the recruiter said you can work on your pullups before you leave.

Dip said, "when do you leave for boot camp?" I said, "October 15th I'll be on my way to Parris Island". He went on to say, "you signed up". I said, "yes you asshole you didn't sign up? "He said, no I didn't sign up. I wanted to talk to my mom first before I made my decision. "Why didn't you sign up too Dip?" I asked him angrily". He did not look at me nor answer me.

I asked him more firmly and he looked away and said "no I want to go to the Army like my dad. He said," I tried to tell you but they wouldn't let me in because you were testing". Well shit Dip said, "you could change the branch if you wanted too. He was right, I could change in fact, not only could I have changed the branch I was entering, I could not go into the military altogether. I said, "I can, but I'm not I'm going too. However, I knew this was my only out and I wanted to become a marine.

I told Dip that I was keeping my choice for him to stand by the choice he made. I was mad because who does that, I mean we agreed to go into the Marine Corps, and he reneged on me.

When we got back to the hood, we went straight to K's house. K was excited to hear if we signed up or not. He thought we were going to meet some girls and we didn't want him tailing along being a fifth wheel. Only if he knew Dip had backed out of the deal and went into the Army. I told him "Yo Dip ass changed on me as soon as we got separated in the office".

K said "what?" I replied "yup" and he went on to ask me "are you still keeping your date of entry"? "Yes, I'm keeping the leave date." I wanted to do my training in the winter. I thought there would be less creatures crawling around.

K knew why I really wanted to go in the service. I was hoping that me and Dip went in on the buddy system. I could not make him change his mind, but mine was made up with or without Dip. I needed this for me.

I was forced into a lifestyle I didn't know how to control anymore, and the rules of the game are always changing. You never know who to trust or who is going to try to rob you. It was becoming too much to bear.

It was consuming me from the inside out. The baptism helped me, but the demons still plagued my life daily. I figured that going into the military was my only way out for a fresh independent start. The military would give me the life I wanted to have plus get help for my mom. I could do more for her and my little brother.

My mom's habit was killing my savings and I refused to get a front because if she had gotten to that we all would have been killed. I Thank God my hood status wasn't destroyed, that was why it is best to leave while my hood balance was at zero. I did not owe no one anything.

I tried to contain her wants but it too had grown way out of control. She was smoking about a thousand dollars' worth of coke a day. I need to get us a foundation before the one we have imploded on us. Now you know with or without Dip I must go through with joining the Marine Corps.

K said, "you're not scared of the United States going to war in shit like that". I began to name all the people we knew who had died or was in jail before they were twenty-one. The people I'm talking about some of them though had died before they could see other cities, cultures, and things other than these same old streets in Norfolk.

The people on the list were not the whole reason either, the reason was to get me and my little brother out of this hell hole we called home.

You never knew if a stray bullet would kill you before your dreams or plans in life could even be formed. That was not going to happen to me or my brother. He is going to have the chance that I didn't have in life. I just don't know how far in life I'll get him but I'm going to do my best. I made a promise to my mom. And I intend to make good on it.

If I could mold him correctly then my family would see that I had only meant well. I just had a different way of expressing myself. I felt if you leave me to figure a way out of a problem and I'm dealing with the situation. Don't try to lend me your two cents. I'm the one to tell you and your two cents where you could go.

I didn't have any problem speaking to you in public afterwards either. Junior prom was approaching. I just got my driver's license. I had to go to the damn DMV off of Military Highway. I failed the test at the one on Wedge rd. out Norview by the Murray's steakhouse. They have a Capital Cuts there now. My homeboy is a real true-blue friend. His name is Gotti. He's maybe the manager or if not co-owner or even owner of the building by now. I worked at the other one. He was at Park Place by the Golden Gate Chinese restaurant.

I wanted to know how to use the black dye that all the stars used to darken their edge-ups and working with Gotti turned up my skills with the blackout haircut. I told him "Good looking" on teaching me the skill. Gotti and I met through my younger cousin. He was more like a brother. He's married to Gotti's sister, and they've been together for ten years now. I've been in with the family ever since.

His sister Cherry passed away; may God continue to bless her. She had developed breast cancer and was winning the battle for a couple of years, but soon lost the war. She did well and survived her first round of therapy. We're praying for it also to be her last dose of chemo. She's strong and we all were hoping she would recover quickly. We all loved her deeply and prayed daily for her to keep fighting. "I'm with you mama'" I would say to her.

Now that I got my driver's license I had to go and pick up the rental car. Yes, son I was so excited. I had a rental we all had put in and got a double joined room and partied all night. Me and Tammy had left before the party had ended. We wanted to allow ourselves some time to reflect on the evening's events.

She had looked so pretty in her all-white gown, with her hair freshly permed and conditioned. It looks soft and full. Her hair was blowing in the night breeze as we headed to the private part of Virginia Beach. If you were from the seven cities that was one of the benefits of knowing the area around the private beaches.

These were houses that were only used in the summer times. And at night these places were totally empty. All the rich people left their toys littering all over the beachfront. Jet skis, canoes and gazebos were just crying to be used or explored. Afterwards We would always return the things we played with or rode just as we found them. (Sometimes I hope one of her friends or even if she reads my book and emails me or contacts me this is so weird.)

There would be a lady at the last street where you could park. It was at the end of the strip of the beach located near the army base. She would stand in the window watching us. When we pull up, I'll hit the lights and look around just to make sure no one would just run up on us.

As we were exiting the car heading to the oceanfront there was this lady who had to be in her late forties or early fifties, white and appeared to be lonely. She would watch us make out on the beach while dancing and drinking cocktails.

She would be dressed in an all-white see-through lingerie nightgown. You could see her silhouette as she swayed side to side to the music. I fantasied I heard her say one day "after you drop her off come up and cool your heels". Some nights when I would go out there alone, I had attempted to go and knock on her door. But being black in Virginia Beach in that rich area they would hang my black ass for that shit, for real.

Back at the beach I placed the blanket down between the boat and the volleyball nets. It was away from the walkways but close enough to see the white caps of the incoming waves. We laid there dreaming and talking till the sun rose. As we watched the sun begin to peek over the Atlantic Ocean I would hold her hand wondering if this time would stay the same forever.

I did want to have sex with her out there, but I didn't want to seem too pushy. Plus, she was all dolled up and I didn't want her to ruin her dress by taking it on and off. I drove her home, we kissed and our love for each other seemed to be tighter. After prom, school flew by quickly. Before you knew it, it was the end of the school testing time.

SAT's had started so the days in class got shorter and shorter. The summer was back in and in full swing. My side job with Jay was paying off good. We ran into a little problem out Portsmouth in Lincoln Village. One of our runners kept getting robbed even when Jeff Brown would post up with him. One would see what went down until he had been robbed. The dope would come up missing when he went to serve a pluck.

So, the first chance Jay had he rounded the crew to watch his back. Once we saw who was robbing him. It was time to go and shake down Lincoln Village. Jay, Fred, Rod, Jeff Brown, me, and Saga. Yeah, Saga had to come. Jay told me to cut him off if he didn't.

While Saga was right in the room with all of us present. So, Saga knew that if he said he was not going he would've been cut off right then and there. And the money he owed Jay for what his sister stole from us would be due on the spot.

He didn't have eight thousand dollars to pay him, so he had no choice in the matter. Saga heard what they did to Lil Jay when he had his stash stolen from him. Jay had him duct taped and thrown in a truck. Then drove him around Norfolk in the hot ass sun.

Then they would stop just to interrogate him and beat his ass until he told who he had at the house. Saga didn't want that, I know he went hard but not against four other bad asses like himself null. We went in four different cars. Once we got through the downtown Portsmouth tunnel we regrouped and agreed to park at all four corners of the project.

We all silently moved into place. Once we had everybody out there that night in the center of the front court, we moved in, closing everyone inside of our scopes. Jay came out with the dude that drove the new Xrt. It was like an escort but supped up on steroids.

It was white and burgundy, and it was kitted up with BBS rims and a loud ass sound system. Jay had the pistol grip twelve-gauge pump to his side. Not showing the appearance of him going to kill the dude but just wound him if he tried to run or fight back. Later he said, "just in case of a misfire, always hold your fire arm towards the ground unless you're shooting it."

The dude he had was not the person who was robbing the crew, but Jay figured since he carried the most weight in the park Jay made him responsible for all loses. Then told him in front of everyone that if our peoples get robbed one more time we were coming back, and it won't be to talk next time.

He hit the dude in the head with the butt of the shotgun. Once it was understood we were not taking no more losses, everyone slowly backed out of the Village. Once we were out of sight we ran to the cars and met back up at the trap house in Park Place. We put away all the guns and separated for the night and agreed to meet back at noon the next day. That night while watching the news a shootout happened out the same projects we were at last night.

I reached out to turn up the volume right as the reporter was saying "a man trying to purchase crack cocaine apparently grabbed a handful of the dealer's stash and the guy tried to pull off with the dope." From what I heard the whole park unloaded on that fool and he didn't die. His statement went like this before they took him away, he said "when he had gotten shot his eyeball had popped out of the socket and all he remembered was looking in front of him and in his lap at the same time."

I was shocked because if those guys would have seen us coming, they could have leveled us with no problem... damn. I said to myself "we were lucky." Around that same time, we had started to acquire a lot of cars.

These cars mostly belonged to fiends who couldn't pay their debt owed to the crew. It wasn't just limited to the fiends, if you owed any money your car and your possessions were up for grabs no exceptions. Then if all that didn't cover what you owed it came out your ass.

Other than that Jay was not a gorilla hustler he was a thinker. That is what pulled me to his crew. We had a mechanic named Pea Pop. He was a fiend, but he was a great mechanic. You just had to catch him whenever you can, but we needed a professional person for this position that could be trusted.

Jay found a guy in the country part of Suffolk, he lived way out in the boonies. It was far out but it was worth the trip. The mechanic's wife would whip up the work (whip up the cocaine into crack) while her husband worked on our cars. They had known each other ever since they were like three years old.

I didn't know how true that was but if so, then I respected it. I had admired her from afar. They had six kids and they were mostly grown by then. Only the two youngest kids stayed with them. They had to be in their late thirties or early forties. He looked every bit of his age however, his wife didn't look a day over twenty-four or twenty-five.

She was gorgeous and from the country, so she had a thick waist and beautiful light brown skin. Her nails were nicely manicured and she always smelled good like a fresh morning breeze mmm. I wasn't even trying to get my nose open because it seemed like Jay was falling for her and falling hard.

I pulled him to the side and had to remind him that you can't fuck with her. She and dude been together longer than both of us been alive. He laughed it off and told me that "I was looking too far into the situation, and it was just business." That's how he left it.

Just before that summer had ended Jay came over and gave me some books to read. They were books that had been written by authors that didn't want to receive any acknowledgements for their work. I didn't know why because the books were good books.

I did not understand why until I had opened one of the books. Upon reading some of the contents they spoke about, how to earn cash without using your social security number. I then saw why the author's wanted to stay off the grid. The books taught you how good living off the grid could be.

At the same time, it also showed you how to rebuild your credit. I didn't know what half this shit was about being so young. I just never had a person I grind on the street with to hand me some books to read. I took them and promised to read them all.

I did, I even took notes. The twelfth grade was nice. I had become the vice president of the gentlemen's club. I was happy about that. I had reduced hanging in the streets by about half of what I was doing before. I had received my date to leave for the marines corps.

The date was for October the fifteenth year nineteen-ninety-nine. I was very excited, and my mom told me I could throw a going away party. That was rare in the hood, you either got a birthday party or a coming home from prison party. Not a going away party but I looked at it as being just what it was that I was finally getting the fuck out of Norfolk. Once I got that chance to leave Norfolk I was never coming back! So for me it was going to be a "farewell for good party".

The first day of school I drove. I hid the car because I only had my permit. I had homeroom then went over to the Norfolk vocational school (vo-tech).

My teacher there was the coolest teacher ever. I feel comfortable saying his name, but I won't just in case he's still teaching. One of my classmates now is part of Pharrell's clique. The one and only Mr. Guns. Yes, we used to shoot dice together in the welding class. Our teacher didn't care as long as our work was done.

I loved that class. We were able to chill after your book work was done. You had to do all your shop work in the booths. In the booths you could smoke whatever you had on you. If you had it, you could smoke it. As long as he didn't catch you, it was all good.

He trusted us to use our own judge. The plan was if you did get caught by anyone he said "he wasn't going to lose his job over us he was siding with that person. We didn't blame him." We just use to play dumb. I remember when he caught me and this chick from Lake Taylor high school in the locker room.

I'm going to call her Barbie and she was bad to the bone. She was a red bone like Tammy and thick like Trina from Trick Daddy crew. She was a little shorter than Trina, but her ass and chest had her beat. See I used to suck on her breast all year at lunch time, but she had a boyfriend and I had Tammy so we only mess around at Vo tech.

Barbie had promised all year that she was going to let me fuck her in the locker room. Only at the end of the school year because she did not want to catch any feelings for me. All I wanted to do was cum all over her big ass breast. We stalled out everyone including the instructor. She had knocked on the door and I let her into the locker room. Two taps on the door was the code anytime the door was locked. Only the teachers would yank on it to force it open.

Not knowing that the force from them pulling the door jams the locking mechanisms. Once they realized it was locked, they would simply just walk away to get the key. I was ready for her and we started kissing at first. Lightly locking lips then it got heavy.

I started to undress her which was easy because she had on overalls. I reached down to put my hand around her waist. She encouraged me by grabbing my arm and pulling it further onto her waist. With the other hand I used to undo her hair.

All of a sudden the both of us were breathing heavily. Her full breast was staring right at me as if they were asking me to suck on them. They were big for her size, damn. As I was playing with her hair in the back of my head, I knew that our time was running out.

I turned her around and lifted her to the table. We started to kiss again. As soon as she grabbed for my zipper, someone knocked hard on the door. We hurried up and got dressed. Then a voice yells out "Tee" you in there. I said "no" and we laughed. The instructor had put the key in the door. Right before he was about to enter Barbie left through the side door that led to the hallway.

Then she made a hard right and followed the wall around to the class garage doors. That is how you get back into the classroom without being noticed. When the teacher came inside the locker room he was like "what in the hell you were doing in here by yourself?" I said "thinking" he gave me a puzzled look and said, "get ready for class".

Inside the class we promised to pick up from where we had left off, but thanks to Tammy she made sure that had never gone down. Even though I was hardly in school. I still had managed to win two things from my graduating class. I was voted best dressed for that school year. (I won it my junior year too, but it had to be awarded to a senior) as well as most likely to succeed.

That year I was supposed to escort the prettiest valedictorian I ever saw but my childhood friend didn't have a date for her junior prom. She was junior prom queen. I could not let her go alone. So instead of going to my home I went to her affair as her escort.

In the school yearbook they had another dude stand in for me with her. By attending Shema's prom, I never had a chance to apologize to the girl I was to escort to our prom for standing her up.

I hope you forgave me for that mama, but a friend needed me, and I went to her aide. Me and my homie K got our pictures in the yearbook. I didn't even know the school press caught me about to skip. The school photographer came up to me and was like "did you mind posing for the yearbook?" Before I knew it, K had come out of nowhere and was like "cheese". I was happy I won best dressed and most likely to succeed.

Though looking back on my graduation from the sixth grade and hearing what my teacher had told my mom about how my clothes were too tight. I wish she could see me now. It really felt good setting a goal for myself and accomplishing it.

I did not have a graduation party. I was focused more on my going away party.

I want my party to be talked about every time my name comes up. This was going to be the last time I see these people for a long time. I had my future planned out. I'm going into the service and then I'm going back to school. Work at the shipyard as a part time welder. That was all I could think about in my head.

Sweet, I had tunnel vision at the helm of my direction. The books that Jay gave me always talked about having good credit and living the American dream. So, if I start off with good credit, I would not have to worry about hustling anymore just working.

October was here I reported to Richmond maps center for a full exam. After being cleared all one hundred of us were bagged, tagged, and shipped to Parris Island boot camp for the United States marine corps.

CHAPTER 13

Parris Island up

While standing in line waiting to get my head shaved, I still couldn't believe I'm in the Marine Corps. It was scary when they brought us here in the middle of the night. They shoved us all on the bus and then off the bus. Then in a classroom then out the classroom. All of us were confused on what to do next.

On top of all the confusion they were still yelling and throwing shit at us the whole time. It was wild and seemed dysfunctional. By the morning they got us up at four thirty in the morning. It was hell but fun and educational. Most importantly it was a way out the hood and for some reason being here had given me a piece of mind.

Now If I had got shot and died my mom would have helped to bury me. If I did not die at least, I'll get a benefit. If you didn't know you would not receive a check selling drugs. The rest would have to live on welfare. I had my little brother. I was raised up on the system that's what I didn't want to repeat in my life.

The next day we were separated into platoons. I was moved to the Iron Mike battalion. That shit was hell. All the drill instructors did was fuck you up. If you didn't catch on to the routines you got your ass whipped. This battalion was located on the back portion of Paris Island.

The brass (officers) did not come out here unless it was time for inspection. The drill instructors had full control of this part of the island. The brass would not know what happened to you until you ended up in the medical unit.

One day still in the same first week of training we had a record-breaking mosquito hatching. The drill instructors made us stand in attention while the mosquitos feasted on our flesh. As a recruit you were trained not to move as an individual but as a unit. What I am saying is you were not allowed to scratch or swat at the insects.

The drill instructors said "you had to eat to survive, so did the insects. If you were caught killing a sand flea or whatever bug you had to bury the damn thing. After standing in attention for an hour and a half trying not to move. We had to do a five-mile run.

I tried to sneak a quick wipe off my leg. We just stopped running. I thought no one was looking. The drill instructors went off on me. They had acted as if I was disturbing a hornets nest. They were yelling, spitting and screaming everything they could to provoke me to get mad. I wanted to swing on one of them, but I wasn't going to give them that satisfaction. I saw the beating they had put on another recruit, and it wasn't pretty.

He had got his ass whipped then he was charged for assaulting a government employee. His jail time was longer than the time it would have had to do to graduate. so, I was no dummy. I let them yell all they wanted.

All the drill instructors ran over to where I was standing. Every one of them started to yell at me to say "who gave me the right to kill gods creatures"? I tried to speak but another one of them would ask me another question. Then my senior drill instructor came over. The wind was blowing strong. Well, his cover flew off and hit the ground. Now here is where I fucked up. I went to reach for his cover, and he went ballistic.

That move there plus dropping out of the platoon run I was recycled. As they escorted me to the physical conditioning platoon or for short pork chop platoon. I was glad to get a break from all this madness. Inside pcp everyone walked around and acted like they were Marine's already.

But in all actuality, they had to meet requirements to leave this part of the training plus continue boot camp training as well. Once I heard that bull shit, I hurried up and changed my tune. I got my ass in gear. After they changed my diet and a lot of hard work, I was released from the pork chop platoon.

I ended up in the first battalion. This was even better because it was located in the front of Parris Island. It was right across from the graduation deck. It inspired me watching the other recruits graduate. Seeing them gave me a reason to work harder. Now I know people did make it off this damn Island.

Training was hard and vigorous but at the end of the day you slept well. It felt strange in the start not hearing guns or police cars and fiends in the hallway getting high. Gods know what else, but I felt deep inside I left my mom and brother behind. No, I told myself I was helping them.

By helping me first I was helping them. As long as I kept telling myself that it made me rest a whole lot better. During the rifle range we all were eager to shoot our rifles. Our group was up next week. I was so happy to show off my shooting skills that I learned in the hood.

They taught us how to fire our weapons from day one. That's all we really did in between drills. Plus, studying rifle knowledge information on how to keep them functional. As we sat down facing the targets, we had instruction to fire. I had let off maybe twenty five out of the fifty rounds. We were given four mags worth starting off. Then the announcement came over the loudspeakers" Lock and unload.

The instructors shouted switch to the prone position. Once again, we were allowed to shoot until the timer stopped. Once again, we were told to lock and unload. The last position was to shoot the target while kneeling when we were told to stop, lock and unload.

I kept firing until the clip was empty. All the instructors ran to me and chewed me out. Back at the barracks the line sergeant came to me and informed me that one of two things would happen to me because of me continuing to fire my weapon. The first was to be court martialed in front of the general or secondly, he said "we can hold court here and now, your choice".

I said "sir" and he continued to say, "So which way do you want to handle the matter?" It didn't take long for me to decide my fate. I was willing to receive the punishment of our line sergeant then go before the Islands commander, and I really didn't want to be court martialed because I heard how those court proceedings turn out.

The accused never wins. If they have you in custody then you're going to jail and that is the bottom line. I've never seen anything good come from those proceedings. At least in a week or two I'll heal from my wounds, but in military jail I'll be there for twenty years.

I witnessed an ass whipping by those drill instructors and it was not pretty let me tell you. When I first got to the new command post there was a recruit in our platoon that got court martialed. He wanted out of the corps, so he figured that if he jumped out of the 2nd story window of our barracks he would break all his limbs. Thinking he wouldn't have to finish boot camp and he would be sent back home. Boy was he wrong... listen to this here. They sent him to the infirmary. Once both of his legs and arms had healed, he was court martialed. Then sent to Fort Levin Worth to serve his time.

Now back to my punishment. The sergeant looked at me and said, "well which one will it be?" He asked again. In a deeper more impatient manner, I said "aloud this recruit would rather hold court here sir". He told me to lock my body (that meant to stand at attention). Once I had locked my body, he hit me in the jaw once for each round I fired. It totaled fifteen punches in all. My jaw was hurting and slightly swollen.

The hits weren't a windmill of punches because they weren't allowed to hit us at all. So, when they did hit us, they did it in a way as not to leave bruises. They had always made sure that the punished did not get one mark, but the hits were still effective nonetheless. I joined the Marine Corps for the brotherhood. The rifle range sergeant had me feel as If I made the right choice.

After the rifle range we were halfway through boot camp. Things started to look better for us as the next fine group of young Marines. They said if you can complete Basic Training here in the corps you can do anything in life. I surely hope so because graduation is just around the corner.

I wanted to finish in the top half of the platoon. I wasn't too strong a runner and the last run before graduation was this Saturday. I was First squad leader until I fractured the tubular and fibula bones in both legs.

On Parris Island all we did was train, exercise, run and read. There really wasn't anything else to do there but hurry up and wait. I finished the run-in with a good time, and I was truly proud of myself. In a few more days I'll be off this forsaken Island and good riddance. My mom, my dad's mom and my mean ass aunt Racheal came along to my graduation ceremony.

The day before the graduation we were finally allowed to walk the Island. It was beautiful looking from someone soon to be a graduate. But from the eyes of a recruit, it was a hellish nightmare. I was so happy to wake up and then say a prayer before retiring back to sleep.

To a newcomer jumping off the bus onto those yellow footprints. Yes, looking back on it all now and knowing what to expect and as crazy as it sounds, I would love to do it all over again. After the speeches they gave us a big welcome as United States Marines my mom ran to me and jumped into my arms.

I was happy to be alive and to have again given my mother something to be happy and proud of her son. The drill instructor who had secretly mentored me and kept my head in the game had seen me and my mom. He came over and introduced himself as drill instructor sergeant Bruno. I introduced my mom to him. They shook hands and said hi to one another.

He went on to tell her all the ups and downs I had as a recruit and how proud of me he was for sticking out with becoming a Marine. He welcomed me into the corps but not like he did before by throwing garbage cans and calling my mother a fat bitch.

It was funny to me when he talked about my mom to get me mad. They tried to take my head out of the game, but it didn't work because I knew he didn't know my mom for one and she wasn't fat. So from then on, I knew it was a mind game they played with the recruits to weed out the weak. This tactic had worked on most of the recruits. It worked too good.

We started with about one hundred and twenty people and we graduated with around sixty or seventy people. So, it works well. He said, "Now that was my job, so it was business, nothing personal." Now I extended my hand to him as a Marine and that was the happiest day of my life.

We had a week to report to North Carolina at camp devil dog. I didn't worry about that at the moment, it's been a long six months and I wanted some fried chicken and some pussy. Tammy was waiting at my mom's house and every stop we came to I called her to make sure she didn't leave.

It was January and it was cold, but I wanted to see her before she left. I was hoping to convince her to stay the night with me. My mom was right, she said, "when I joined, we were going to go to war". I had hoped she would not be right but while in boot camp all the training we received was for bio and chemical warfare. She was right we were going to war to save Kuwait.

President Bush (the father) had reactivated so many reserve military personnel they gave people the option to go full-time or go reserve while in boot camp. I chose to go to the reserves. I had no plans on going to war at seventeen. I'll stay and fight right here at home if they make it this far.

Tammy and I sat down and talked; I had gotten so drunk we didn't even have sex. She left early the next morning. She wanted to beat her mom home from work so we agreed to meet up later for dinner.

The next day my mom had me touring the whole city of Norfolk and I was getting tired. We only had a week off and that didn't include travel time so really, I had two- or three days tops before I had to report back to duty. I didn't want to spend the remainder of my time in the car with my mom visiting relatives. All I wanted to do was get some rest and lay up with my girl. That was all I wanted to do.

My mom had asked, "if we could make one more stop?" She wanted my great granny to see me in my uniform. I was gamed because I loved her just as if she was my grandmother. She had raised me too. The last place before I got to see my baby, we stopped for gas at the seven eleven on Ballantine and Princess Anne rd.

The manager there at the time was known to start fights in the store with people, especially Marines. He never gave me a problem, it just so happened that night everything changed. Let me tell you I'm at the pump and I'm waiting for my mom to pay the cashier for the gas. So, we can go to my great grandma's house.

After about fifteen minutes or so Sharon still had not come out of the store. I peeked around the gas pump to see if I could see her, but she was out of my view. Well as I'm standing their bend over the gas pump on the intercom, I hear white noise then I hear someone say, "look you drunk crackhead bitch you already owe me for gas so together with the beer you owe me twenty three dollars".

I stepped back from the pump to scan the store. I wanted to see if there were any other people inside shopping. I hoped that he had not been referring to my mom. After I noticed that she in fact was the only person in the store other than the manager I was pissed. I removed the top to my dress blues and walked inside the store.

I asked the cashier "why was he talking to that lady in that manner?" Like he must not see me drive up with her. He said, "this drunk bitch pumped some gas and tried to act like she just pulled up and never got gas". Well, I said "I'm with that drunk bitch and she did not fucking pump no gas.

She came straight into the store to get the beer before twelve o'clock. I stayed at the pump while she went in to pay. He looked at her then looked back at me then said, "no that bitch" and before he could finish his sentence. I took the six pack of blue bull beer she had on the counter, and I threw it at the ice cream and frozen food glass case, and it shattered the two glass doors.

Then I told him "That drunk crackhead bitch was my mother" and asked if he wanted her to pay him anything to come and get it from me. He did not want to come from behind the register. In fact, he refused to come, then as I was talking to him a security guard came out from where the atm used to be and grabbed me up into a full nelson.

I didn't even know anyone else was in the store but that didn't matter. As soon as the guard had snatched me up then the manager came from behind the counter. He rushed towards me and as he was approaching me, he raised his fist to punch me in the face. I could not move, the guard was about six nine and he had my feet off the ground.

I was kicking my legs trying to get some leverage so I could break free. Then as the manager got closer, he swung. Before he could connect his jab, my mom went to catch the blunt end of the force from his swing. I kicked her out the way and he caught me square in the mouth. The impact was so hard that my tooth went through my bottom lip and chipped on his ring.

I had a hole in my lip for a month. I said I invented the piercing under the bottom lip first. But I wasn't tribal or gay not that I have anything wrong with any of them I'm just being me. I let the hole heal up and didn't try to wear a ring. The security guard still would not release me. So, I didn't struggle anymore by trying to loosen his hold. I was mad.

I grabbed a handful of his balls and as soon as he let me go, I turned around and kneed him again in the nuts and punched him dead in the nose as he went down. The manager tried to run back behind the counter, but I pushed the cash register onto the floor, and it had blocked him from retreating.

I went to the manager, and we traded blows and I caught him a couple times with my elbow linked to my blow. He could not handle that much impact repeatedly. He retreated to the back of the store and called the police. Norfolk's finest arrived on the scene. They separated us and once they had me outside the officer asked me "when did I graduate from the corps?" I had told him "Two days ago".

His partner asked me "did I pass with honors?" I said, "no" then I looked at him confused and he said, "Did you get your dress blues for free?" or "Did you have to pay for them?" I said, "everyone paid for their uniforms as far as I knew". Oh, he said "well when we graduated you either paid for your uniform or they were given to you for graduating with honors.

You received everything else for free. I said, "all that has changed is you get a debit card and everything you did but chow was taken out of your final pay". When you left the Island, they put your last pay on the card no more checks. They were impressed that I was a squad leader.

After a few more questions they told me "I had to go to court and that the manager had a history of harassing marines whenever they visited this seven eleven location. Anyone else he felt that he can take advantage of without having anyone lashing back at him. But tonight "I think he knows it was not the night for his bullshit. He came across a true-blue marine.

Ok have a good night devil dog". Kool the brotherhood do work. I had turned to my mom and said, "you know it's too late to go and see grandma tonight." She replied "I know baby. She then began to cry. I didn't want this Tee. I just wanted to show your grandmama how proud I was of you.

Plus show her I did a good job raising you." I wiped off her tears and told her "Not to worry about anything. And that I know how good of a job she has done as a mom" she smiled. To myself I thought I'd show her, and she could then see how much I loved her when I bought her a new house.

She smiled, she knew as a little kid I had always told her I was going to buy her a house. She removed a handkerchief that I had inside of my dress blue jacket and wiped away her tears. I then kissed her on her forehead. I said to Sharon "I love you mom, let's go home". We got in the car I drove, and she looked at me and said, "baby you know we still don't have any gas".

I know mama I wanted to say "I told her I didn't want to go out at all, but I didn't want her to feel any worse than she had already felt. And this is what happened for her going against my wishes, but I knew she meant well. She was all I have in this world and I will never let anyone, or thing happen to her ever.

One of us had to be the strong one. We went to court before I had to return back to mct (marine combat training).

This was just a preliminary hearing to allow the judge to hear both sides. And to see if there was any reason to either enforce the charges or to drop them after he heard both of the stories.

He dismissed the charges on both sides but he told my mom off the record to file a lawsuit against him and the Seven Eleven Corporation because they didn't train or allow the managers to verbally or physically attack the stores patrons (my mother had to handle the lawyer and to get in the motion because I had to return back to training. If not, I would have been considered awol.

They said "no exceptions" on our behalf. (However, her being a crack addict she never even got a lawyer to file the suit. The statute of limitation had run out and forever left us again without any future endeavors). We thanked the judge and left the courtroom. And as we walked to the car I "said ma did you hear the judge we can sue them".

She said, "yeah I heard him". I said "we can own that damn store. She wasn't too happy about what had happened that night and she has been trying to put it behind her ever since. I hoped she would follow through with this shit, it could really help us as a family. I know she's going to fuck this up too, watch I said to myself.

I had explained the situation to my first sergeant and frankly he didn't give a shit a war was coming and a lot of the enlisted soldiers weren't reporting to duty. They were not playing when it came to reporting for duty. Going awol was a very serious charge that goes for anyone, I mean anyone not showing up for duty.

Whoever didn't show they were slapped with abandonment charges that carried a fine, jail time and a dishonorable discharge. I finally got a line to the first sergeant, and I wasn't allotted any more time. I had to report back asap. I was mad not to be home to push her to get a lawyer. She had to follow up on filing a lawsuit against the Seven eleven Corporation.

Once at camp devil dog the combat training was really reinforcement of what we had already learned in boot camp. We just had used more live ammo and weren't treated like we were kids. The training was only for thirty days. Once arriving at camp we all were separated again into platoons. They were really rushing us because as we were entering into our third week of schooling.

President Bush Sr. had recalled damn near the whole marine reserve back to full duty. There were so many marines there at one time. They started to send people back to their home bases to replenish the ones who were called to serve full time.

So basically, he called the reserve back to full service and had the new reserve to replace the old marines on the frontline. With the last week coming fast I wanted to call home and ask my mom did she find someone yet to handle the case for us. She said "yes" and she paused as if she wanted to say something else about the case, but she had changed the subject asking "when will I be home again"?

She said she missed me so much. I know she didn't file anything. I just had a bad feeling about the whole situation. She knew that when she'd ask me stuff like that it had made me blush with anger. I was not in the mood for that now. I wanted to know what was going on with the lawsuit. She said, "we'll have fun baby and I'll see you soon".

CHAPTER 14

Back to the Hood

Returning home always makes me feel like I have to adjust to my surroundings. Sharon doesn't want to be rich, she didn't even call a lawyer. If she wanted some crack, she could find that but couldn't find a lawyer. That's some bullshit man. Slim with the jag from down the street knows I'm back home. I'll holla at him later. I may need him to front me an ounce to get back on my feet.

The fourth of July was coming up soon, my first holiday since I became a marine. I've been away for a while, but he will still throw work at me if I need any. From what he has been telling me he had slowed down too. Ever since I went into boot camp.

I had seen Jay and asked him about "the chick who was married to ol boy who fixed our cars." He said "he wasn't seeing her anymore". But she was in his car the last time he told me to come through to see him. He would never be exactly where he would say to meet him. So then at that moment, when he told me exactly where he was it did not make any sense to me. That was not like Jay.

Well apparently, the lady's husband caught Jay with his wife and chased them to a dead end. (It was Westminster Avenue in Norfolk behind Norfolk State University). Once he spotted Jay and his wife he crashed into Jay's car. He then got out and shot Jay in the head four times and five times in the chest. He then shot his wife in the head three times and twice in the chest.

The only way they caught that fool is because after all the shooting he was walking over the Campostella Bridge with a broken leg. He was lucky he did get caught because he had bounties on his head all the way From New York City. After that Rod had caught a murder charge he was sentenced to ten years.

From what I heard the charges came from an innocent by standard being shot in the gun fight. It was a little girl, but she didn't die. The same judge was not having that shit. And if I'm not mistaken the charges from the original shoot out where the dude he was shooting at got killed were dropped.

See in Norfolk if the police thought you were in the game, then you chose your own fate. However, the little girl had nothing to do with that and that's why he had received the time for shooting her. The oldest brother Porky was killed trying to sell some fake weight in coke. The marks had come back to the hood and blasted that ass.

His death was the third that had links to our crew. Then Ro was charged with murder as well. He had just got his AK-forty seven. That afternoon some Jamaican dude was coming up the wrong side of the street. Ro nor dude refused to give the right of way. Well, they had exchanged words and Ro being the hot head he was, he shot the Jamaican and he died on the scene.

Now I know the corps saved my life or saved me from doing life either way I'm happy. Now that the holiday was here, I wanted to be extra careful. because the last four murders of the summer has either been someone I knew, or they was the one who did the killing. I just didn't need to join them either way. But in Norfolk you will always have someone trying you or wanting to be you.

None of the above was healthy, not living in the hood anyway. I missed the ride to go with my aunt where the rest of the family was attending the cookout.

So, I had decided that I was going to stay home and get a grip on things. Our connect Jay was dead and we were all falling off one by one. I was preparing to go sit outside to smell the food that the neighbors were cooking next door on their grill. I didn't want them to see me, so I sat near the stairs by the sidewalk.

I know if they see me looking, they'll invite me over. They usually did not do things like invite non-family over. I didn't blame them for that it was a lot of fucked up people out here. They have known me for so long that they trusted me not to be disrespectful.

They fucked with me from time to time especially during holidays. What is it that people get all extra friendly one or two days out of the year? It's like we did not know you were a dickhead all year round, so I just wave and keep on walking. And that's how I treated them.

They had their own little world however complex it was, and I did not care to learn the inner workings of their family. I had complexities in my family that I'm dealing with already. It was overwhelming enough. My cousin called and asked if I wanted to go to his brother's house for the Fourth of July cookout. I wasn't in the mood, and it was already around two in the afternoon. I had a lot of shit on my mind and partying was far from being on top.

He was like "I'll come and get you" and then. he hung up the phone. I knew what that meant. He knew if he would have stayed on the phone any longer, I would have lied to him and told him I had plans. Which I could have gone to Tammy's house or the bitch out Norview house. I was not in the right mind to be around a hugging and kissing atmosphere.

My mind was on filling these orders I was getting since the other members were gone. However, with limited supply of coke it was sickening to see all that money coming to my pager. I can't get all of it. This was some bullshit. I heard a loud ass car pull up. It had to be Lil C. "Come in" I shouted, "Yo I'm almost done" I said. He sat on my bed and started to look at my shoes. I had a sick shoe game from air maxes to top sides.

I told him don't even try it and stay out of my closet too. When he came around, he always acted as if someone owed him something. But he won't offer anything he has. We all have one of them in the family. He asked if he could bring this, he picked up my nine mm. I said, "hell no you don't like to return shit".

Fuck no and put it back in its box. He said "we're going to the park Tee you know it's always some bullshit popping off out there." He was right, it's always something jumping off out there, but his brother Savage was crazy.

Let me tell you he went into the army after high school. Once there the drill sergeant said some fucked up shit to Savage. He went berserk on the whole command and ever since then he was labeled insane by the state. Wait, it don't stop there when he came home, he started to offer his services to local kingpins as their bodyguard. So, I did not feel we needed a gun.

Besides the last time someone out the View tried to set Savage up to get gunned down. One time was when he went into the apartment to see the guy that owed him money. A person jumped from behind the door and shot him in the head. He turned around and chased the guy down. Savage got on top of him, he shot Savage again in the side. Savage still beat the shit out of dude and won.

Let's just say he survived twice from being shot in the head and lived to talk about both shootings. Now you see why I felt confident that whatever came we could handle it with no problems.

Then I said to Lil C "did not you just come from out Roberts Park"? "Yeah" he answered. I then said, "Lil C you have been out there all day long and now because you see my guns, we need to bring one with us huh?" Well, I said "you don't need any of mine guns, so the answer is still no"!

He was mad but what was he going to do? Nothing. However, I grew up out that park. It was rough but there were a few people out there where if shit got to that point, shit would get dealt with fast.

I wouldn't say that my back up people were workers because I did not front them any coke. They bought everything they got from me. Let's just say they were independent contractors. Workers did not buy drugs and hustle for themselves. That makes a difference between the two groups.

I liked dealing with them because their money stayed straight. No shorts, not like this fool who is with me now. He's family and all they did was rip me off. I know you might know him, but I tried so hard to help this motherfucker. Here is a short story real fast.

I gave him a hundred sixteenths to hold for me. Just to hold them and I was to come back re-up as needed. While I was out on the block, he took it upon himself to go to the bootlegger's house by Booker T. Washington high school. Well after I ran out of dope I went to him at the car.

My car was not parked outside where he was supposed to be waiting. I knew I was at the right house. I couldn't find him and he would not call me back from my pages. That was the first mistake because I had sales and I had missed all that cake.

Since he wouldn't call me, I had a bad feeling something may be wrong. So, I went and tracked him down to all the known hang outs in the area. I lucked up and found a chick that saw him going into a bootleggers house on VA beach Blvd.

Once I found him, I cussed him out. He did not care about none of the money he made me miss. I was heated with him and I wanted to fight. I just said "man give me my shit. When I grabbed the bag from him it was light as hell.

I asked, "Lil C what the fuck is this"? He said, "that's what you gave me minus a couple twenties". "A couple of twenties" I said. He looked at me puzzled. "Twenties" I had repeated and told him "They were not twenties in that damn bag! They were all eighty dollars bags apiece". He turned white and then said, "they told me they were twenties". I was mad as hell now for real. I demanded him to tell me who had told him that bull shit. He pointed upstairs to the bedroom.

I said, "take me to them". He was trying to explain I was not trying to hear that shit. Someone owed me money and I wanted it now. At the top of the stairs, we turned right, and he went into the last room on the left. He introduced me to two pretty young ladies, and it was a third one in the restroom.

When she came out, she said "hi". I looked at her with low eyes and said "hi". Well, the older of the three reached her hand out. then said, "it's nice to meet you. Was that your product?" I said, "yeah, it was and you knew that they wasn't twenties?"

She said, "yes but I told him we would make it worth his while" so he did get paid for that coke baby". They were all redbones thick as hell half-dressed and looking like they were ready for round two. I had done the math in my head and figured they had smoked up a grand worth of work.

They owed me for that shit! I said, "how did you pay him?" Because I haven't seen not one dime. Lil C looked at the mom and turned to me and said "Cuz do not act like that I told you I will pay you back". I heard him but little did he know I already charged him for that bill it was their turn to pay. The mother asked, "which one did I want first"?

I looked at Lil C and told him "Cuz you can wait downstairs this is going to be awhile. The older one looked as if I was joking, and she was like "all of the coke he gave them was gone they sold some and did up the rest" and if I wanted the something Lil C had that I would have to give them something to get in the mood with.

I agreed and handed her one of the bags. They had it going on too. The mother would lead the marks to the house promising him sex but when they would arrive to the house, he would see three and the price has now tripled. To the marks it didn't matter because all three was down to party. That's when he goes broke.

I saw the trap but unfortunately for me the door had already been opened. I saw right through their little scheme. I just wanted some money from all three of them. Yes, my eyes might have been as big as my wallet, but I wasn't going to EAT NOT ONE OF THEM BITCHES! The mother said "we could all party but pay us before we get started. I know she didn't want to share with her daughters, so I gave them a bag to split.

I was hesitant at first but then I thought if he gave them twelve bags, three bags each. Ok now I timed that times twenty it came out two hundred and forty dollars. Two can play this game. Lace went downstairs and I showered with her daughters first. Once we all got out the shower. We went straight into the bedroom.

I smoked some skunk weed and they had their coke. We partied and drank all night. Their mom came back upstairs she walked in on me fucking her daughter. She came over to the bed and grabbed my dick whenever she could get a chance. After their mom was catching her breath,

I started talking to one of the twins. While the other one got a cloth then began to suck me off. After I bust in her mouth she got up and went to get us something to eat. Man, I had a ball. Afterwards on the way out she asked me "if I thought it was worth the money". I said "yes," it indeed was worth every penny.

It was a dream come true: a set of twins and the mom shit. I did not blame Lil C anymore but however the mother wasn't too happy with me because I only gave her eighty dollars' worth of coke. She told me to hold on "that this was not what he paid them earlier". I said, "hold on ma you told him they were twenties right"? She said "well yes" trying to see where I was going with what I was saying.

Well then I said "I gave up what you originally asked for from him he was the fool not me. "It's my shit don't you think I know what they're worth?" She looked at me and smiled. She asked me "did I have a girlfriend?" Even though she was pretty as hell, and she had the body of a twenty-year-old I don't get down like that ma. Maybe another day and time but not now.

I told her "I got a girl". She smiled and said, "come back and see me sometime" and she pulled me close and said, "Next time come by yourself and it'll be free.. all three of us". I looked her in her eyes and said, "you got that ma" and then we left.

After that I should have known not to hang out with him anymore but here we go I said, "I'm ready yo let's go!" On the way out I asked him if we had to pick up anything for the cookout? He said no, everything is there already so we're good. We arrived while the sun was setting. It was not hot, but you still knew it was a July summer day.

I had worn this new blue Polo short set with the shoes to match my outfit. I felt a little overly dressed because the other guests had on new outfits as well however, it was not as expensive. So, they were about to play football. Clearly I wasn't dressed for that, so I stayed in the house watching all the sports that were showcased for that holiday.

Everyone came in the house cussing and arguing about why they were bringing the cookout in doors. I took my attention off the television and focused on the conversation between the other guests. Something had happened to someone's son. He had gone to the store and as he was returning, he got jumped for the change.

His mother took him to the hospital only to find out his thumb was broken. The boys who did it came back by the house taunting the other kids until the parents left the cookout. Well all hell was about to break loose.

See the dude Moet and Savage use to run together. Savage was Moet's bodyguard. When Mo got killed Savage went on a rampage. He already had a chip on his shoulder. If you were family or not, if he thought you disrespected him you paid dearly. Some had even paid with their lives.

After that happened to his homeboy, he got sent away to the insane asylum in Richmond. He just came home on the fourth of July like I had. The party was like his home coming party as well as a holiday celebration. You could tell Savage didn't want to get all gassed up over the small incident, so he told everyone to bring the party inside to finish the fun and games.

Well, it was getting late, and everyone left the house but Savage, his old lady and their three kids, me and his brother Lil C. Savage was upstairs helping his old lady with the kids putting them to bed. His girl was pregnant, so she needed his help getting them in and out the tub and changing them into their night clothes. Their children were all still toddlers.

Me and his brother Lil C were in the front room. Now listen closely. Remember I said "as long as I can start off life with no bills and have good credit I'm not going to hustle ever again." Well here's where that dream all goes south. I was sitting on the sofa ten feet from the front door drunk off vodka.

I was fading in and out of conciseness and Lil C was five feet from me sitting in the recliner. We were watching the news waiting for Savage to come down and have one last drink with us before we left for the night. Then something told me to sit back. As soon as I pushed my back into the sofa (luckily it was one of those old fashion sofas that had wings that were upholstered to the arms and was reinforced with wood) bullets flew past my face.

The wings of the sofa protected me and silhouetted me from the shooters. Once I felt they had stopped shooting I looked up and they had started again. For a split second I saw five different red dots at the door.

Me just coming out of marine combat training I realized it was five people or five guns being shot at us at the same time. Again, the shooting had stopped. I Immediately jumped up and removed the long nose thirty-eight Taurus Lil C had brought with him and returned fire. I was glad for once he did not listen to me.

By the time the gun had emptied Savage had run down the stairs. He jumped over the sofa all in one motion he slammed the front door on his way down to stop the bullets. There was a loud boom then he hurried to secure the lock. He was like superman or a hero. I was relieved to see that everyone upstairs was ok.

That was the only reason I had returned fire. See I did not and probably will never care about dying. However, there were children upstairs and I was not going to die and let whoever was shooting at us get past me to those kids. It would have been over my dead body. I had to reload so as soon as he locked the door it gave me a chance to yell to Lil C to throw me the speed loaders. I had hollow points and dumb dumbs in every other chamber.

I looked at Lil C and said "you ok" he said "yeah man shit." He was in the chair but somehow, he had answered me from behind the television fifteen feet from where he was first sitting. Savage was like "what was that all about"? Before I could respond I had reloaded my gun and opened the door.

I ran two both corners and the building. I did not see no one outside, so I turned around and went back to the apartment. As I started telling Savage what happened, I felt like I was sweating from all over my body.

I had figured it was because I had just run around outside. It had to be from all the excitement my adrenaline levels were depleting. I then wiped my forehead and there was no sweat that was strange I had thought to myself. All that running and I'm not sweating. I felt like the sweat was dripping down my shirt now and my back felt sticky.

I felt Like I had jumped in a swimming pool fully dressed. I went to wipe my back. I looked at my hand to see how wet the napkin became. That's when I realized I had been shot. The napkin was not just wet but sticky too and stained red with dark blood.

I did not pay any attention to it at first because there wasn't any pain, and I didn't feel any exit wound, so I figured I had just gotten grazed by the bullet.

Then Savage said "Yo Tee turn around you've been shot. I told him it had to be a graze. He replied, "Tee it's a whole in your back man and you're losing blood fast". From there I cannot remember anything but bits and pieces of what had happened that holiday night. Things had started getting blurry, but I could hear Savage tell Lil C to take me to the end house.

He said "call the ambulance for Tee and he'll be over after he locked his house up and checked on his kids". Lil C helped me to my feet then we walked over to the neighbor's house. She let us in while she had made a call to 911. She told Lil C to "lock the door after we left, and she went upstairs where it was safe.

Lil C had sat me on the love seat in front of the downstairs window. He then went to lock the back door. As soon as his neighbor went back upstairs Lil C was coming from the kitchen back to where he sat me.

He was talking to me asking "If I saw who was shooting at us" and right as I started to try and form the words in my head to answer his question. Trying to ensure I did not sound as if I was not mumbling. I lifted my head up to respond and in the corner of my left eye I felt someone looking through the window at me.

As soon as I started to turn around to see if anyone was at the window a dude raised his arm and swung his gun at the window. The gun slammed into the window shattering it all over me and the love seat. I fell immediately to the floor then rolled as close as I could up against the front of the love seat.

Lil C had tried to run from the kitchen to the living room. As he came in view of the front room window there were three shots. After the shots died down. All you heard was motherfucker. He shot me. He had got Lil C too.

Damn where the hell is Savage ass at, I said to myself. Then we heard somebody say, "put the gun down" in a loud but forceful voice. I sighed a sound of relief and then I heard POW, POW, POW, POW, POW. I was in a state of shock. Why? You may ask. Because I didn't know if that was the shooter or Savage?

I was like "oh shit" and I told myself if it was the shooter I was going to lay here and pretend to be dead. That would have been easy. I had already felt dead anyway. I said, "is that nigga about to come in here now?" Savage had my gun and all I had was a pocket full of bullets.

Damn, well I had no choice but to play dead if he came inside here. I laid perfectly still and waited for a sign that everything was clear. While lying there I was still coming in and out of conciseness. At one time I thought I heard Jay talking to me from the dead.

He was "telling me to just let go and it was better on this side. It felt bright and warm. I got curious to find out if that had in fact been Jay. In fact, I wanted to see if he was in heaven. No homo I had really missed my homeboy and I was tired with my hopes of getting out the hood. All my dreams I had were now lost. I at the time wanted to go wherever the voice was calling from, especially if he was with God.

However, the closer I got to his voice the more I looked around and I couldn't see him. Pausing for a second to get my bearings another voice came to me. This one was warm as well, but it had told me that if the body dies so does the spirit.

That had taken me back to a verse I had read in the bible. It read that it was better to have a living dog than a dead lion. Because the dog can protect you now, but the dead lion cannot do anything.

His spirit has moved on. Once I realized that voice couldn't be Jay's voice I came too. In the back of an ambulance. To this day I have always wondered what would have happened if I would have gone to the other side. Like if I had followed my best friend's voice. "Would I have woken up?"

I saw Savage in the back of the police car. Lil C was in the back of the other ambulance. The E.M.T guys had me strapped down to the inside of the ambulance and said to the driver "let's go."

As we were pulling off, I saw that I was naked. To myself I was like "this was great my first day wearing my brand new outfit and I got shot". I laid down for the rest of the ride to the hospital. Damn they had cut my clothes off to get me undressed. "Why didn't I wake up to stop them?" I am glad I had on clean underwear.

I dropped my head back down. Whatever they gave me for the pain was working.... I was out. That was the first time I had morphine. It worked good for the pain. I could not fight staying awake. Goodnight. I woke up in the operating room in Sentara Norfolk General hospital. With IV's in my arms, feeding tubes, neck brace and two detectives waiting for me to come completely too for questioning.

In my room they were trying to interview me while I was still drunk and now high on morphine. It's not happening. I played sleep until they gave up and left. They placed their cards in my room on the table by the phone. Before they left, they told the nurse to tell me to "call them" as soon as I came too.

The doctors that were to operate on me had finally come in; they moved me to the MRI unit for a sonogram. They then pumped me up with dye that would stick to any foreign objects that may have been left from the gunshot. We were in there for hours and they still couldn't find the bullet or an exit wound.

Perplexed at the discovery that the bullet may be enlarged in the base of my spine. They did not want to adjutate it by probing the wound any longer. So, they told me eventually the bullet would work itself out and there was nothing else that could be done.

At this time, I was not in too much pain. It felt like I could still walk. The doctor's didn't know what to say other than until the bullet became dislodged by itself that it wouldn't be wise to try and remove it. Without knowing the exact location of the bullet, they didn't want to cause more damage that had already been done.

However, they told me in the process if by chance it moved and shifted in the wrong direction it could cause me to become paralyzed for the rest of my life. Damn I said, "I'm about to be eighteen and not be able to walk, that was not in my plans." I was a hair length close to becoming one of my home boys who have passed before they have seen outside little ass Norfolk, USA.

I wasn't having that shit. They moved me to my room and a code blue came over the intercom. I asked the nurse "was there anyone else that came in on the same case as I did"? she said "yes" he had been stable, but they were having a hard time stopping him from bleeding internally. Then she turned and left the room.

Later, that night there was another code blue, this time he didn't make it. I did not know how to feel. How could I feel for someone who tried to kill me or leave me paralyzed for life? Wow just last night before the last code blue I was on the phone with the girl from Norview. She was on her way to the hospital with my gun.

Once again death had paid me a visit. This time, he missed me by inches. I thanked God; he had only left me his calling card again. It has been a week since I was released from Sentra Norfolk General hospital. The same two homicide detectives were coming by my house on the regular. I just wanted to get away for a while. Just to get my head on straight and now the military wasn't an option.

I had to hit the streets and hit them hard. The last five murders of the summer was all aimed at me and my crew. I would have been the last one now, that was a sign to get out of town but "where could I go?" We did not keep in touch with our family like we should. We would only see them at family reunions that were out of state.

In fact, they were out of the picture too. That would not be good because that would be the first place that the killer would look. I need a plan and a place to lay low until my wound heals. Meanwhile Lil C came by the house and said that "they had Savage in custody, but they were going to give him a bail". Kool I said. That meant they were probably going to give him a self-defense charge. Lil C said, "he was using Mr. Robinson for his lawyer". He was like Johnnie Cochran in his day. Everyone used Robinson. Hell, that was the lawyer that Cannon used in his case. He was a good lawyer.

Lil C had got shot too. If it was an inch more to the right, he would be called stubby. The bullet had just missed his groins by an inch. Boy, he was lucky. Then I asked, "who was shooting at us?" He said he found out It was "Ikey, Boo and three other dudes." Boo I knew him. Then when I found out it was them. I was very upset they were my go hard crew.

All of them were straight killers. Everybody in that house was lucky me and Lil C were the only ones shot. They had some fire power they could have leveled the place if they wanted too. Let me tell you I got half my guns from them. It was like that and now he was gone (R.I.P Boo). I was shocked and very upset over being shot. Now finding out who shot me made me even madder. It was my stepbrother's cousin.

His family member had confirmed what Lil C told me. Except they had spoken to him personally and he told them to tell me that he did not mean to shoot me, he was aiming to get Savage. At first, I was hurt. He was my man and we were tight. We never had any beef. He used to buy weight from me. I was speechless.

Three weeks of not answering the door when the police came isn't going to keep working. Tammy said her "dad wants us to come visit him". How bad can South Chi town be, I thought to myself. Boy was I in for a shocker. She'll be here tonight. I had enough money to hold us for a month or two. Ro sent word from jail for me to clean the apartment for him before the landlord took everything and changed the locks.

For payment I could keep what I found in there. He was still being held for shooting that Jamaican dude. That had happened in the early part of the summer. Well, I went to clean the place. I bet I'll find something to increase my pocket change for our trip to Chi town.

I wasn't walking too well. It was more like a slow stroll. I made it up the block to the apartment to see exactly how much shit was in there to throw away. I had to jimmy the door open because I did not have my keys. They got lost the night of the shooting.

Inside the place had already been cleaned out. Oh shit how in the fuck did Saga know I was coming here? Yo Tee, he shouted, "You In there"? I replied, "Yeah man keep it down and don't call my name". "What are you doing here?" I asked. He said, "Your mom said you were coming up the block". I thought this had to be the only place you would have gone.

Ok Sherlock! I told Saga "Ol boy asked me to come up and clean the place." It looks like it has already been cleaned. Oh, hold on right here. I went into the kitchen and investigated the pantry. Inside of the door frame there was a slot where you could remove the molding. There in between a tight thin gap was a good way to hide work. "I almost have it". I said to Saga just a few more inches. Got it!

I pulled out a rolled-up gallon Ziploc bag. Inside was at least five ounces of crack. I rolled it back up. I looked in the hidden crawl space in the back bedroom and there it was an AK forty-seven. That joint was sweet, but I cannot take it where I was going. So, I left it in another one of our stash spots and later I was told Lil Jay came and took it.

I went to the front room and when Saga saw the coke, he asked me if that "was that dope". I told him "Yes and told him here you keep it". He had a son on the way and at the time I was leaving town. I had a plan to help raise him with Saga. After all, he was my only nephew.

I did not care I was not going to try and take that shit on no plane. Hell, the airport would send me straight to jail. I did not have a kid so he would need it more than me. He said he was going to open a barber shop. When I got back, he would give me the old furniture and together we could open shop number two. Either way he meant well but I know it was just talk to ensure I was still giving the dope to him. All I cared about was getting the fuck out of dodge.

CHAPTER 15

Whipping it in Gary

Tammy had called her dad after I got shot and he was happy his baby girl was coming home. He seemed thrilled to have me tagging along as well. When we first arrived, we flew to Alabama. In the cab on our way to the hotel I was not impressed. She was excited until on the cab's radio had a breaking news flash. It was a police chase that ended with two men driving their car into a river.

Shots were fired but no one was seriously injured. Once the news break had finished, I looked at her and said, "ok it isn't as country here after all huh?" She said, "that her family was from Alabama which explains why she was so thick. Plus, this is where all the red bones were born.

A lot of them (red bones) always have roots from the south and she was not any different, but like all families from the south to become free or lead a free life they had migrated to the north which for them was the midwest now Chicago.

We were in Alabama for about a week then me and her father flew to Chi town. Here everything was fast and big. The Chicago Bulls were on their way to winning their first championship. I am here to see them live. I couldn't believe it.

We drove from the O'Hare airport to Indiana. That's when I learned that Gary was considered the suburbs of Chicago. Here is where they came to play. Gary was the leading producer of steel until the early nineteen eighties. When the steel plants shut down the whole city became corrupt with violence and crime. It all started with the local police department going rogue.

The reason I was brought to Gary was to help my father-in-inlaw with the family business. Around the same time, I had gotten shot. His head man was gunned down and robbed. So, Mr. Lee needed a new right. This was perfect because I needed a new playground and a place to lay low and regroup. When I was introduced to one of his friends, I had recognized him as the Puerto Rican dude that had got busted in Miami.

You know the one who had the million-dollar house and the Excalibur's well that was him in the flesh. I wanted an autograph but I did not want to seem like I was the feds. So, I stayed in my lane, introduced myself and shook his hand and fell back. He and my father in-law had some business to discuss, and I did not want to appear to be ear-hustling.

I told them I was going to the car. As I was leaving the room they had begun to talk. Now I see why every time me and Tammy's father had talked he kept asking me "if I got high or if I used coke over and over." In different ways to insure he was getting the answer he was looking to hear. It was as he was interrogating me.

I did not know it was to take me on as his head man. Hustling was just one of the family's form of income. He wanted me to be one hundred percent sure I was drug free before even bringing me down here from jump. But I thought it was Kool. I had a father in-law who I could get money with and show me how to elevate to a higher level in the game.

After we left the pizzeria, we drove to an old car lot back in Indiana. A tall older man came out and he had a Jerry curl. Accompanying him were two young ass chicks. They were high yellow with miniskirts and halter tops on with thigh highs boots and they were hot.

It was the ending of the summer and the temperature here wasn't helping. We went inside his office and there were two more young ass hotties. They had on booty shorts and tank tops. Their shorts were so tight that you could smell the sweet scent of pussy and roses.

He introduced us as 'goodfellas', he said. As We walked further into his dealership you could see he had a lot of older cars. They were classics like Cutlass, Cadillac Ciera, Thunderbirds, and Mustangs. Mr. Lee was talking to me about going to the car auctions here. The next time homeboy goes, we will just go with him.

The only thing we would have to pay him is fifty dollars and the taxes on the car. There we can bid on any car we want at the car wholesale auction. Yo "how are you doing my main man?" he said to my father in-law. My father-in-law was a Kool ass country dude he replied, "just the same old same I can't complain". So, the plan was to take ol boys order and let him know that payment was due upon delivery.

Mr. Lee didn't like phones, so he planned all my deals in person and in advance. So, if you want to do business you'd better listen and remember because he won't call you. And if the bread wasn't correct or you didn't show he'll never deal with you again! No matter how much money you wanted to spend. The game taught him the hard way. Once as a young man he had moved to New Orleans, and he rose fast to the top.

So fast he fucked around and met this white chick. "What's wrong with that?" You say well let me finish he made so much money fucking with this chick that he moved to the super dome before hurricane Katrina came thru and leveled the place. Now he is balling but one thing he now doesn't have time for this young pretty white bitch no more. Well, you couldn't have guessed what happened next? Her daddy was not just any daddy, he was the governor of New Orleans.

Let's just say this after almost fifteen bullets and five years of rehabilitation later he was back. After almost losing his life, he didn't take chances. Hell, I couldn't get into the family until me and his daughter were married. Good they finished their little deal. Mr. Lee "if we only have four ounces left how are you going to fill his order"? I asked him.

He looked over at me and reminded me of the talk about cooking the product up to crack. It was on from there ever since. It hit me. I had always seen Jay do it and knew if I did it right that four could become seven depending on the coke and how much cut was on it. I was driving and I said, "Yes, I do remember what we talked about".

In my head I was still thinking to myself however, if the coke is bad meaning all cut up then a whole lot could be lost, and we'll have nothing. I said, "I'll have to test a little out first to see what you have?" But if it's strong enough to hold in the hot water then we could triple its worth. He was a little concerned at first, so he showed me their mid-west style. He took that four and made eight. That's when I learned how to cut.

That was how the power re-rock game went and I was amazed. It was a crash course, but I caught on fast. Ok one more time he said "to keep the strength of the coke. Only put four ounces of cut on it. If the whole kilo can take a two then the four can take a two then you look at the quality of cut. They had a cut that smells like coke, looks like coke, and numbs you like coke.

The only thing it is not coke and it didn't get you high like coke. It was called Miami Ice. He wanted to turn the four we had into eight dump that and we got a half kilo. From that half of kilo nine will get re-rocked to give us eighteen ounces of powder. Then with the other nine I was going to cook it up into crack. Now if the coke quality is as good as they told us then the nine I'm cooking up will come back at least eleven and a half or twelve ounces.

That Miami ice shit was expensive, it was one hundred dollars an eighth, but it was worth it. Once you open it you can smell the odor of coke. If you tasted it would numb your mouth just like real coke. I will sell eighths for one hundred and seventy-five dollars. Sometimes you can double your money and get two hundred and twenty-five.

It all depended on your buyer and what they wanted to do with the coke snort or smoke it. He had all the shooters and snorters. I had to go out and find the smokers. So, since he had just lost his last man due to his head getting blown off. He wanted me to continue his runs and of course bring in new clients as well for his powder. That was not the problem. I told him how I moved, and he seen to be Kool with it.

But for some reason he wasn't convinced about accepting how I did it or how far would it go before his daughter would find out or get hurt behind my methods of operations. I had told him that as I'm out in the city I'll be hunting for a new girlfriend. Once I found her, I was going to put one of her family members on board as a partner.

That was how I moved. Then that side of town will be used for the crack operations. We agreed and gave me a house to use as headquarters complete with metal shutters. Yes, that's how they got down here. I slept with them down all the time. It made me feel safe. even if my car was on fire. you'll still not be able to reach me. That house looked so intimidating.

You'll be like oh well let's just rob the next house. Let these nice people rest. His niece's boyfriend was a fast-food manager and I promised to take care of him even more if he showed me the ropes. At first, he seemed upset that Mr. Lee had given me the promotion. I told him that if he just keeps his Kool do not take offense. I will move you in my place as soon as the crack sales increase.

I was married to the boss's daughter so of course I'd be next in line for the job automatically. After the dick pissing contest, we became good friends. We moved all that shit the powder and the crack in two weeks. We doubled everything with the last way we had prepared the package. Now it was my turn to meet with the connect. He would never talk to me before. He would only talk directly to Mr. Lee. and then Mr. Lee would fill me in later.

We brought eighteen and he gave us nine on consignment. The new coke can take one to one which means we could take eighteen and make thirty-six mmm let's get to work. We got to the lab on the south side of town by the car wash. Inside I knew I couldn't put one on one if I was going to cook it up. I could put a four or six on it and hope it would come back.

I could not spare no less the twenty-six or twenty-seven ounces off the eighteen and I'll just take the extra nine he fronted us and re-rock them. That would give us eighteen ounces of powder and twenty-six ounces of crack, not bad. So, eighteen plus thirteen equaled thirty-one ounces from the goal of thirty-two my father-in-law said, "that would work". And I got to cutting and cooking before I knew it. By the end of that month, we were up to two kilo's.

And then we were cooking one and re-rocking the other. We had the midwest jumping. Things were fine. I had a new town house in Alabama. It had three levels and it was further off the grid then Dover. It was nice Tammy stayed home a lot. I traveled mostly alone. I never wanted her around me, especially if I was dirty.

Every time I came home, I would return with twenty thousand dollars at a time. The trips became so frequent that I started sending the money home in cashier checks taped inside oversized birthday and holiday cards. Eventually I had to purchase a cash box and a safe.

It would prove to be useless to think it would protect my money and the things I held dear. It would be soon I had to watch both the trap house in Gary and the one back home in Alabama. The trips had started taking a toll on my body.

We had started dealing with some big boys and they knew my face but not my name. That's how out of towners played it. So, it was now time to bring the dude in to step up in my spot and I'll open a trap house in Birmingham, Alabama. I thought to myself that would keep me closer to Tammy and I can have a little extra coming in while I was out of town.

I had started to get paranoid. The police were kidnapping hustlers from their trap houses. Making them hustle for them twenty-four seven without the option of leaving. I'll keep my spot down south to avoid them assholes. It was getting crazy up there I kept two pistols on me and after I had just gotten shot a mother fucker wasn't getting another chance.

Things were going well and the money was stacking up so much that I was starting to look for a barbershop of my own to just lay low plus wash my money. Not to mention to have a place to go to when it was slow on the block. Some bullshit had happened between me and my father-in-law once I had the city on that hard cook up.

Even though he knew from day one how I moved my coke. I began to wonder if the secret was safe with him anymore.

The crack was catching on so much we were losing powder sales and he asked "if we should switch to just hard" I said "yeah but we're going to need more help at the trap house.

The block was good, but it was getting hot being out in the opening. My little Purdue chick had me on that and she didn't even know it. I had her twin in charge of the runners. They all had headsets and operated as an ice-cream truck driver. I monitored them the whole time from the Purdue chick house.

While we fucked all day damn this is the life. Not knowing it was all about to fall. I kept her protected. She was my little baby. She was really smart and cute too. I had loved a woman with brains. She was a twin and after her I promised myself never to date another one. They really were on some same shit it was scary.

I had never seen two people finish each other's sentences and thoughts. that was to me too much sharing amongst siblings. Seeing the game was simply meeting the girl in the right neighborhood I wanted to pump from. Then spice her up but don't fuck with no one in her family.

At least not until you find the family member that no one in the family would fuck with. Now if he was shady, I wouldn't fuck with them either. I dealt with the quiet and the loner in the family. Or the black sheep like me. then I would bless them and put them on hard in the game. Show them some king pin love, no really show them some king pin love way before Jigga my nigga.

Her brother fit the bill, so I blessed him, and we got paid. See I had two cousin-in-laws that stayed in the apartment right across the street from Coral and her brother Cortez. When I go visit them, I would hit Cortez off. Then in the meantime he would supply my cousins.

Without my cousins knowing it was my coke. Because they would get their shit from Tez. The whole hood was now all mine and all in one swoop. Tez would keep them supplied with my coke. Then I wrapped it into a present and he passed my money to his sister. She would hold it until I re-upped her brother.

Most of the time she would hold it until I came to tuck her in for the night. Either way was fine with me. Now Tez helped cut out half of my foot work. Even better, he was respected in his hood. So, I didn't have to worry about the bullshit jack boys. It was the police that I kept an eye on. They were playing for keeps and I wasn't up for grabs.

My wife's cousin's boyfriend... They called him Derail. He was working less at the job and more with me. He took me to all the client's that brought four ounces or more. In return I taught them how to cook up and now we both had the city on wrap.

It was nearing my court date. I was hoping for the best knowing it was a self-defense case. My cousin had pulled the trigger. I still had to go to court. He told them that it was my gun, but he had taken the murder charge. And threw the gun on me. It didn't matter to me though all my guns I had brought were brand new. I knew they were clean. I told him when the judge saw that the gun was clean, he would throw my charge out.

I guess that's why I did not get upset with Savage for that shit about saying it was my gun. He did save our lives that night. I just did not have a chance to register the gun yet. I was going to court to save his life, so I had planned to go to court. My date had just come two weeks ago. However, Tammy did not want to come with me.

As she had any other time, and I noticed her dad hanging with her more as my court date became closer. The cousin that had gotten shot the same day I did at the cookout I had flew up to help since things were going well. We had the same court date, so I wanted him to drive halfway and I would drive the other half back home.

He was a good for driving at least I knew he could not fuck that up. On the way down we talked a lot and the first question I had for him was who he was fucking that had put antifreeze in my damn fire bird's gas tank. He paused for a minute and said "she thought I was you damn" he was up to his same old shit again.

I told you people are riding around acting like they're me. I just did not know my own cousin was a frenemy too. Then he started to say, "how he does not think Mr. Lee likes the fact that he was here." I started to think, and I noticed things getting a little strange too. Like Tammy popping up at the O'Hara unannounced and Mr. Lee always wanting a cash count at weird times of the night.

I just could not put my hand on it, but I did not want Lil C to think he was on to something. He tended to take things way too far. We arrived in Norfolk just in time to park and run into the courthouse. As we were entering court it was just about to start. At court the charges were dropped, and Savage had received time served.

The judge gave me my gun back then told me to get it registered. I left that gun downtown in the courthouse. It had a body on it, it had to be retired. I tried to reach Tammy to tell her we beat the murder charge, but she did not answer the phone in Alabama or the phone in Indiana. I hoped she was ok. I told Lil C once we were back up top to take me to where the work was stashed. We got the money for the coke I fronted out before we went to court. I had needed that doe before the weekend.

As we entered the driveway back in Indiana. I noticed all the cars were here and the garage was open. Good everyone was here, yes. As I reached the house, I also noticed my father in-law's car was here too. He never took the Bentley out oh shit here we go it hit the fan. Ok inside I saw Tammy. I reached out my hand and motioned for her to come here.

She grabbed her coat then she said, "you did not get the message"? No, I replied. Call your mom. I just left Norfolk. the phone rang ma "what's wrong?" "Your father had an overdose." I just saw him. When is the funeral?" She said, next week ok I'll be there. I put the phone down. I could not cry because I didn't know him like a father.

However, I was sad because I had always wanted to know him. He was supposed to move up here with me, but I guess he wanted what he wanted. He had to have his heroin. That was the reason for leaving his wife and his real kids his life insurance money.

He never gave me shit plus he told Sharon that he was worth more dead than alive to them. So how could I cry he committed suicide. He was weak for that. I thought all I wanted to do was just see him off. Tammy rode with me this time and she tried to cheer me up as much as possible. It worked for a moment. I wasn't mad, I told her I just could not understand him. He could have had the house to himself.

So, fuck it he's always been selfish. He got what he wanted. it was his wish, so I just had to accept that and move on. We pulled into the grave site. We arrived late due to an overturned eighteen-wheeler on the highway. It happened when we were merging onto interstate nine five. I did not want to interrupt the service, so we fell back until the proceedings were over.

Once the service was over, I waited for the crowd to disperse to approach the casket. I started to walk to the casket but once I got there the name wasn't my father's name on the tombstone. Now I was mad, embarrassed, and upset all at once. Tammy said to call your cousin. I was so upset I forgot she and her dad had just flown In from London. Her dad was on his way to retirement from the air force, so they traveled the world.

Deanne picked up and said, "they had buried him in Hampton memorial cemetery". Shit I'm not driving all the way over there. I'll wait till y'all get to the repast. She said "ok" and we hung up. In the meantime, we went to have a bite to eat and get a nap at my mom's house. Deanne called a couple hours later and said, "they were at my uncle Sam's house". "I'll be right there" I replied and woke everyone up so we could at least show our respect before going back west.

I entered the house and the house fell silent. The whole family was saying that no it can't be oh Tee damn he looks just like his dad. All the voices in the crowd murmured. That's all he ever gave me was my fucking looks. I suppose that's why he never gave me anything else. I said hi to everyone.

I did not choose any person to single out. Then I turned to leave. I had a little brother. He was like my dad himself and my sister has his stubbornness so, either way they were getting what he left them. Their college was taken care of. I still had to go out here and get mine. I'm glad they have each other to lean on. Perhaps one day I can join them but who was I fooling I would never fit in so fuck it?

I like where I am in life so if they do not want to come on my side then I think our relationships should stay the way they are, distant. But as I got older, I thought his family deserved that money. At least it could help heal the pain that I heard he had put my stepmom through. She didn't deserve that bullshit either. So I was happy for them all. He left her like he left my mom a single woman with kids.

I just hope they used it for something that would last because that would be the last thing Robert Williams would be giving anyone for a long time. And the craziest thing about it is he killed himself (self-lottery I called it lol). He went out the way he wanted too. I just hope I will be just that lucky. He followed through so he must have really been fucked up. His death made me promise myself that whenever I have kids to make sure all of them get something from me.

To show that even if I wasn't in their life the way they may have wanted me to be there for them. At least they would know I never forgot about them. They would always be on my mind. See I told you he taught me how to be a good father. By showing me how to be a fucked up one like he was to me. On the way to the car, I saw Deanne. She ran out to me and asked, "if she could come back to Chi town with me?"

I had felt a bad vibe about having her and Lil C together in the midwest. I told her "It would be best if she stayed here, and I'll be back for you soon I promise" she smiled with an uneven grin and said "ok". I wanted her to come but because I had a bad feeling that I wasn't going to be out there too much longer there was no reason for her to tag along.

I was going to be returning real soon. Things just did not feel right back west. I wanted to figure it out before I brought anyone else there. It was too late. About halfway back to Gary I wished I had brought her with me, but she would have been a weakness in my armor. If the competition had gotten their hands on her I would have been done.

She was very pretty and green in nature as far as playing in my game. All I kept seeing was someone trying to ransom her to me. I would have killed for her safety. Back in Indiana Lil C would handle the daily tasks at hand.

Things for the most part of the business were going well. A call from Carol and all hell broke loose she was upset saying "she was pregnant, and the baby was mine". I had no doubt about the fact that the baby was mine. It was keeping the baby from my wife that had me nervous. In her hometown I had gotten another bitch pregnant. That had been all she had wanted from me. Now I got another girl pregnant.

I'm hit. This is a big problem. Mr. Lee kept asking me "If I had decided on the location of the barbershop that I was going to open?" I said "Yes, I wanted the shop to be in Indiana." I wanted it to be a source of income for Carol and the baby once I left the city for good. I would have Cortez run the place and the side business.

"No," he insisted. That's when it all came to me in a full circle. He flew to Indiana and called for an emergency meeting. At the time of the call, I was in the motel with this little hot white chick. I had picked her up at the grocery store three blocks from the house. She was sucking my dick while I was on the phone. When I hung up, I didn't know the next time I would see her.

It was dark in the room. I reached over and grabbed her by the waist and flipped her over. She landed onto my lap, and she rode my cock until I came. As it was shooting out my dick, she hopped off me and began to suck out the cum. Damn she was good. After she stopped sucking me off. I said, "baby turn around" and I fucked her doggie style till we were both were covered in sweat.

She could take whatever I threw her way. In the car, on the porch outside it didn't matter. Once I had found out her father was the local sheriff, I thought the next place was going to be in his car lol. I did not get to get that far because this as I felt was never going to be the same because I was never coming back this way again. I got dressed and had one of the boys in my crew meet me at the trap house.

Then I called the rest of the crew to be on standby in case I needed them there as well. I told them they were to come armed. I had found out later that they had talked to each other about what was going to happen when I left town.

They had wondered why I had them go to all the workers and collect what they had fronted out. Either the cash or the coke. Bring it with them. But to leave the coke and the money in their cars? I did the same thing but since I dealt with the bigger boys I got work and cash unknowing to Derail. That's what I was blessing him with when I left for home. Believe me, what I was leaving for him was beyond his wildest dreams. I promised him that by showing me the ropes I would leave him in charge.

I keep my word. That's why I had everyone meet up. After me and Mr. Lee had our little talk, I'll have my talk with them. My first stop was to Doug's house. He was the guy that put me on about the cops kidnapping everyone. They caught Ivan the other day. He was another person of interest. Indiana's finniest wanted him badly. He was more flamboyant than I was. He had driven a yellow Lamborghini around town.

He stunted every chance he got to get one up on the police. Well right before I got my BMW, he brought the lambo. I was even taken by the shit. I had brought a BMW three twenty-eight i. Black on black chrome package with bbs rims. It was a nineteen eighty though, but she was fast even with the four doors.

Well apparently, he was at a stop light and the boys ran down on him. They immediately took him out of the car and handcuffed him. Now I told you they were corrupt, but they did not fuck with him like whipping his ass. His dad was a bigtime fucker so they had just fucked with him every chance they could got.

He was in the intersection of MKD doing donuts. When he hit the brakes and smoke was all over the place. The officer's then got out and they took his whole car apart right there in the middle of the road. After they were done embarrassing him, they uncuffed him and left. He was standing over his car fuming.

Ivan was so mad that he had gotten a stripper that was in her early stages of aids (the package that's what they called it in my day). Anyway, he had got the bitch a job at the damn police station. Her being an ex-stripper all the men were up her ass. Well, she fucked half the department, and they had all contracted aids from the bitch.

She was found later with her head chopped off and her body was found in the gutter. That was the first to my knowledge of the police going bad.

The sheriffs had taken over the job of the police department. It seemed as if all of them were fighting for the top position of running the city's underworld of drugs and violence. Because they both were going for themselves in the streets.

It took the FBI to bring order back to Indiana. Doug told me he was even leaving for a while until things blew over. He was from here, he just said it was getting too far out of hand. That told me it was time for me to leave as well. So, we had a plan for when I told him I was on the way to him.

Since we had already done our business, he knew that was the queue to have my traveling bag ready. Yes, he remembered. He asked, "where I was heading?" I looked at him like really. He grinned and said, "well did I still want him to give the other kilo to Derail?" I said, "Yes, every gram of it please!" We shook hands and I left him to do his business.

I was going to miss D. He was a true soldier and looked out. I had to go back to the house and that's when the truth jumped up and bit me right in the face. On my return from court, I had a feeling things weren't right and now it's about to explode. I thought to myself I do not have time for this shit. As I entered the house, I saw Derail and his right-hand man.

His boy had an AK forty-seven. Mr. Lee was holding a three fifty-seven magnum in his hand. Lil C was standing across from Mr. Lee holding a tech nine in his lap. My wife was on the sofa crying and shaking her head. Mr. Lee said, "I heard you were leaving town, and you planned to take all the bread with you". There was only one person who could have told him my plans.

Pillow talk gets you into shit every time. I thought I could trust her no matter what I did. She was my wife for better or worse. I guess I was wrong.

My neck liked to have snapped from how fast I spun around to look at Tammy. I looked into her eyes as if to say, "why baby I took care of you for four years and you turned on me for your dad?" She remained silent, and she lowered her head. I turned back to her dad and said, "you never gave me a chance to expand.

Then you tried to cut me off. I just beat you to it." But out of respect I did not touch your stash at all Derail tell him what's going on. Derail told him where everything was and how much was left. The product and the dollar amount matched his records. I told him to look in the safe and he'll see it's all there.

He looked at my cousin and aimed the gun at him. Then Derail's man raised his AK. My gun was in the fucking car. I said, "wait" I had a bad feeling that Lil C deserved whatever was about to happen to him because he was that gorilla hustler. I told him he did not have to do it like that here. Fear makes a nigga get strong off your food then knock you off.

Then fill your shoes. Playing it smooth builds the loyal niggas. You allow them to grow then they will spend their earnings with you. He never understood and he could not figure out that's why all his cars (my cars kept getting egged, scratched up, shot up and shit like that).

He stayed fucked up and his money too. I learned in the game that no trust from your crew equals no money for you, the pusher. Mr. Lee said, "your cousin was trying to fuck my wife". I looked over to Mr. Lee and said, "No offense but what?" I looked at Lil C and he was like I just said, "a few things to her. I did not think she would have been offended by my actions." I said, "C I knew you was going to fuck shit up. I just did not know how long it was going to take you to do it."

It was not like I bitched up but right was right and wrong got you killed. Mr. Lee did have a pretty ass girlfriend but that does not give a member on the team that right. But to try to mess with the wife that shit was disrespectful. His girlfriend would have been wrong as well. You just do not go behind a friend.

I may have turned my head if it was the girlfriend, she had a donkey ass. If anyone he would have hit on, I thought it would have been Joanne not his wife. "Yuck Lil C" I said to myself. Mr. Lee had cut me off before I could finish talking to Lil C. He said, "So I took it upon myself to tell Tammy you had got a girl she went to school with pregnant." I was like "what?" So now I see that's why she was crying and not even trying to come to me.

On the table in front of her were all the titles to my cars and a small bag I kept in the safe. It contained all the fucking cash. I condensed the cash whenever I got a chance. to just hundreds. That's all it was and it was easier to hide. Now everything was clear, and I understood. "Ok Mr. Lee," I said. I did not feel like explaining myself. He knew how I got down and instead of letting shit be as it was, he had to tell her. Now my wife is going to ride with him fine. They both can stay here and wait for the FBI.

Lil C I will deal with him later back in Norfolk. Yo fuck it! You got what you want your daughter and all my shit take it I'm going south anyway. Lil C, Derail and his man looked at me and then Derail nodded his head and so did his boy. They turned to Mr. Lee and lowered his weapon. Derail knew this day would come ever since I told him Mr. Lee had wanted me to move my barbershop to Alabama.

That is when I had to plan a way out and have a security blanket to cover my ass. By moving D to my spot gave me that leverage. If Mr. Lee would have killed me, he would have lost the money and the stash. This made D the next man to control Mr. Lee's empire. I did not want to leave him with bad blood on my or his hands.

When he nodded back at me, he knew to contact all my people and he'll be straight. The shit in the car was what I owed Mr. Lee. It was small compared to what I had left D. Look I turned to Tammy and said, "I'm leaving Tammy you coming or are you staying"? She didn't even look at me and just simply said "she was staying" and I left.

Before we hit the highway, I wanted to scoop up the second part of my plan, MeMe. She reminded me of Ms. Shella from NWA except her voice wasn't as ignoring as the real Ms. Shella's voice was lol. She was short and thick like oatmeal, she had coco brown skin. She could ride a cock boy. I'm getting hard now just thinking about her damn. It was a few girls I had in my life that were mind blowing and yes Ms. MeMe was one of them.

She said she had her eyes on me from the first time she saw me move to Indiana. She lived right behind me off Green St. The day I brought the BMW she wanted to be open to me. Then she said "she wanted to fuck me ever since she saw me move in. Now guys truthfully what she said could be true. I'm not a bad catch myself but I would be stupid to think the car did not play a major part in it too lmao. She was already packed to leave. She said, "she had never been to Norfolk, VA before and she was looking forward to the vacation." She still lived with her mom, nothing exciting.

And when she did get out of the house she left with her mom. Both would visit her aunt in the projects of Chicago. And she'd always be stuck with her all the time. This was her first trip without her mom. And I wanted this vacation to be all she hoped for. At least I'm going to do the best I can to make it enjoyable anyway.

CHAPTER 16

Hell's kitchen

Back home and yep moms light on. "Mom," I shouted at her bedroom window. I did not need her to let me in; they never locked the hallway door. "Hey baby you home?" Sharon yelled. It was like three am and I had taken six no doses. The caffeine had me going. My body was tired but I for some reason could not get comfortable. Me Me said "I'll calm him down Ms. Sharon."

She was blunt. We'll be alright and she led me into the bed-room. Like that she was not disrespectful, and I think that's what made me attracted to her. She spoke her mind and did what she wanted to do! Nor did she bite her tongue for no one. She was only like four foot eight too lol.

We came out of the room and I felt a hell of a lot better. She sucked my dick so good I had forgotten about everything. I didn't know if it was for me bringing her to Virginia or if she was happy to be with me. Either way I wanted her to do it again. The only problem with that was I had to wait an hour because she wouldn't let a drop spill out her mouth.

She showed the cum to me and then swallowed it. And afterwards she licked her lips and said, "thank you daddy." Wow I thought to myself why I didn't marry her. I said, "you welcome you fucking slut". She leaned over and kissed me on my cheek. I smacked her on her ass as she had passed on her way to the bathroom.

I'm in fucking love. I told Lil C to take the car home. He was living with his pops out the beach. His dad lived in the

200

fancy rich section. Out there the BMW would fit right in unlike in my hood. Shit it was not a foreign car out here until you hit the downtown Ghent area. I think there was a Benz, but I was the first one with a BMW.

Me and MeMe got settled in and fell asleep. As I was drifting off, I thought I had to flip what I brought down with me. The cash I needed to stash it fast. My mom thinks I was up there remodeling houses. I told her that I brought the car with all the money I had minus gas and food.

She didn't mind that I was home. Now first thing first I had to find a connect. Second, find out who's in charge of things? And thirdly set up shop yawning and now It's time to............

Damn I sleep well Yo where is Me Me? Is someone cooking? I knew it was not Sharon. After I passed home economics, she had completely stopped cooking altogether. So, I knew it was not Sharon in the kitchen. Ok it is Me Me. Good morning you pretty thing you. Let me find out you suck good dick, fuck good and cook. I told her "If I was not married, she would be my bride".

Yeah "is that right?" she said. I looked at her and we laughed. She had told me she loved me. If she had ever caught me cheating on her, she would chop my dick off. Yelps! Well, I hope she doesn't find out that I was going to see my lil Norveiw bitch today. Ever since her mom made her have an abortion, she been bugging me to have another baby.

And that was by far the last thing on my mind. I was too young and she did not care. She just wanted a baby, so I still fuck her whenever I was in town. I just made sure I shot my load in the bed or fake having an organism. She was allowed to drive all over the seven cities now. Not just back and forward to school, work, and home.

Damn I had told Me Me that I needed to go around and check on a few things "ok" she said. Here is some cash, go shopping or whatever and I'll see you around dinner time. She said "ok" and after breakfast she took me in the room again. We showered and I waited for Lil C to come and scoop me.

Well all my questions were answered Lil C said, "What you mean big Cuz?" Well Todd is still in power out Park Place.; the

Bremerton boys fell off the feds pick them niggers up. When we were in Chi town. That fool with the burgundy jag down the street from me got the best powder in town and the weight was good.

Slim was his name ever since beat street all he kept saying he had family in New York. He's a dick rider for sure. I fucked with him because we had one thing in common money. I did not want to dress like them, I just wanted to get paid like them. That's all, nothing moving but the money. I hooked up with my Norview bitch for two reasons: she was a straight whore plus she listens to me.

I paid her car note and tricked up her ride. She will let me hold the whip while she's working. I can let the BMW sit up. I'll use her car for my sales that need delivery so I'd like to spend time with her and give her this dick until my phone rings.

Over her house she had company. She knew I did not like her dorky ass girlfriends. They were ugly as hell and nosier than a mother fucker. I mean she was too, but she had the body of Nicky Minaj. Ok you got me on this one. It was before the plastic inserts, but shit Nicki was fuckable before the operation too.

I could never tell her about Me Me. Because she would have had a fit and tried to kill Me Me. It did not matter any way Me Me was leaving soon. My nigga Derail was coming to get her. He blew up. We had still stayed in touch. I did that so, whenever Me Me got ready to go back home. I knew he would be on standby to come and get her.

She was cool with that because if I was not going to be married anymore to Tammy, she was down for whatever I asked of her. I went back home with two out of three of my problems solved. At least I had a solution to fix them. Except for the most important one. Where can I pitch from?

My mom's house was out of the question. From the start I never sold from her house, and I was not going to start now. Lil C said, "why not out his grandfather way behind Norfolk State?" "Null, that's where Jay was killed" I said to him. I did not want to be out there at all. Plus, I did not want him to be that close to my shit.

Or for that fact know where I was pumping it from. I'll bring him what he needs. I felt the less Lil C knows the better off the world would be for me. I had a client that stayed around the corner from Red Ball. I saw a light on in his bedroom. Good he was up. "Yo Lil C" I'm good from here "where you going"? He asked. I replied, "Mining my business" and he drove off.

I went into the store until I couldn't see the rear lights of the BMW. Then I walked over to the apartment building. Once there I tapped on the downstairs window. A tall dark-skinned fellow came up to the window. He looked then I heard someone say, "is that you Lil Tee?" I answered back "yeah" open the door it's hot out here Yo.

The hallway door opened, and it was Black. He used to work for my cousin Roy on summer jobs doing demolition work. That was a long time ago. He said, "what's going on Tee?" As we entered the apartment. The place had looked the same. The curtains were old with flower prints. You know the ones you get from the dollar store.

These clearly needed to be changed because you could see the discoloration from all the years of smoking cigarettes and crack. The house had a dungeon smell to it as if it was a giant ashtray. I guess since they lived here, they were used to it. "Yeah, black how have you been?" I asked him as I sat down.

"Not the same since I no longer could do construction." He replied. "His old back injuries were becoming more painful every day." He said, "he had to do odd jobs and work part time to make ends meet", I asked "how would you like to make two hundred a week?" Shit he said, "I would like that a lot! But I cannot do real work Tee, I'm all fucked up"! I said, "That's the beauty of it, you just sit here. I will pay you and save your money". I will take over the apartment. He looked at his old lady and she agreed. "When do I start?" he asked. But the look on his face seemed as if he wanted to get more info before fully committing.

He frowned and said, "do I have to live here to make that money". I saw where this was going and said, "why?" out of curiosity and he went on saying "Well I have to be out of here next month anyway and I figure you wanted to work out the house right?" Not really work from here but use it as kind of like my safe house slash office" I told him.

"Shit isn't going to be all crazy in here is it?" You know I do not even get down like that right? He was a little nervous at first because he had two young kids here and his old lady too. However, I convinced him to stay here.

I wanted the house to still appear normal. The house had to have a real family to throw off the cops and jack boys. He had time to save the first month's rent and deposit up for their new place. We both agreed and I left for my place on foot. I hit Colonial Avenue to see if the cook man was home.

In the game he was the closest person I had that would listen to me. I needed him on my team. He was the coolest dad in the hood as far I was concerned. And If I was going to be back on the set again, he is the best man for the job. "Cook man," I yelled from the outside of his apartment.

Hector or Slug was not home either. Those were two of his sons. They had hustled out here too. Slug was the oldest. They were good kids. Hector just played sports. He stayed off the block other than to joke around or to go to the store. Now Slug on the other hand worked. If he had got money, it was on the low and out here that's where it always should be if not niggas will come knocking at your door.

Today niggas was getting bolder and bolder by the minute once that crack shit hit the scene. That's why I needed a cook man. "Damn" I told him I was stopping by to see him. Oh, shit there is his daughter. You remember Loraine from the movie House Party that started Kid n Play.

Yeah, the dark chocolate chick with the phat ass. And her uncle was the fat dude that always was offering people Dick Gregory when they wanted something to drink. Yeah, you know that's her, well their sister looked just like her but shorter.

I would have had a chance, but she was wifey material and now it was play baby time for me. Oh, shit man "what are you trying to wake up the whole hood?" Cook yelled from the upstairs window "what's up man"? I asked then I yelled "its back on we going to that four-family house around the corner from Red Ball".

"Ok" Cook said "You moving up huh?" I laughed and said, "what you mean Cook?" You not taking any more chances over at the rooming house at Red Ball no more huh? I said, "Cook after I saw them bring Lil June back to life after he overdosed, I was done." You know he was on that heroin. It reminded me of Robert too much and I wasn't trying to see all those needles and shit.

I did not want to be around people who used needles. I mean do you after my dad died from an overdose, I did not want any parts of it. Naw Cook man, that wasn't my kind of show. He asked me for "twenty dollars." I never asked why? Or what he needed it for I just gave it to him. If I had it, he could get it no question.

I tried to give him more, but he said, "He didn't ask for that amount." I smiled and replied, "no you didn't". Then well what are you giving it to me for then damn it?" he said. Then he turned and started towards thirty fifth and Newport. He walked away until his dark blue jacket had blended into the night.

Me Me was going to kill me. I should have been back hours ago. She thought she was going to ride the bus all the way back to Gary. Little did she know Derail was driving down to scoop her up for me. That was right on time. He was happy to hear from me when I called him. He could not stop telling me how thankful he was for putting him in that position.

I said, "Yo D chill man it's Kool just be here by Friday". "Ok" he said and hung up. See Tammy's father used her by telling her all my shit. He knew she would be so upset he would turn over all my assets to him. I know he realized I took the BMW and all he had was a copy of the title.

Then he would cut her off too. He would not have anything to do with her just like before when I met her. She was still my wife and I would give her my support either way with Me Me in the picture or not. I wasn't going to deny her if she wanted to come back home.

I think the bitch out Norveiw is pregnant again. I do not need Me Me to end up the same. So, she had to go. D pulled up and we went to get a bite to eat. Afterwards we walked outside and kissed. I see you later baby it was real. D walked over to me and asked about Lil C. I told him I sent him to work out the beach.

He fucked up a lot when he is around me for some reason and with me rebuilding, I'll have to hurt that nigga Man so, he asked "you not coming back Mr. Lee misses you man." You turned up out their homie. D was telling me and how the fellas were asking about me. Derail I'm going to stay right here and see where this leads me.

Ok he said, "and if you do want to come back you got the number, I'll see you later". I did miss the money, sex, and drugs. but Mr. Lee was from the old school and even though I did not steal anything from him. Like that young dude did from one of Mr. Lee's partners and they found him hands cuffed behind his back with his head cut off.

That's ok I like my big ass head no thank you. That was that and I finished talking. He did a couple donuts in the rental car that he had and they were gone. Things at the trap house were going so well I paid dude sooner than I had planned. Plus, I paid three months in advance on rent as well.

He was like I might as well take over the apartment yourself. I was like "you sure?" He said, "I had found a good job near the new house and I no longer had to come out this way." He thanked me again and gave me the spare key with the address to the rental office.

I knew exactly where the office was located. The picture popped in my head immediately. That was near where those three red bitches had stayed. The ones who had got Lil C for all that dope. Damn I hoped to run into them on my way to pay rent one day.

I was always closed on Sundays. My cousin's ex-wife mom would come over to cook every Sunday. Even though I did not open for business she'd come and cook and serve everyone who did come to buy from me during the week. People in the hood. The other hustlers at first did not know my angle; they looked at me as a goody two shoes or something.

But when they saw I had done it every Sunday they even started to come by and get a cold beer and a plate. She could cook her ass off and you could smell it throughout the whole hood. It was getting busier by the day. Especially with Cook screening the sales, it was money coming in hand over fist.

Then I met her. She was the local trick her name was Barbie. She had class about herself. She was not like any of the other tricks I ever met before. The way we met was crazy. She came to cop some coke and when our eyes met, I told her to come inside and have a seat while I get your order together.

I usually don't have people come into my trap house but it was something about her that said she was a good person. I returned to the front room, as she was taking her coat off. I said "hold on Miss Lady" I did not expect her to get comfortable right off the bat.

She said "I'm sorry." "No you did nothing wrong. It's just that I had plans this evening." In my head I was thinking of her. She was this Lil young chick from the hood. (She was crazy as hell we have not fucked yet. I told her she had to wait until she graduated before that happened.) She was coming over and I promised her I'll be free tonight.

Shit I asked her "was she free the following evening?" she said "Yes", and we hugged. While hugging she said it will not take that long baby or it is free. Damn that young chick was in the way. I did not want her to drop out of school. So, to make her go to school I would give her money.

She never kept her curfew, and she would pop up at any time. Cook be letting her by too. I did not want her popping up on us, not tonight and not with Barbie. Me and Cook needed to have a serious talk. Back to Miss Barbie. So, "What did you have in mind?" I asked her.

She began walking over to me with her breast out. I had asked her "so you out here all the time?" She said "Yes, but not like the other bitches" and she stood up over me and said (while bending over and exposing her ass and though her underside the crotch of her panties was smiling at me). "You typically do not see people that smoke crack as thick as I am. Do you?" "Hell No" I answered while she was unzipping my pants.

She said, "because I check myself into the rehab before allowing myself to shrink away to nothing." And then I started to see stars. She was sucking, pulling, and choking on my cock.

It was so hard I felt like I was about to pop .... And then with one big slop she swallowed everything.

She was our neighborhood super head. From then on, a beautiful relationship had formed. She would bring her tricks to the house. I did not care, it was only for a couple hours a day. Plus, the money she made with whoever she was with (which was usually navy boys) she gave it all to me.

Man, she was hot and thick with sex appeal. She did not look like Halle Berry in 'Jungle Fever' either. She looked like Halle Berry at the Grammy's no shit. When her days were slow, which was rare, she would stay with me at the house. We would fuck all day long. Eventually I had started to rent the upstairs apartment as well. I keep my unbagged work up there.

I had only brought out a small amount of work to sell downstairs. While up there we would pretend she was a college school girl back home from school and I was her high school sweetheart. I mean in our world all we really had was fantasy. She had this short cheerleader dress she used to wear during the escapade. We played fantasy games like that every day. It was like having a small vacation from all the chaos around us.

I liked this time of the month. It got me out of the hood for a few hours. It was rent time. I loved going down there and seeing Mr. Bloom's hot secretary. I know he is fucking his little assistant. She is going to own all his shit one day. I know I can fuck her. I see the way she looks at me.

See she be staring at it all the time. Watch as soon as I enter the office. "Can I help you?" she said, from behind her desk. "Yes" I'm here to pay rent on these three apartments. "Ok one moment please" she said, then went in the back to get me a receipt. I hope she does not get the wrong impression of me.

"Excuse me sir, are you renting all three of these apartments"? No ma'am, one is my mom's and the other two are coworkers of hers. I take their rent payments when I pay my mom's rent for her. "Okay" she said, looking strongly at me as she wrote out the receipts. When she handed them back to me, she said, "I didn't mean anything by that, you just looked too young to be renting three apartments".

I replied, "thank you Ms. Judy" and left the rental office. I got outside and walked to the car. Saga and whichever chick he was clinging to as a wife this week came to borrow some money. So, I had him run me around on a few errands. "What are you doing back there?" Saga asked me "Yo snorting some powder?" "Why you want a some" I asked.

He asked me when did I start doing that? At first, I was going to blast him with all the mind your business and fuck off shit! I said "you do not know what I have been through these last few years let me just say it has been hell!"

(Speech) Then I realized he was asking me these questions to make me feel guilty so I would do him a favor. I knew exactly where this was going. So I said, "Look if you do not want me in your car you can let me out right here! I had a car, but I left it in Lil C's father's garage.

It drew too much attention so I didn't drive it a lot. I was always at the trap house anyway. So having the car parked out of the hood was always better anyway. Between Saga and Lil C everyone thought it was their car. It did not bother me either because that too kept the haters and the police off my trail.

Both had stopped claiming the BMW once I had shown them the bill for the alternator, parts and labor receipt. They changed their stories quick. Hands down they did not have the money to fix it. So, I guess it was back to being my car again.

I decided I wasn't going to have it fixed either. Just to have them driving it all over town no sir. It was going to be stored and nothing else. He took me to get the rest of the errands done. Then we ended up back at the house. He wanted to come in, but I told him the house was not clean.

I had to catch him later. Barbie was stopping by to see me later. I did not know when she would be arriving. I did not want Mr. Saga over when she arrived, he would never leave. Work at the trap house was going smooth until everyone was having a shortage. You were lucky to get some good coke. But be warned niggas see you getting that cash they coming to rob your ass and that's some shit.

We were all criminals but just because you did not get off your ass and put food away for the winter, they'll say fuck it and come by and steal your food. I could never understand the hood but that's all we had. You had to love it. I stopped fucking with that nigga with the jag. He seemed as if he had too much going on.

You owed him a dollar. He would sweat the hell out of you. Even if you had owed him a dime, he was on it. I needed a new connect, and I did not want it to be someone local. That's too easy, them niggas will get desperate and send people at you. I saw it all in this game. If you did not learn from other people's mistakes you were bond to fuck up sooner than later.

It could cost you your freedom or your life. So, I started hanging at the club on Military Highway across from the mall. it was called the Big Apple all the out-of-town hustlers hung out here for some reason New York niggas the most. Whenever they came into Norfolk you heard about them, they would end up here by night fall.

I felt lucky this weekend because I met this dude last week from Queens. He had a cousin in New York with coke for the low. He said "his name was SUPREME" the name (at that time didn't mean anything to me but now as a grown man I knew exactly who he was CEO of Murder Inc.)

Did that ring any bells? For some reason I trusted them more, so I always dealt with people from Harlem. Well, he said "he was going back up there before Thanksgiving." I said, "Kool, by then I'll have my money right." I'll take about five stacks with me. The date was set for the seventeenth of November. Me and Lacey had started fucking around the young chick that come by the trap house unannounced all the time.

Well, she stayed in school and was about to graduate. I had to prepare her for college, and we got down to business. Graduation was around the corner. She had done everything I asked of her for school.

She had given me my first gun. Since I had been home, she was the only girl I trusted. Out of all the chicks I was fucking Lacey and Barbie were the only two allowed in the trap house. I told her to stay here while I go to New York and hold the house down for me. I'll get my man Cook Tee to watch out for you.

He'll be here with you till I get back. No, she insisted then said, "I do not want to hear you got killed or locked up from nobody else. I want to be by your side." "I'm going to be right back," I told her. I had admired her for her heart. Last week this dude came to the spot after he found out that her new boyfriend (me), can go suck a dick.

Well, he thought he was going to come to my house and confront me about it and I would let him slide. The next day he came over it was on. I invited him in. He then asked me "if I was the one who told Lacey, he can suck a dick". I said, "yes I said it and what are you going to do about it motherfucker"?

As he turned to the front door, he said something as he was leaving, I couldn't hear exactly what he said. Then I heard him say he was coming back with a tech nine. I reached for the trophy that was by the front door. I grabbed it and bust him in the head like three times. He turned to me and charged.

I was like one hundred and fifty pounds soaking wet dude had to weigh twice that easy, but I did not back down. Hell, no he was in my house and disrespected my girl in my hood. He was coming towards me. I lunged into him, and we collided in midair.

Once he saw that he could not get me in a bullshit wrestling hold we got up and we both started to throw blows. This is what I want. I had the advantage of this big ass burrito. I had caught him two or three times in the face and he could not land anything. He then got enraged and he charged me again, this time the momentum of thrust that he had accumulated was so strong that he had caught me off guard.

Then he lifted me up until my back was at the kitchen window. He was trying his best to put me through it. June he was about a hundred pounds if that was just standing right there watching. I yelled to June "hit him man, shit he's about through my ass out with the trash." As he was pushing me, I had to extend my wings and traps under my arms to prevent him from pushing me through the window.

Suddenly out of the corner of my eye I saw June and he had something in his hand. Boom he struck dude in the head. He did not let me go, but he did turn his head and once he did that, I relaxed my traps and opened the palm of my hands like huge symbols. I slammed them over both of his ears. He dropped me onto the floor and ran out the house yelling that "he was going to get his gun and come back and shoot us both".

I told June to put everything up and he should leave. I wasn't worried about them shooting me. I was from out here. They did not want no smoke. My family would kill those niggas. As I was walking June to his car this boy Big Ears came with a tech-nine and looked at me.

We locked eyes for a split second. Then I just saw the gun. He raised it in June's direction. Then I looked at him. He didn't hesitate when he did not recognize June. He had let loose. See they all know if Big Todd my cousin found out who had shot me, they would not have a chance in hell to leave Park Place alive.

He would find out and get revenge on their whole family. Believe me he would be there waiting for you. Big Ears ass could not afford to cash that check. He and Fat knows how Todd's crew gets down. So, he turned from me and focused his aim on June. Once June saw he had stopped talking to me and his gaze had then focused on June.

June took off through the front yard of the apartment. I hoped he remembered that there was a fence there. I wanted to laugh but this had not been the time to do that, not just yet. Dude that I was fighting in the house was still kind of new to Park Place, so he didn't know me and Todd was family. I didn't care, I wanted his ass. We wanted to finish what we started in the house so we headed out to the street in front of Red Ball.

I still can hear the gunfire, good he got away. Big Ears looked at his boy and saw that we were about get it in again, so he ran after June. Once I realized June had got away, I was ready for war.

Then I looked up and fat boy was running at me full speed. I braced myself for the impact and that was when the first one came. We belly to belly right in front of Red Ball. All I could do was grab him as tight as I could and brace myself for the impact of hitting the concrete.

I raced to get to my feet first and get his ass before he charged me again. I got up as soon as he released his hold on me. While he was bending with his hands on the ground, I kicked him right in the face. By this time my cousins from thirty fourth street had us surrounded. They had started edging me on to fuck him up. Todd came out from the crowd and said, "let someone else shoot at my family again you won't be eating turkey this Thanksgiving".

Finally feeling that family bond was in place I turned to fat boy and grabbed him. I went to belly to belly him, but he reversed it. Bam! One more time we went down and once again I got up before he did only this time, I didn't just kick him in the face. I kicked him in the nuts then in the face. again and again, I went ham on that nigga he was done.

The fat boy was at least three hundred pounds easy. I was dumb trying to belly to belly him but, hey I had my family behind me. I had gotten a little cocky. Who cares I won. It was getting close for us to go to New York, and I was cool. I had put shit from last week between me and Fat Boy behind me. For some reason someone kept parking a fiend rental car in my trap spot.

I did one in one of coke. Then went outside and tried to open the car door. When I realized it was locked, I stepped back and with my left leg I kicked the driver's side window out. Then I reached inside, unlocked the doors. I broke the gear shift and moved it too neutral.

We watched it roll backwards into the intersection. The car hit the telephone pole. Then Lacey ran out the house and said, "what happened to your leg, it's bleeding?" I hadn't even realized I was bleeding. I hopped to the house and wrapped it in a towel.

"I told Lacey to drive me to DePaul hospital". (Once these books are published, I'll be reimbursing you guys for the good job). As we were driving, I told her what had happened. She wanted to kill Fat boy. Inside the emergency room I filled the paperwork out with a fake name. When it was my turn to be seen, the doctor was shocked.

"He asked me if I was on any other medicine?" I looked at him and "said no!" He then led me to the back of the er. As soon as he saw how serious the injury was, he was amazed at the fact that I was not in pain. Once we were alone, he asked me again but this time he asked me more seriously. "Are you on anything"?

I said, "What we talk about is private, right?" He said, "yes". I said, "I had snorted a couple of lines of coke before and after the accident." He nodded his head and said, "it must have been strong because one centimeter more and your leg would have had to be amputated.

I opened my eyes then and asked, "If I would be ok now?" He said, "other than the blood loss your motor skills seem to be fine. We will have to wait for the CAT scan to come back to see if that's all clear. We will close you up and you'll be on your way." "Thank you" I said, and he left us in the back while he retrieved the results from the test.

When he returned, he said, "looking at the charts everything seems fine however, the gash is so long and deep in width we're going to have to use staples to close the wound." After saying that he shoved a needle in my leg to sterilize and numb the area. Then he cleaned out the wound.

Then he reached for a plastic bag with this stainless-steel stapler and retrieved a box. Inside that box were carriages filled with surgical stainless-steel staples. Then without warning (unless you consider this a warning, hold something) he started to close the wound. It felt like a stapler.

That shit hurts. He had to use at least three hundred staplers. I was still high on coke so he could not give me anything right away for the pain. I was done with the coke I thought to myself, I could not wait for the effects to wear off. He gave me a prescription for the pain and I ran to get them filled.

Back home all Lacey kept telling me was to "postpone the trip". I wanted to but I had no choice. This shit isn't going to set me back. I have a lot of people depending on me. A baby on the way here and one in Gary, Indiana. Recently I just found out at my mom's best friend's grandfather's wake, that I had a two year-old daughter. by the name of Ms. T.

My bills and my mom's house bills were adding up too. I threw Lacey's mom a couple hundred here and there for her and her siblings. So, I was spreading myself thinner and thinner by the day. I did not want her to know my habit was getting bad too. I really did not want to get to the point where they both ran out my money or my coke.

They both held me down. I'll be fucked for real without both in my life, so I thought. The night before we left, we stayed at the driver's house. He lived in Linden Wood right before tidewater drive with his mom.

Right off Tidewater Drive. You turned off twenty-six street onto the back road on the left. Before we had reached Tidewater, I told Lacey" do not worry you are with me ok." That night I prayed that the trip would go well and if things did go wrong, I prayed that the jail was not like the ones on television. I turned over, did one more line and lit a cigarette.

Lacey was asleep right beside me. She looked so beautiful. I hoped I was doing the right thing by letting her come along with me. God, please watch over us. I put the cigarette out. Laid beside lacey hugged her as I fell asleep.

CHAPTER 17

Going down a Dark Path

I wanted to leave her in Virginia, but I did not plan on driving the coke back home. I was going to catch the Greyhound. That's the driver's job. I told her "Ok, you can go." On our way up the road we passed Mr. Grand Am's house, the dude that took my high school girlfriend Ms. Texas. He told her that I was a player lol. The whole time he was telling her that I was in the back seat slick motherfucker.

After that shit, I always made my girlfriends ride in the back seat. I did not care who we were getting the ride from. I hoped it was worth it because I was a good friend to him. He was a nerd ass nigga and no one in school even like him. I had always had his back.

That's why to this day I did not trust another dude around my girl. I did not tell another nigga none of my business.

They are still married. His first piece of pussy and his last piece. It must be nice. He came out one pussy to be given life and he stole another person's pussy only to die in that same piece. Well better him than me I thought to myself.

After passing through I told the driver to pull off. I had let her ride in the front only because I had those staples still in my leg. I needed room to stretch my leg. Having it bent for that long ass ride would not have been too comfortable.

His radio didn't work anyway. The whole trip all Lacey talked about was the thought of her being pregnant. I was not trying to hear anything. All I wanted to hear was two words: New York. No matter what I had dope to sell and I was on my way to meet this Supreme cat. So, he could have been kicking game to her or not I probably would not have even known.

We arrived in New York kind of late. I wanted some coke. My leg was killing me, but I could not let Lacey know that I had bought any coke with me. She knew I snorted but she did not agree with me using it at all. I did not want to explain why I used cocaine. I guess from so many years selling it we all fall victim to the drugs one way or another.

She had just liked to smoke weed and drink. That was cool because if she was on anything harder I would have left her alone a long time ago. Frenchie told us to drive through Central Park and wait in the car. I did not care because my leg was killing me. Even though I did not drive I was exhausted. Back in the car Ty said, "they had gone to an abandoned apartment complex."

In the trap house niggas rigged up the electric and plumbing from the city for free. You had to put your money in this hole and the weed came out another hole on your way out of the complex. "Damn" I said, "OK Frenchie where were the hotels located?"

He was like "how much you want to pay for a room?" I thought about where we were, I said, "nothing cheap!" I did not want any bed bugs and shit crawling all over me. Well, he said "that's a two hundred dollars a night kind of room." I said, "well you two niggas sharing a room. It was not like they had pussy coming or something. Me and Lacey were getting our own room". Franchise had stayed with some people he knew in the city.

The next morning, he came to the hotel and woke us up early to allow us to get used to the work traffic as cover. We hit Queens Bridge and Lacey went wild when she saw that we had finally hit New York. I was excited too. It was different from what I was used to seeing. I mean you see it on television, but it was something about being here in New York in the flesh that gave you goosebumps with all the busy streets.

It brings the big city life curiosity out of you. We parked downtown near the train station. About a half hour later this navy-blue MVP pulled up. And if as it was yesterday, I can picture him parked across the street facing in the opposite direction. Showing only a side view of his face. "Wait he turned yep that was Supreme" Franchise said and he walked slowly to Supreme.

He returned and said, "his cousin is going back to Hampton University and he was taking five birds with him." So, to be safe I told him "I'll deal with him back home." Frenchie showed us some raw coke that weighed out to be one and a half ounces. He said, "Supreme wanted eight hundred dollars for it. He said since you are going to deal with his people back home, he gave it to you for the low.

So, we didn't have to ride back home hot." Ty was like "man for that is the same shit he is sending you back home." I said, "yeah how much did he want for it" I said, "eight hundred dollars". He was right, that was a good deal for one and a half ounces of pure coke.

It could take a four on four and still be raw. I told him "To go ahead and get it but if anything, go wrong he had to take the weight. I would come back and bail him out." He knew I had like twenty bands put up in my stash. He just did not know where. Nobody knew and that's how I liked it.

Franchise stayed behind, which was strange. I had thought to myself, but he was from here so fuck him "Go Ty" and we peeled out. It was like nine or ten in the morning. I asked Ty to stop as soon as we hit the New Jersey Turnpike.

I needed to use the restroom. We saw a rest stop. Everyone got out of the car to use the restroom then got a bite to eat.

When we returned to the turnpike something did not feel right like I had to pee again. I had just come from the restroom. I just ignored it and we continued driving. As we merged back onto the turnpike I saw the state boys weaving in and out of traffic until he was right on our tail.

Ty was nervous and he began to sweat hard. He made the car slow down then he would speed up. I told him "To keep his speed with the other drivers. As soon as he shifted into the far-left lane the state troopers lights went off. I bluntly said "yo pull over Ty". Lacey was up front with him. I was in the back seat like damn this was the bad feeling I felt.

I was not worried about being stopped. We had all remembered the story we all had agreed to say. We were up here taking a friend home for the holidays. We all had got his name right. It was just one thing Ty could not stop sweating the state trooper asked, "if he was ok" or "if he needed a doctor?"

Well from there in the report the trooper stated that's what gave him probable cause to search the car. Ty agreed to let him search his car. As soon as the trooper went in the car, he was right back out holding the coke.

It was as if he knew exactly where to look. I leaned over to see where he retrieved it from. When I saw the radio was hanging from the installation wires, I knew exactly where he had stashed the coke. Right under the radio I mean it was not even bolted down. He must have placed the radio on top of the coke. I looked at Ty and under my breath asked him "if you had it that close to you, why didn't you throw it away?"

He said "he did not want the state trooper to see him throw the coke." At the station I said to the trooper that "the coke was mine." He was going to let Lacey go since I had calmed the drugs. However, she needed an adult to come up to the station and sign for her. We did not know anyone in New Jersey.

I called my dude June to get her mom up here. He said he could not come until the next day. Now he did not let Ty go because he had really thought that the coke was his.

So, he booked both of us and said, "as long as I'm still willing to take the weight when we see the judge, he more than likely would let Ty go too." The next day at the jail I met with my lawyer. He gave me the rundown. He said, "Your girl wants to take the weight." I said "no." He agreed because she was a minor, they still would have charged me but would have given me even more time for using her as a drug mule.

However, since this is your first offense, they will be easy on you. Think about it and let me know what you want to do." "Ok" I replied and went back to the card game. Ty did not want to take the weight he was saying "he had just signed up for school. He did not want that on his record. Son I told him that from here on out that this was school right here and right now.

You and I are all we have in here. it's two to nine hundred and ninety eighty so get your shit together. It was the weekend and I called my aunt Lillian as soon as I got there. She was mad but I figured I will deal with that later. One sign of weakness in here and you'll end up being everybody's bitch.

My first plan of action was not to show any sign of weakness. That was not going to happen to me. One thing that stayed on my mind was I'm glad I went into the Marine Corps. They said if you could be a marine, you could do anything. I was ready for war. A good example: one dude just got in here and he was talking shit to this Spanish cat.

Before you could hear what was being said between the two. The Spanish dude spit a razor into his hand. Two seconds later the other boy was holding his face in his hand just that fast. They rushed him to the emergency room but I don't think they saved his ear.

I minded my business and watched who I kept company with too. Because people retaliate and are quick to anger in jail. Come to find out that dude had dated his sister and beat her up. That's why he was in jail and the brother said, "as soon as he saw him, he was going to cut him exactly where he had cut his sister." Shit like that didn't bother me simply because I did not know none of these niggas.

As soon as June comes to pick up Lacey I'm bailing out. I'm going to let the judge cut Ty loose. Shit since I did not feel bad for making bail. I'm taking the weight, he is going to get a free ride. I figured with fare exchange there's no robbery. I had to tell June where my stash was, he said "I'm broke and could wait for you to get home." I had to tell him where the money was hidden.

I would not have told him but since they were getting Lacey, we had a time frame in which the offer could expire and we all would wear the charge. Her mom had only two days off before she had to go back to work.

I had no choice. I said, "Yo June, listen, it's all in the shower rod at my mother's house." He shouted, "the shower rod?" It sounded like there were forty people around him. The only two voices I heard clear as day was Moonie's and Sharon's.

They were discussing the hiding place as if they never thought to check there. Like I couldn't hear them. Then he got back to the phone and said to me "how in the hell you get twenty grand worth of work in the shower rod?"

I told him it was "half money and half work." "Oh" he said and went back into the bathroom. I still heard them saying to each other I never thought about the shower rod. Then I heard Moonie in the background shouting "do not drop the soap motherfucker." I do not know why he was so happy because he better have that money from all the fronts, I gave him when I got home.

Or I will not give him another gram ever. June came back to the phone and said, "he got to the stash". I continued to tell him that "I have a person who'll take the coke wholesale. His number is under the television in my room. With the money he makes and the doe that was in stash would be plenty for the trip good".

"Ok" June said then right as we were about to hang up, I said "Yo hold at least five grand for me but take Lacey out shopping for her and her mom. And lastly, I told "June make sure the spot stays pumping you'll hear from me soon" He said "okay" and we hung up the phone. Once Lacey got out November flew by then December came and left.

For fun we toilet papered the pod. Most of the tissue hit the guards; they were mad as hell. Some of the inmates however were throwing batteries at them too. This made the goon squad get called in to calm everyone down. Luckily for us they did not have to use the pepper spray on anyone. That shit was lethal.

After that little stunt things inside had started to drag and I was hoping to be leaving here real soon. But I wanted to take advantage of the remaining time to seek some answers about religion. It was information on every religion you could think of inside here. I found some material that was saying how all the religions were man made. I was stomped. How is a person supposed to know which one to follow?

This has gotten confusing now. From here on my beliefs will be based on how I will treat people, how they treat me.

I may not know my creator name, but I will still give him all praises and acknowledgements. I felt fulfilled in my newfound reformed way of thinking.

However later that night as I was trying to get comfortable enough to fall asleep. I was awoken by a force on my chest that made my breathing difficult for me. At first, I thought I was dreaming, and I tried to sit up in the bunk hoping it would help me breathe a little better.

I woke up and turned as if to get out of bed and I could not move. It was like I was stuck to the bed. Now I'm fully awake, but I feel paralyzed. I started panicking. I looked over to the other three guys I shared the cubicle with. They were all sound asleep. Fearful of the thought that I was having a stroke, or something I tried to call out to the guard on duty.

He did not even turn around to see if I was ok. My mouth was moving but there was no sound. I yelled again but nothing came out this time. It was as if someone had their hands over my mouth muffling my screams. Then just as I started to pray, I saw him. It was a small but powerful Entity. I do not know where it came from.

But earlier that day I had read about them but why me? Why in here, right now? Most importantly, why me? I thought to myself and right as I was looking for an answer to help me rationalize or give me some kind of clarity to what the fuck was going on....

It spoke to me. He did not tell me his name (I did not want to know either). I wanted him off my fucking chest. He said, "you were looking for something or someone earlier in those books huh?" Before I could answer he went on to say, "you wanted to get locked up so you could try and kick that snorting habit too huh?" As I attempted to ask him "why was he doing this to me?" He again cut me off and asked me "if I liked the powder, he sent me from the pod next door?"

My eyes popped wide open, and I wanted him off me now. He was scaring the shit out of me I was bucking and thrashing my shoulders back and forward to loosen his hold on me, but to no avail he rode me like a raging bull. It seemed as if I was being tormented for trying to seek the truth.

Am I being punished by one of the devil's minions? Once I figured out where he was from, his hold had loosened on me. Finally, I could breathe again, air rushed into my lungs I felt so relieved. It was as if he had given me enough air to stay awake but not enough to move. It was like it knew the right pressure to apply. He did not squeeze enough so I would fall back to sleep. Realizing he was doing this to allow me to speak with him.

I did not want to lose this opportunity to ask him a few questions. I knew from the teachings I had received while I was attending church that if you knew their name you could gain control of them.

I only heard one side of the story. I thought to myself that this was the time I could hear what the other side was straight from the horse's mouth. This is when the demons I believed had entered my life. I had mustered enough air to ask him a few important questions.

I asked, "Out of all of those religious books, what was the truth of the universe?" "Where did all life forms come from?" "What made the wind blow? Most importantly, who did I owe thanks too for my life?" He pulsed and answered, "Why did I care if I continued the path I was on it would not matter anyway?"

He said, "you prayed for incarceration so you could stop snorting coke right?" I shook my head yes. He went on to say, "well when the guy next door knocked you did not hesitate to take the coke did you?" but you did?" I said, "I did not ask him for anything! He could not read or write so I agreed to help him."

I wish I didn't help that dude. He had got caught on his boat with a hundred and twenty kilos of coke. He was with his wife and her girlfriend. He had bailed the girls out, but they held him.

The friend was so spooked by the fact she was arrested. She was going to turn states on him. That was what the letter he had wanted me to read to him stated. After I read it, I wished I had never gone to the door. The letter he had me write for him was crazy. At first, I thought he was bullshiting.

You know to get attention in his pod for being a tough guy or something.

You never really knew who was in here. If you had listened to everyone's story, they all were kingpins. Some say they were here just waiting for their hoe's to come and bail them out.

But this was not the case with this guy, he was the real deal. I continued to help write a letter for this Louise guy. He was to go to her house and cut her tongue out.

After that if she still wanted to testify, cut her head off. I had thought nothing of what he had me to write. I took it as just talk and he gave me an eighth of some raw ass coke. Then he told me to "look him up when I came home."

I thought to myself he was never coming home. Especially with all that shit he had on him, but positive thinking was the key in here. I thought he was delusional at first and agreed to look him up when I was released. Well, a week after that letter was sent, we would talk from time to time. He would pass me some more coke and things went well.

One day a dude was calling at the door and asked "where was the guy who I used to read for the old man?" I went to the door and said, "why what's up?" He said, "he just wanted to give me something." Then he shoved this envelope under the door. I looked around first to make sure this was not a setup. Once I figured it was legit I reached down and opened the letter. It was not a letter it just had a phone number written on the flip and some coke about seven grams.

I asked him "what was this for?" He said, "the old man was released today, he had wanted me to give this to you." I said to myself well whoever he sent that letter I wrote to must have carried out the old man's wishes. I was glad for him but sorry for that bitch when the old man catches her ass. I was wondering how in the hell did he know that a dude in the next pod over was giving me coke. Before I could ask him the demon said, "So how was my detox coming along?" He started laughing out loud with his mouth gaping and showing its fangs. Right then I knew I should not have even exchanged words with this thing. I had stopped struggling to escape and a calm sensation came over me.

Something told me to not be afraid because that's what the demon wanted. I had relaxed and focused all my faith and energy on heaven. Then said this to the Entity "I rebuke you in the name of the Lord my father of the son and with the holy ghost." "I command you to unleash me. Leave me be from here on."

At once the calmness of the being had changed from taunting to malevolent. He tried to test my faith to see if I would crowd down. As I had displayed earlier. I stood fast. I did not know how he knew about me wanting to quit using coke! How did he know I was getting coke in here? The curiosity has faded, I wanted him from me and out of my face forever.

I raised my head (that was all I could do anyway) and looked him square in the eyes and said "I may not know his name, what he looks like physically hear this I know he is out there and he is real. He was acting as if he was going to attack me. I closed my eyes as tight as I could. I spoke to the lord: in my heart dear lord my God if this be your will so let it be done." I opened my eyes and right before the entity was about to bite into my face just like that he was gone.

Now it's January and still nothing. All the courts were closed. Damn I thought to myself getting busted over the holidays was hell. The whole government shuts down. I can't see no one till the fifth of January. I was telling my mom "Go and borrow the money from someone." She said, "they had to use the bail money on bills."

I knew her and Lacey were trying to keep up the business. I felt all alone by myself. Hell, if hustling was that easy then I would have let them do it a long time ago. I finally got a bail reduction since it was pure coke the judge originally gave me a hundred-thousand-dollar bail. A ten-year minimum with a twenty-year maximum sentence charge.

Since it was my first offense, she reduced it to fifteen thousand with ten percent. That made my bail fifteen hundred dollars good. Later that day I finally got a chance to catch up with Sharon. She said, "you have to wait till my income taxes come."

You know how long that could take to come. I was confused and I felt dizzy all of a sudden. I asked her "what do you mean I had to wait?" Before she could respond I went on to say, "mom I left you at least five grand to flip, a place to flip from and you still didn't save anything for my bail?"

I know what happened. They all got fat Christmases' and forgot about my black ass. I was fucking heated. If they were in front of me, I would have fought each one of them. I fussed and cursed her, Moonie, Lacey, June the Norview bitch and everyone I had helped till this day out.

Again, in the background Moonie tells my mom "To let me stay in jail she should buy a new car with her income tax!" I told them "To go fuck themselves!" I hung up the phone then I returned to lay down in my bunk. I was fuming. I took care of all of them and now I really see who had my back.

A week later I was playing poker and the guard came over to the table. He said "congratulations you had a baby boy" damn. I wanted to be there for his birthday. I did not think I would have been here this long. "Yo Kip" he was a white dude in the pod that did tattoos. I went to him and told him "I have fifteen packs of cigarettes. I wanted my son's name tattooed on my arm.

As soon as we were done, I felt better. I felt like he was with me and I was with him. After finally talking to my grandfather, he reassured me she was going to bail me out. Sharon was just waiting for her check to clear. We said goodbye then we hung up. I had opened a store in here and it was doing fine. Ty on the other hand was having a difficult time fitting in with the other inmates.

He did not get along too well with them. They were going to get at him a couple of times. I would not let that happen to him. How can we be co-defendants and I did not have his back? Next week a call came through that Sharon's check cleared.

Now I had to arrange for one of these niggas to play as my uncle and let their wife bail me out with their address. I only can make bail if I have a New Jersey address. Once I secure that I'm good to go. I wish the dude next door was still here. I had lost his damn number too. Oh well.

I walked over to a couple of new guys who were older, and I asked if I could talk to the older of the two. "Yo I'm about to make bail my mom on her way now from Norfolk, Virginia. I needed someone with an address from here to say they're my family so they give me a bond."

He looked up at me and said, "what's in it for me?" I had a grand on my books. (The state trooper did not take it. he said, "he liked my attitude". He told me he was going to let bubba fuck me. I told him "He did not want bubba to die did he?" Then he laughed and I was serious. I was fresh from marine combat training and I was waiting to use some of my new moves on a motherfucker".)

I was ready to pay anything to get out, I thought to myself. I said to the older inmate "I'll give you half of what's in my locker." He was like "what was in your locker?" The question was really what I didn't have in my locker? My shit was full of cigarettes of all kinds. I had the second largest store in the pod.

My partner was a kid named Henry. He was from Trinidad; he was about to be deported back to his country. He was only nineteen, but he had the heart of a lion. I was leaving the other half for Ty he was going to need it. The old man was like "Kool!" The fact I told him "I'll give his old lady a grand for her coming up here so late."

He was happy as hell so now I was set. they are going to visit me first then I can give them the ladies information. I didn't want to say it over the phone just in case they heard the plans. I did not want them to rewind the phone tapes and get all the details. Thank God the outside never looked so sweet.

I went to the trap house only to find out a new family has moved in. Everything was gone, you know what else was gone, my bad little habit. I did not snort coke anymore. I guess it was an even trade. How can I stay clean if it was always in my face? My son was getting big as hell.

All those books Jay had given me came in handy. I had named my son the same as mine. I now had a whole new start in my life with him and a new me. My whole existence was to leave something for my kid. My life was their life and now their life is my life. Since I had left New Jersey, they considered me as a bail jumper.

Two months after I got out I called the bondsman up and he said, "I can either pay him the remaining ten thousand dollars and only worry about the cops. Or don't pay him and you will have both of us on your ass. It was my choice."

I hung up the phone and said I will take a year then turn myself in. Until then I will pay up when they catch up. That year had come and gone so fast. Before you knew it my son's first birthday had arrived. I had arranged to turn myself into the bondsman after his party. They did not pick me up until after the super bowl XXVII.

The Dallas Cowboys had hosted the game against the Buffalo Bills. It was on the thirty first of January it was cold out. To me I was warm and in fact I enjoyed it as I knew this was going to be a long time before I was going to be able to walk outside free like this for a while. When he came to get me, we hit the gentlemen's strip club on Granby.

I found out that Lacey was not pregnant. The day we all got arrested, that was all she thought about. The following year, she did get pregnant on the same fucking day we got arrested. After we left the club, I had convinced him to take me by the house so I could see them before he took me back to New Jersey.

He agreed only If I could take him to get a bag of weed. At first, I thought he was bullshitting me. Then when he asked me "if I wanted to see my son or not?" I said "Man I cannot pull up to my peoples house in no damn handcuffs are you kidding me?" He looked over at me and said, "just remember you called me so, no funny shit." I was not trying to run. I had four kids now and that's why I called him. I had wanted to get this shit out of the way.

We got a box of Dutches on the way to get the weed. After getting the weed I took out a Dutch and started rolling it up. I looked over at him as I pulled on the blunt. I was savoring every breath as if it was going to be my last blunt.

I asked him "What type of bounty hunter are you?" He said, "I am one of those who understands people have ups and downs in their lives." He went on saying "No matter what they have done as long as they show me respect, they get respect back."

I couldn't argue with him on that because I felt the same way. At the jail house in North Brunswick, New Jersey we smoked one more blunt. As he was about to pull in, he looked at me and said, "Wait, do you have any more weed on you?" I did damn he remembered and if he would not have asked me I damn sure was not going to tell him that I put two of the bags in the front part of my underwear.

He asked for them back and took me in for booking. They booked and processed me into intake. It was going to be a long night. All I could think of was my kids, their mothers, my Lil brother and my mother. I fell asleep then I woke up in a cold sweat to them calling my name. Then I realized I was in jail.

I was so high earlier that it did not seem real or at least I did not want it to be real, damn. Ty had been sentenced to one year. They however gave me two years. The judge had the nerve to ask me "What do I do for a living? Apparently, I was not very good at it huh?" I had thought to myself as they had led me out the court. She may be right but it's not like I had a road map on what to do in life or what not to do in life. I'm in here now. This is the last time I will ever take other people with me to score. The court sentenced me to eighteen months before I could be released. Then I must serve one year on parole. "Ok" I said to myself "I can do this."

After a week of intake, I was looking forward to going to population. The other inmates said, "in population we can have more movement plus we can get jobs to work. That helps the days go by faster." The good time gets added to your workday." The extra dollar a day helps a little too. That's what they paid you for working in jail. Yes, a dollar a day.

I didn't have to worry about the money. My granddad had me on everything I needed. I'm just upset I had put this shame on him. To be his oldest grandson and I ended up in jail. From the time I could remember he never let me forget when he had locked himself out the house. I was three years old and he said,

"Tee had got a chair and reached up and unlocked the dead bolt for me to get back in the house."

He was really nervous because my mom was on her way to pick me up. He did not want her to take away this time we shared together. Because he was locked outside of the house, she would have known I was alone. He was so proud of me from that day on.

Finally, they placed me in the "K" unit. It was a regular pod in the North Brunswick prison. It had three levels. Each floor had twelve blocks on each. In the twelve blocks were four bunks. "K" unit was not a working pod. If you kept your nose clean when a bunk became open you would be taken into consideration for the working pod.

It was just my luck that they had paroled many inmates. The parole board had sent a hell of a lot more down to the penitentiary in Trenton. Once inside it was no different in here than the working unit. The working unit stayed half full all day because everyone worked in the jail helping in day-to-day operations.

The others work at businesses around town and on the outside of the jail. This was the sweetest part of the bid. If this was all there was to doing time, I see why half the people keep coming back. Half of them grew up with the guards. Some of them were even schoolmates.

Some even were family in some way. Being here to them was a vacation. Damn I got a visit today. My bitch from Norview was coming. I told her not to come. I did not want her and the kids to see me here. I did not want them to think that being here was Kool.

I didn't want them to think I could leave when they left. I think that thought had hurt me the most. I asked my Bunkie, who was a barber, "Could I borrow his clippers so I could freshen up my Brooklyn fade plus tighten up my edge up?" He slid off his bunk and handed them to me. He said, "make sure you clean them and I want a pack of smokes for you using them."

I retrieved the smokes and threw them on the desk. Now I'll be Sharp when she comes to the visit. I went to the third floor and got the clippers out. I removed his mirror and I began to cut my hair. First, I faded it. That was the easiest part. Now I closed the blades on the clippers all the way then opened them just a centimeter and followed the outside of my hairline.

Just an inch all the way around my hairline. Starting on the right side of my head above my right ear. Then I would open the blade halfway and cut an inch above that line I had just cut. After that I would open the blade all the way and put the one guard on the clippers and blend all the shades together. The blend would remind you of butter. Only ending with a milky middle... perfect. Now, I removed the one guard and closed the blade until a millimeter of the moving blade was visible. Then I would follow the outline of my fro imagining a basketball was in front of my face. With only the outer shape of the ball showing I would trace cut off the loose ends.

Excellent now to clean off the clippers. Get out the edgers. I would trace my outline first in my head to make sure I had a good handle on the Edgar's. This helped, they would run hot fast. I used them only for edging up.

I don't run them while trying to practice holding. Kool, I looked myself over. Then I cleaned up my area and showered. I returned his tools and thanked him again for letting me use them. Ever since my mom made me learn how to cut my own hair, I did not feel comfortable letting anyone else cut my hair. That except dude G from the hood.

"How does someone make you learn how to cut your hair?" you ask. When most people cannot even shave without fucking up their mustache let alone cut their hair? To the point where people are stopping you asking you "who did you go to and get that cut?" Or who was your barber on the streets? As a kid I was ashamed to let people know that I cut my own hair.

See everyone else went either the shop on church street or to G. At that time I did not have the money for either one. My mom made me learn at eleven how to cut my hair. If I did not do a good job she said "She would beat me. If I do not cut it at all she will beat me."

Either way I did not have a choice in the matter. I did whatever cut she had wanted me to cut. I thought if people knew I had cut my own hair they would pick on me and my skills. I did not want people to know so I would lie. I would tell them my grandfather had taken me to his barber in Roberts Park.

Well over the years of cutting my hair in reverse I became very good at all haircuts. Not as much in textures. Well at least not until I had met the head barber in the prison. His name was Goose. He had come from a long line of master barbers and he was locked up running the prison's shop. He told me when a spot came open, he would let me work in the barber shop with him.

When they moved you to the work pod everyone started in the kitchen. I have been in the kitchen for about six months now. I could not wait to get in that barber shop. However, it was not that bad in the kitchen. I even managed to befriend the two ladies who were civilians. They ran the kitchen for the culinary service.

I do not know why they had made the name of the company sound so exotic when no matter how you said it the food was nasty as hell. They had used an additive called soft Pete. This hey used to numb sexual stimulation between the inmates.

I hated working the third shift in the kitchen. but I learned fast that the kitchen supplies play a big role in the inmate's social structure. More than you would think, the hustle they made helped their bid go by with any help from the outside. And you say "well how is that? Well the jail did not sell ground coffee in the canteen. They did not sell sugar either, nor fresh sliced meats and cheeses.

Well, since these things were not sold in house. They were however sold on the black market in the jail. I mean everything was for sale and no one liked the jail food, so if you worked in the kitchen, you had access to the same food as the officer's. And if an order came out for anything everyone in the kitchen worked together to deliver the goods to the buyer.

Whatever was earned in the sale was split evenly. Like I said I was ok. I washed the dishes. Then helped on the line with putting food onto the trays. That part was fun because everyone came online. We threw the food onto the trays every meal. It always would be some Idiot that would start a food fight. I always stood by the opening to the officers dining hall.

So, I could see this one lady that worked in the medical office. Man, she was a thick and chocolate chick. Her ass sat up so high that you could place a laptop on top of it. The laptop would not fall off even if she stood up. I was picturing that in my head.

Then this inmate next to me said, "Yo that's my cousin." I had hoped not because he would pick his nose all day long and I was not looking forward to seeing him at any family reunions. He was the reason I really wanted to get out the kitchen. But with no other skills the only other thing I could do was sweep and mop the jail.

They left those jobs open for the older inmates so that was not going to happen. Normally after I left the kitchen the whole shift would go back to the pod and play cards. Most of them would play bridge but the hustlers would play Tunk or poker. I knew how to play Tunk already. I did not really sit around that table to watch.

They would always end up the same either someone thinks they're the lowest and drops their hand. Or they were running, they would hit you to stop you from tunking. Even though that's how you play the game. When you're playing twenty and fifty dollars a hand, I want better odds than they were giving out.

A lot of the players at those tables were the older inmates that had been coming in and out of this place since it was a farm. As a matter of fact, that guy right there with the scratch on his throat yeah him. He's been in here back when this place was a real farm, they grew the food and animals they ate.

He said "The inmates had started fucking the animals. They were raising for food." I guess the warden and the staff found out their food was being fucked, plucked then served to them on a platter. That ended that work program. Poppy seaw when I first came here. He had schooled me on saving my money. By the end of the week, he saw me making a picture frame out of the cigarette packs.

At the same time, he had also seen me folding twenty-dollar bills into the folds of the frame. If it had been anyone else, I would have told them to mind their business. That's why I was on his tier because he was one of the few in here that had minded his own business. Later that day we were alone in the kitchen. He had asked me "who I was sending the cash to every month?"

I said "I still had promised my girl I would pay rent on our apartment while I was here. Every time I hit a hundred dollars; I would send it home. I had made some of the money from moving goods up the turnpike (the hallways) from the kitchen. I earned a pack or two cutting hair in the pod after work.

The packs I sold as cartons for a hundred dollars cash each. Hector had gotten visits from his girlfriend at the time as Poppy. When he would kiss her, she would (with her tongue) push a small package in his mouth and he would swallow it.

He then would fish it out the toilet and sell it to the other inmates. He said "it's usually heroin" because you did not need a lot to get high. The amount he sold them was the size of a needle head. And you could get fifteen packs of cigarettes for one bag. Then he'll take the cigs and sell it to a new inmate that had a dope habit. The rich kid's parents would smuggle cash inside to help their kids continue his usage while he was in jail.

He was making way more money in there than I was, but he was also taking bigger chances too. He, like Goose, had taken a liking to me because they saw that I was a young man doing my time and still taking care of home. Poppy came to me Sunday and asked me if "I wanted to go to the church service?" The pastor came to the pod and held a short session every other Sunday.

We spoke on trials and tribulations the first day I had attended. After church, Poppy told me that I should not mix with the other inmates. If they know one another from childhood and they're in jail screwing each other over. They don't know you at all, so they would not hesitate about fucking you over. I went back to my tier and watched the floor.

I did this after work for that whole week. Taking mental notes who to watch and who to steer clear of in the pod for the remainder of my sentence. This was my first time I ever went to jail. This was a real life college.

See in college if you failed you could just pick the course up next term. Oh no, in here the guards do not listen. So court was held in these walls daily by the inmates. And if you did not mind your business, you could inherit that person's debt and end up like him or worse. At church the following week I saw Poppy and I told him "While watching the pod the last week I saw brothers fighting brothers, cousins warring with cousins. I wanted to thank him for that information he had schooled me on.

He did not have to share that powerful information and let me find out the hard way. I read a lot of Donald Goines books while in jail and if an older person came to you with an ounce of interest in this cold world you listened to them.

I thanked him and walked away. See in here unlike college there was no start over. If you fail a course, you either lose a limb, your manhood or even your life.

These lessons were important, and I listened. I wanted to just do my time and go home. My second child was born while I was in here. First my son was born right before I made bail. Then as soon as I turned myself in my daughter was born a week later. I don't know but that Norview chick, if she's around when I get out, I'm going to try and see if we can have a normal life without hustling.

We'll see I thought to myself as I laid in my bunk waiting for the guard to start my shift in the kitchen. I started to think about my kids and tears filled my eyes. How did I let this happen to me? While waiting for me to answer I drifted off into a dream. From the start in a flash, I saw myself being shot ending my military career then jail.

I felt like my life was all over. The military had medically discharged me. That means I had lost my job and college fund. The shooting had left me with a fifty-thousand-dollar hospital bill and I have three boys and two girls that need more than money to survive in this world.

I had to hustle. If I did not, how would my family have survived this long? A voice said in my dream "the same way they are surviving now." When you can go home don't feel as if the world has to rest on your shoulders. I woke up at the sound of the guards quietly walking around and waking up the other inmates for the shift.

I could not wait for him to come to me. I got up and walked to the restroom to brush my teeth then went to work. As I walked the turnpike on my way to the kitchen, I'd always pass the prison barbershop. It was located right on the corner of the hall as you turned to the adjacent cross way by the jail's entrance.

That day everything felt good, but I was on a crash course with Chance. See no matter how far you go out of your way to just mind your own business it is always one person in the crowd that must try you. Right then as I was washing the dishes and preparing them for chow.

This light skinned dude approached me and told me "I stole his kilo of sugar and coffee." At first, I was confused as if this was a joke. But somehow, I knew it wasn't because he was sweating and looking around as if he was waiting for me to make the first move. My first thought was to grab him and just choke him out, but I knew of him and his family. They were huge so instead of making an emery I made a friend.

I said, "Yo I don't know what the fuck you're talking about!" Then I said to him (just to make sure that he wasn't trying to shake me down by making all this shit up to get me to steal that shit for him for free. I played it Kool. He was not pulling that shit on me.

I wanted to go home to my kids, and no one was stopping that from happening.) How do you think I had anything to do with it missing?" Then he looked under the sink and said that "he had put it under there so when the juice for the pods went out it was to be placed inside the juice and you're the only one that was over here at the time."

The trustee in the pod (once the juice was done) had to remove the coffee and sugar before the guards came to inspect the food carts and juice containers. It was three packs of cigs for a single cup of coffee and two packs for a cup of sugar. It was important and expensive for that package if I had to replace the product.

It may even be a reward for it so I said, "if I find out where it went, what I get?" He looked at me and grinned then said, "find it and we'll talk but I better not find out you had anything to do with it" and he walked away as if to say if you do have anything you will have problems.

I knew at first, he did not care too much for me. We both were after the same chick in the kitchen. She would go in the freezer with me after they all have left for the day. She showed him love too. He may think I am trying to move in on her. I did not care about that shit.

I had cut some of his boy's hair. He was still questioning my skills before he sat in my chair. Me and his partner looked just alike. He was a Kool ass nigga. He reminded me of the comedian who played in house party, small world and we had the same hairstyle. A Brooklyn fade so, I'd cut his hair for two packs of smokes. I would tell the rest of them I did not know how to cut their hair. I did not want the other barber hating on me for taking their clients.

Then I learned if you had a talent or knew a work trade you did a service for free one time. Then let everyone see your service as free advertisement. It was good for business. The only drawback was the inmates would expect you to cut their hair every other day.

That's why I would only cut afros. By dinner I had found out who had hijacked the shipment. It was the juice boy I confronted him with and he tried to deny it. So, I watched him when we had dropped off the juice to our pod.

As soon as the juice was done, he walked over to the service area to clean the container out. As the top came off the last container, I had signal Goldie to go over to him by the sinks. There he was drying off two big green blocks they were duck taped. Damn they wrapped them just like kilos of coke or dope. The shit was funny but useful. Well after they divided up the bounty between their crew. Goldie came over to me with a cup of each sugar and coffee.

And he said, "thank you". I saw it in his gesture that he had meant well, and I accepted his apology. We became close friends afterwards. I thought to myself a plan well done. I started to cut his hair until I was paroled. The barber job had come open. Goldie ran to the kitchen and got me. I went to Goose and asked if the position was still open?

He said "yes if you wanted the job." He looked at me and asked, "can you cut white people's hair?" I said, "hell yes I could but not as good as I can cut black people's hair!" He then said "well we're surrounded by crash dummies. I'll teach you the in's and out's you got the spot". I did not see why I could not learn while on the fly. Shit half of the white people did not even care how their hair was cut. They either wanted to be cut either short or faded out in the back.

I knew he was great at cutting their texture of hair. I caught on fast. I had planned to keep my eyes on him then I knew I could not go wrong. I had wanted out of that kitchen anyway. He told me which correction officer to contact. His name was Barry. tell him "You are next for the barber job".

He said that he knew I had the job. On my way back to the pod I saw her again damn she smelled like fresh air. Her hair was braided and pinned up in a bunt. She let the back hang down to her waist. She had worn this tight dress with slits going up both sides. I looked over to the guy that was walking next to me and said, "I'm going to make her my wife one day" and at that moment she looked my way.

Oh, shit she heard me, and she smiled. I winked my eye at her, and I kept walking until I passed her by. If this was the block, I would have stopped by her and "asked her what her favorite place to eat?" Once she would have told me I would have offered her to join me on a date.

Then that's where I was just heading. Even though it would have been a line. It normally works. I mean who turns down a free meal at the restaurant of their choice? But we are not on the block, and I have nine months left to make her mine.

Back at the pod I found out from her cousin her birthday and whatever information he had to offer. It had cost me a pack of smokes plus listening to his long ass story. We were in jail all we had was time. However, I did not want to spend all of it listening to him while he picked his nose. Damn note to self never invite him over to our house for anything ever. I received the clippers from the correction officer at the barber shop. And at the time I had wondered why the last barber had given up his job?

Not like I really cared because I was not going back to the kitchen. So, it did not matter. I just wanted to know. Well, he said "the last barber had got shanked and he was shipped down to the penitentiary." I was like damn that "inmate must have really taken his hair cut seriously!" He said" that a lot of them are coming here from other jails to answer for charges that they had received from passing through the county.

"So, when these inmates go to trial because their charges are usually high profile cases. The reporters are there photographing their trial so, they want to look as if they're innocent" he said. I then said to him "so all of them are in the daily newspaper"? he looked at me with a shocked expression and said, "where have you been all of them are usually on the front page". or on the front page of the local news section and they want their pictures to look good while there on trial".

I knew I was not going to give this job up. I pictured all my cuts on the front page of the paper. I looked at him and said, "I'm ready." He was like "good the inmate who had shanked the last barber still needed his hair cut." This cut was going to be my first assignment. After rechecking all my equipment, I heard the sound of the doors opening. "Open the outer doors of upper B pod," he yelled into his shoulder intercom.

The doors cracked open and then the heavy chains began to slide the outer door open. "Step in," the guard said. Once inside the pod it was totally different then the pod I was lodged in. All the cells had steel mesh in front of them. The small tray slot was for meals. It was only four showers but from what I'm told they shower by their cell numbers. showered every other day for odd and even cells units.

This Spanish guard led me to the cell. She was exotic as hell. Her hair was long black and wavey. It was waist length, and her uniform was so form fitting you could count her ribs. Her breast was so firm that if she had lifted her shirt they would stay right in place. It looked to me from here that her girls were perfectly fine. They were ready for a stroll on a nude beach.

Once we locked eye contact, he asked me "if I wanted a drink?" I was like "sure" thinking he had meant a soda or bottled water maybe. I did not know they had special privileges because of their status. He looked at the guard and shook his head. She had returned to the cell with a bottle of Henney.

I was in aww. I have not had a real drink of liquor in almost a year. We had drunk like half the bottle. Then I just came out and asked him (I did not want to bring it up but after he had told me about his last stop before coming to Middlesex county he was in Norfolk. I had been curious to know who he had known down in my city). "Who did he meet while hustling in Norfolk"?

He did not answer me right away. I did not push for an answer either. We started talking about the clubs and the streets. We had also brought up the women he dealt with while in VA. It was one chick we had both known. And believe it or not he described my oldest daughter's mom to a tee.

I mean the times he is telling me that he was with her when I was in Chicago. He could have been Ms. T's father, but I wasn't going to let that stop me from being her dad. I've already taken her in as mine and that's all she will know that I'm her father. As I looked at him more closely, we did favor. I could see that's why me and Ms. T looked so much alike. I started counting back the months I was with her mom and it added up to me as being the father.

Me and T's mom were not a couple. She got pregnant the first time we had sex. I told her she did not have to tell Ms. T anything and things have been fine ever since. After we laughed, I asked him "why did he cut the other barber?" It was a taboo thing to ask another inmate, you never asked someone what they did, or did not do?

You just don't unless you're ready to take whatever the person does to you for prying into his business. Sometimes nothing happened but it was always a rare occasion when some had got bad news or their parole did not go through and a question like that would send them off their rockers. He looked at me and said "yo man I do not blame you if you do not want to shave me and line me up."

I told him "That wasn't the case, I just did not want to make the same mistake the other barber did!" We laughed again then he told me "That the other barber had told him he could do a good job on my hair cut," so he gave him a chance. Then he went on saying, "he went too far up on my beard, and I got upset then I stabbed him."

I looked at his shape up and said, "I can see what you're talking about." He assured me that I did not have to cut his hair if I did not think I could do the job. I said, "I can, that's not a problem. Plus if I don't cut your hair, I'll be out of this job." See you stabbing him is the reason I got hired.

If I do not cut you up it is back to the kitchen. He was like "I hate to cut your ass too." I said, "man this is what I do." I have never cut anyone's hair until I got locked up other than my own but one thing I did know was my hair always came out good. If it didn't my mom would be whipping my ass. So, I was going to pimp his edge up out.

It was going to be on the front page of the newspaper for the new year. When I had finished his haircut I hurried up and passed him the mirror. I waited to see his facial expression. I used that to see how the client would like my service. I kept his hairline sharp and his beard lines to the letter. He turned and with a big ass grin and said "yo now this is what the fuck I'm talking about." It felt good.

And from then on, I felt like I had to go to jail to find my calling. I could not wait to tell my granddad. I wanted to become a licensed barber when I got home from jail. I'm not going to hustle anymore. I'm going to become a barber, open a shop and make him proud of me. When I called to tell him my plans, my mom came on the phone she "told me that grand dad had died two weeks ago.

No one wanted to tell me because I was so close to being paroled." She stayed out of contact with reality so much that she did not realize what she had just told me. She never thought about how I would take the news. All the times he was in my life flashed before my eyes. As if I was in a motion picture movie with the film that was stuck on fast forward.

Then the movie ended. I hung up the phone without even saying goodbye. I went to my bunk and cried out to myself not wanting anyone to ask or hear me. I wanted somebody to ask me how long did I have left? I was going to show them more than I could tell them.

Then a voice came to me and said, "the last time when we talked son, I told you I had to leave. I did not say where or when I was leaving. You asked me why I had to go? I could not tell you I just knew it was going to be soon." Then the voice went on to say, "I waited for your return as long as I could son, I heard your plans and I will watch over you and your dreams until you come here to me."

From the sound of that voice, I had recognized who it was. It was my grandfather's voice. I got up and asked, "who wanted a haircut?" Later that day before the first shift had ended in the medical unit, they called me down to the office. It was a procedure to talk to anyone receiving news of death in their family.

To see if they will become suicidal. There she was my future wife. She oversaw the inmates in the medical unit. I wanted to talk to her and then it happened, she told the psychiatrist she would do my interview. She called me into her office and told me to "shut the door behind me." She asked the same old things they would always ask you whenever you were sent to medical.

Once the formal work was done, she asked me "if I felt suicidal?" I thought to myself no, but I did not want this time to end. Not that fast and I did not want to say yes either. They would give me a paper suite then throw me in the crazy pod. All the people there were drugged up.

Believe me no one wanted to be in there with them. All they did was sleep and that pod smelled like shit. I told her "No, I did not but the way I do feel now that I lost my granddad is alone. While being in here if a person farted and did not say excuse me, I'd kill him."

Her eyes got big, but I think something else happened and then she told me "I was free to report back to the pod." Before I got to the door, I turned my head and asked her "if I would

GET OFF THE BUS

be able to see her again?" she said, "of course I'm going to be your wife right." I laughed and that had made me feel better than I did without taking meds.

Back at the pod the Spanish guy who worked the medical unit came to me while I was cutting hair. He told me she said "I better call, or she was going to tell the warden I had sexual harassed her." I said "what?" He looked at me without a smile on his face. Call her tonight excitedly I said, "Ok I would."

He walked to his area to prepare for dinner. I called her right before the phones were to go off for the night. Just in case the phone conversation went in the wrong direction the phone would save me by hanging up on its own.

She accepted the charges and said, "I thought you were too afraid to call me." My dick got hard as hell. I said, "I wasn't scared, I was just making sure this wasn't a setup!" She was like "if I was not interested, I would not have given you my number." I wonder why she gave it to me anyway. There were at least fifty guards that wanted that ass too. She was hot. Why me? I wonder to myself. She went on to say, "I am in the tub."

I like to have exploded in my pants. I looked around for a chair and I was too late right before I could say "hold on" the phone hung up. She had passed word to me again to call her the next day. This time she had me call her office for my glasses. When I got to medical the guards were all in my face. Looking me up and down like I was selling drugs or something.

Anyway, they were just jealous, and I did not care. As soon as I shut the door I went to her desk. We began to kiss. I was sliding my tongue in and out of her mouth slowly until we both were exhausted. She wore a dress again today, this one was above the knee, and it was made from a netted material.

I started to finger her pussy. Damn I thought I was in heaven. For a minute I felt free. I did not want it to end. I took her big ass breast out and pulled on her nipples. She came and I was just drunk off the smell of her famine essences as it ran down my arm.

We did that for the remainder of my time, and she helped me out a lot. I had lost my granddad but meeting her and having our secret visits was all I needed for my outro. When that day came for me to be paroled, she picked me up from downtown New Brunswick.

We went to her mom's house and we fucked for the rest of the day. That night I was supposed to go to the bus station, but it felt so good being in a woman's arms that I wanted to stay forever. That morning she flew me home on a private flight. We promised to stay in contact. I did not know that we would be back in each other's arms sooner then what I had expected.

CHAPTER 18

Not falling for the Bull

I had to report the same parole officer as my boy Saga. I had grown my hair out and he was jealous as hell as usual. My hair had grown so long that when I had it braided into cornrows the tips would hang to the center of my back. Anyway, at the time I didn't have my own set of clippers.

Saga was a so-called barber himself. I had asked him to come over and give me an edge up. Man, I could have killed him. He took the clippers straight through my braids. then said, "we had the same parole officer and she did not like braids."

I told him "You should have let her tell me that shit man." I was mad as hell and told him to just cut it bald. He was always jealous of me and for what I could never understand it. I had a feeling we were on a crash course to that road real fucking soon. Being back home things had changed. Not so much the buildings, the people seemed different.

Not the same faces on the block either. I'm just trying to get a job. Me and the girl from Norview have a little spot out Little Creek near the ninety-nine-cent movie theater. Things do not seem right. I can't put my finger on it, but after work she runs out with her little girlfriends every night. I know she's creeping with Duce.

He was a dope head that went to the same school as Saga. He was no real threat, plus I was here for my kids. I must get out of the house. I cannot get a job sitting here. I decided my mom could watch the kids while I job hunted.

As I'm cruising the hood, I see all the old crew. The talk is all the same. See my whole family get money and that's all most of them knew how to live. When you asked for money for gas to look for a job or for diapers for your kids, they would give you dope. With me being on parole I was not going to take drugs.

I had no plans of going back to jail with a new charge. Then being obligated to finish the time I owed in New Jersey, No thank you. The new time I politely turned it down and niggas shouted "Oh he thinks he better than us."

A lot of the family I wrote off and a lot of them had done the same to me. It suited me fine. I didn't care. I did that time in New Jersey alone. None of them fuckers sent me any money. Not even a visit. What they were saying went in one ear and out the other.

That's when I knew I was tired of being in Norfolk. One thing in jail I learned was that new people, new places and new things kept you focused. That was going to be the only thing that keeps me out of trouble. Well now I need to put that shit to use ASAP! Norfolk and the seven cities were designed to trap you off.

It was like catching fish in a barrel. These niggas did not care because they hustled until they went to jail. They would do five or ten years. Then come home all swollen up with no skills for employment. Then they just repeat the same thing that got them locked up for the first time.

I knew that was not for me. That's how I knew I needed a change. I gave the Norview chick a second chance at trying to raise our family. We had an opportunity to manage a dollar store, the first in the state. I felt that the concept was catchy. In time we could buy into the franchise.

That would have been worth the hustle, but she did not want to give the idea a chance. I knew from there she did not want me to do anything but sell dope. I was not interested in that route anymore. From there on I was plotting my departure from this rat race. I stayed in contact with my New Jersey thing from the prison. She had come to Virginia from time to time and stayed for the weekend. We would go out and have sex all night long.

The next time I'll ask, "How would she feel if I told my parole officer that I wanted to go to New Jersey?" I had wondered if she would accept me living with her until I could get on my feet?" She told me she'll help me in any way she could so I'm going to see what type of help she is willing to provide me.

She called me the other day asking, "if it was ok for her to come and visit this weekend coming up?" I told her "That was ok." I was not doing shit anyway. I did miss that pussy. When she gets comfortable, I will spring it on her, after I put this dick all in her stomach. That always worked on them hoes. She would be happy for me to come and stay with her. The only thing was that I had remembered she stayed with her mom.

I was excited until that came to mind. She told me before that if we were married, she would not have a problem with me moving in with them. I hope that offer is still on the table. The last conversation we talked about saving up to get our own place. With the both of us working we would not be in her mother's home for long. That was if I did decide to come.

When she came, I told her the plan I had. Then I asked her to work on making it happen. I felt if I do not get out of here soon two things are going to happen. Neither one of them had a pretty ending. Before she left, she had asked me the next time she came down to Norfolk "would I marry her?"

I said "yes" then it was set. Two weeks later she flew down and we eloped at the Justice of Peace. They held the ceremony at the county clerk's office in Norfolk, VA. This I felt was a new start for me. Now all I had to do was tell the Norview chick that I was leaving. That wasn't going to be easy.

As I walked through the door that night, she was in the front room crying holding the marriage license in her hands. She said, "this is the second time you got married on me!" She screamed and shouted at me as I turned to lock the door behind me.

"Why?" she asked me. I told her "She was a follower, and I needed a team player." She cried and said "she could be whatever I needed her to be" but it was too late. I said "if the deal with the dollar store could have been rekindled" it might have been a chance for us to work on our relationship. The opportunity was gone and now so was I.

I told her "I'll send half of the bills and money for the kids. Now she had all the time she wanted to see Duce." I was free again and New Jersey bound. We stopped at the parole office for my last report date before I had to move to New Jersey.

She called us into the office and she asked for our marriage license. The parole officer made a copy and returned the original to my wife. She informed me that "since Norfolk did not have any charges on me it was not a problem for me to be paroled out of state. However, if for any reason (this is when I should have declined to go at that time and wait for my parole to be done, but trouble was all around me in Norfolk. I said to myself "not going was going to be worse than leaving". I'll take my chances in New Jersey.) you get in any trouble while you're up there and your time is not up once you get here your time would start all over." I said, "all three years?" She said "yes, so I advise you that if that's going to be a problem you may need to rethink what you're about to do here."

She left us alone for a couple minutes to make sure I wanted to still transfer my parole to New Jersey. We looked at each other and I told her baby I wanted a change and inside I knew I had to make it work. My whole family was telling me "I did not know her. I should take it slow."

Hell, I told them "Life is fast and before you know it, it will pass you by." She looked at me for a while and said, "I love you and whatever you want to do I will support you the best way I can because you're my husband." With my parole officer walking back into the office. I looked over at my parole officer and said, "ma'am I going to New Jersey!"

From that point on I would regret that decision for the rest of my life. We drove back to New Jersey and for the most part other than boot camp and the trip to New York this was my second longest trip I made as a young man on my own. We got to her mother's house. She had lived in New Brunswick, New

Jersey. Down the street from her house was a restaurant that one of the most famous crime families owned.

After entering the house, I greeted everyone. Her mom was nice and very caring. She had been very happy for us getting married. However, her sister the Grinch was not happy for her big sister at all. She did not give us her blessings right away. I thought in time she would come around. My wife worked two jobs, one of the jobs was where we met at the North Brunswick Correctional Facility.

She also worked part time as a home health aide. She made good money, but I wanted to get more involved so we could save up faster instead of just helping around the house. I was doing odd jobs here and there in the neighborhood just to make a few dollars. Her son and her nephew shared a bedroom at the house. I'd cut their hair then play with them afterwards.

We did their homework everyday at the same time. I finally got into cosmetology school in Perth Amboy, New Jersey. I loved it! There were exotic chicks everywhere. It was only three guys that went to the school and one of them were gay, so the pickings were vast.

Things were going well until one night she came home upset. She did not want to talk about the incident. Then I said, "we should not go to bed angry." So, I insisted she tell me what was on her mind? She wiped her eyes and said, "She heard I was seeing a girl at the school." I said "yes" there were a lot of pretty girls there, but I was truly happy with who I was with. She smiled and hugged me.

She didn't know how bad I needed this to work. I have to get my little brother. My mom was running loose again on those mean streets of Norfolk. Ever since my dad had died, she was staying out more and more. My brother's father was allowing her to trick so he could share the coke with her. This left my brother to do whatever he wanted to do. Even skipping school.

I have court for my two kids in Norfolk. That Norview chic was scorned, she had given me and Duce the choice of marriage or jail. I was already married so I said "I'll take jail even if I was not married, I would have still chosen jail anyway. She wanted me to do something (hustle) that only benefited her, not me. But if I went to jail, she would tell my kids I chose to sell drugs over being with them.

So, I chose to support my kids without her being in my life. When I got back to New Jersey later that day me and my wife's mom had got into a very deep discussion about me and her daughters future. She asked me where I saw myself in five years with her daughter and her grandson.

I did not blame her because with all the arguing that we had been going through lately, I started to think if there even was a future with us at all. My wife was seven years my senior and it had played a major part in our fights. I told her I could not make her feel any more secure than I was doing.

No other women called my pager or visited the house. So, I did not know where the source of her doubt came from. It was placing a dark cloud over our relationship. I explained to her mom that I was going to finish hair school and get a barber shop. I was going to send Dina her daughter to nursing school. Then help her get a nursing agency of her own.

We had found a condo we wanted to buy. With the baby on the way it really was not enough space at her mom's anymore. We saved enough money for the deposit plus closing cost. Since she was in the service, we used her veteran's loan to secure our purchase. We were just waiting for the approval from the banks. By this time, I had worked for Taco Bell and Payless Shoe Source as an assistant manager.

I had gotten a tip that the Burger World around the corner from the new house was hiring. They were looking for an assistant manager. If I could switch occupations and work there I would be set for life, I thought to myself. We moved into the condo in November around her birthday. I used that as a good excuse to give her the house as a birthday gift.

"It was good that we bought a house instead of having a big wedding. See if we were to break up at least we could use the equity in the home for the both of us to have a fresh start. She smiled but we both agreed not to let that happen to our marriage. We were broke after the purchase of the condo.

With the baby being seven months away we had to hurry and recoup our funds for the next big investment... him. I met with the head manager of Burger World. All I needed was the second interview with the general manager and the job was in the bag. I still had school and a job at Payless Shoe Store as assistant manager.

I was going to stay there until the call came for me to start Burger World. As soon as we had settled in, I went and got my brother. Her mom's baby sat for me when Dina could not watch him for me. I did not know if it was the pregnancy or her just being hateful but she hassled me the whole time through her last trimester.

To the point my little brother had to stay with her mom while I was not home. I did not trust her with him. He stayed with me on the weekends. It hurt but I had him close to me, not at that crack house in Norfolk. I prayed to God please watch over us every second of the day. After the birth of my son, she had tied her tubes without even asking me. That was a sign to me that this was a one-sided relationship.

I hoped she changed her attitude but in reality every woman in the industry was all male bashing that did not help much at home. I got into an accident and broke six ribs and fractured my chest plate.

She did not even come to see if I was ok. When I had to report to my lawyer's office to receive my insurance check, she was right by my side. I received fifteen thousand dollars in the settlement. The first thing I wanted to do was get a barber shop. She had a cousin who owned a beauty shop on route twenty-seven. She told me to ask her if she would rent me a space.

That would be Kool. I did want to rent a space from her, but it will be a big difference until I can build up my clients. One thing I could not take was a salary change. Not now with the new house and the baby on the way. But just as we were leaving her cousin's shop I heard a voice call out "Yo VA" (that's what I went by when I was locked up in the county jail).

I said, the only people calling me VA were the dudes I was locked down with. I looked up and it was Goldie. He was with his three cousins. One of them was always singing all the time everywhere you saw him. He was going to get signed one day and he sounded like Luther Vandross.

He was young too. The two other cousins I had never seen before. He was a sight for sore eyes. I knew if I started cutting hair he would definitely come and get a cut. Most importantly he would also spread the word that I was back in town. The next day I placed a sign outside it read five-dollar cuts.

Maybe twenty minutes afterwards I heard the door open and no lie Goldie came in with ten people for a haircut. The rest was history. It was all gravy from there. I mean people that I had cut on death row their family would come to get a cut and talk about the days I spent with their loved ones before they would get shipped back to prison.

A lot of people remembered my hair cuts from the newspaper. I think that's what brought a lot of my clients in. Plus, the fact that the barbershop next door to me had been open for forty years. The owner was retiring. He planned to move back to North Carolina. He was leaving the shop to his son.

But it never panned out. His son wrecked his car the first week of his father's retirement. Then the following week he went to jail for messing with this white chick that was a minor. And when her parents found out about their relationship, they pressed charges. He received a football number from those charges.

He got his boots smoked. He had to be a year or two older than her but in New Jersey that did not matter. They did not play the mixing of the races too well, especially with one of us. Well that there was the last straw and the store owner had refused to renew their lease.

Then I had the whole block to myself. I raised the prices on the haircuts to fifteen dollars. Then I moved in for the kill on the competition. My wife's cousin had received "the calling" she said. She left the shop to me and that was ball game. I joined the masonic temple and was flying through the proficiency as fluent as if it was a second language.

I was asked to run for the head worshipful masters seat. I told them I would think about the position. It kept me away from home and my barbershop. They do a lot of charity drives and raise money for the lodge and our sister lodge in Summerville.

I liked the fact that I could use the club at times to hold private parties for my clients. My wife really did not mind the strip shows. She made sure to be at every last one of them. Talking about "she wanted to count the money," yeah right. I just went with it to save face. Those shows had boosted my clients by twenty five percent every time we put one on.

The shop was rapidly growing. I needed to open something else to keep the money rotating. Since I was a mason now and only masons were allowed upstairs. All that carpet... then it hit me. Why not open a carpet cleaning business. Shine bright Carpet cleaning and restoration was born.

I enjoyed opening businesses. It gave me time to release some steam making something out of nothing. In less than a week, I was doing carpets all over Brunswick. After I left the shop for the evenings, I would clean carpets at night.

At Dina's graduation she told me about a job at this new nursing home. Two of her friends from class had already got hired there and she said "she was a shoo in for the other position they had available." She asked me "how did I feel about her working in a nursing home?" "It was okay with me" I said "go for it."

But inside that was not the plan. The plan was to get a nursing agency of our own. She knew what she wanted to do. I left it alone. Well, a girl from her school offered her a job in her agency. She had been in competition with this same lady all through the school year.

They both had tied for the highest grades. Apparently, Dina was not too happy about tying for first place. While she was recruiting for employees, she saw Dina. This lady gave Dina a card. She wanted to hire her competition, but I guess to say come work for me. Since you do not want to work for yourself, well come and work for me.

One thing I learned in New Jersey about Africans is that Africans did not like American blacks. They love the white Americans. I asked "why did they feel that way to one of my African clients?" And he said "that they had it hard at home.

While here in America we are offered all this opportunity. They feel as though American blacks do not take advantage of all that's offered to them."

When he told me that it dawned on me, he was right. That's why I pushed so hard not to be one of those blacks. I did not look down on them either. Different people want and have other things that take priority. Doing what's considered to be the right thing to do at that moment. That's why they're in the situation there in now.

I was poor all my life, I knew that's not what I wanted in life. I aimed high. Well, that African must have hit a nerve. She came home steaming mad. She said, "we have to open our own Nursing Agency. Where do we start?"

Before she turned it down, I had stopped communicating with the chick at the Insurance Company. I said, "let me call the Insurance people again and we can go from there." I knew what they wanted. They needed five grand. Not up front but in installments over the first year. Then the payment would be twenty-five hundred the following year.

I needed a Registered Nurse as the nurse on call to cover the other nurse's. Plus, as a contact for emergency medical calls until the ambulance arrived. We did not need her for a first responder. Our nurse's would be working directly in the nursing homes. There are always doctors on duty onsite.

All our nurses would work inside a nursing home. That was the sweet part. That way our insurance stayed low, and we did not have to pay the Registered Nurse overtime. There would be no cases for her to have to assist on. It all went well and after the first check came it was around fifty or sixty thousand dollars.

After she knew how big the checks were going to be she had the consecutive ones sent to a p.o box. at the mail store in Governor's landing, right across the street from our community. She came home and opened the second check, and it was for eighty-eight thousand dollars. She was gone on power. She looked at me and she was like mine. She had forgotten that first agreement that we had.

If I used my child support payments to put the money up for the agency. The first checks were to catch me up to date before anything else was to be done with the money. I mean how else I was going to get the money for the agency. Well when the money came, I was going to pay up the tab.

She could have the rest for herself; that was the agreement. It was her business. I had my barber shop and the carpet cleaning business. I was good.

The money went to her head and the fact she had to share was not in the strip. She told one of my clients that she was not going to give any of my kids shit. After seven years of marriage, I now wanted out. I just happened to be walking the dog and the mailman was delivering the mail.

I was high as hell and I was trying to avoid him but he already had the mail sorted. He handed them to me. I thanked him and went on walking the dog. I swear on everything I loved I was not prepared for what I was about to see.

It was a letter from a divorce lawyer. I opened the letter up and from what I gathered she had this in for a while. it was in the dismal stage from me not showing up for the first hearing... that slick bitch. I had to beat her in her own game. So the next day I had reached out to a lady friend I met through the Internet.

I would get advice from her from time to time. Well at first, she said "I should leave the house," but that was not an option. She had all the accounts in her name. That way child support couldn't take money out of my account again like before. So, the only funds I had was what I was making from the shop on a daily basis.

I hit Lil Tight up and he loaned me five grand. With that I went to a lawyer to fight for my rights. I moved out after the betrayal of my wife. I could no longer trust her anymore. One of her girlfriends from work had liked me and she confirmed what I was told. That was she was not sharing my insurance money either with his kids if I died.

That had hurt me more than anything else. She knew that's all I wanted in life. That struck a nerve with me. I had hoped she had another man on the side. I wanted to move on.

I was doing all this shit for her and my kids. So, if she wasn't going to give my kids their share then my love for her now was truly gone. I wanted out!

With the money I had from Lil Tight I used it for the lawyer and a few things I would need when I left that bitch. At the lawyers office after waiting for four hours he finally let me in the back where he was with an assistant. Inside were also two stripers. One was sitting by an older gentleman on a leather loveseat. She was talking to him but he clearly wasn't listening.

He had his whole body turned so he could watch the lawyers back. "Sit down. Sit down." I looked around and all I saw was another striper on the desk. Her head was hanging off in the direction of the door and her legs were bent at the knees. There he was wiping his mouth with the sleeve of his suit.

"Hi I'm Kenneth Wiener and from what I understand you are going through a divorce?" "Yes sir" I replied. "And did you bring the retainer we talked about?" (Not the whole thing he wanted thirty for the whole hearing but he took pay installments) I had put five thousand dollars down already last week.

Today I brought another five bands. I had some questions for you that I needed answered. That's the only reason I had agreed to stay after hours. If I was empty handed, they probably would have turned me away. He said that "he was a better criminal lawyer then divorce Attorney." then went on and asked "what did I think about killing her?"

The thought did cross my mind. He said, "You'll do six months, your son will go to a boys' shelter and you'll get out, have custody of him, the houses and the businesses will be all yours." He said, "think about it." I did for a second and I told him that "my son deserved his mother no matter how fucked up she was" and I walked out the office.

I still needed him to represent me in court but I said to myself before I wasted my son's college fund paying these lawyers by dragging this divorce out and draining my pockets. I'm going to wait till court ends and tell the judge I don't want anything unless she sells one of the properties or one of the companies.

If she agrees with me, I want half the profit from any family property sold. I know she will not pay up unless I pursue her for the funds. I told the judge I would like to have the money that's owed to me. If she drags me for my half from sales, I want to receive the current interest rate. She agreed. I knew it was going to be like pulling teeth from a baby trying to get her to pay up.

She had shown that in court when the judge asked her "If she had sold the house yet?" she lied and said "No." In fact, one of my clients saw that the home had been sold already. She already received a check for one hundred sixty thousand dollars.

All the days leading up to the divorce she had me locked up repeatedly. She would call me and if I did not come home to her, she would call the cops or tell me the date that I was going to be arrested and it would happen. When I finally learned that's how she kept me getting locked up, I had stopped even picking up the phone when I saw her number.

It was hard because I had to know when to get my son for the weekend. Then when she knew I was on to her she started coming to south Jersey and telling the police I was following her. Now realize that one. I had just beat this trial. Every man was a suspect. I could not escape grasp.

You could not keep count of all the times I went to jail behind her. It had gotten so bad the sheriff would not even lock me up anymore. He started making me wait in the lobby. He made me walk over to the court on my own accord.

I ended up being the first in line before court would start. The judge was mad that I was quitting the fight. She was to the point of locking me up in contempt of court for not answering her questions. I was mad and I had enough of this bullshit to the point murder had crossed my mind.

The murder would not have stopped at my ex-wife. I was going for the sheriff's gun and giving everyone in there one shot one kill. After court later that day my shop manager came to me when her daughter had passed.

She said "My pastor from Atlanta was going to be in town for six months preaching out of the hotel on twenty seven."

Then she went on to say, "If you're open for church this Sunday come by and see what you think of him." She had advised me that "If I didn't have an open mind to stay home and just pray either way the lord will hear you." I was intrigued by the chance to have my soul read. I had listened to my manager because I was going through a divorce and it was difficult.

She had just lost her five-year-old daughter. It all happened the week before the divorce had started. The day of her daughter's birthday she told me her daughter asked her if they could go to the mall for some shopping. Her daughter was so peaceful and beautiful that the rest of this story is a little disturbing. It is hard for me to share with you guys. However, this was a significant reason why I went to see the profit. When they arrived at the mall she asked her daughter "What are we shopping for?"

She said her daughter looked up at her, smiled and said "My burial dress." She said, "She looked at her as if to say why would you even think like that baby?" Then she said to her mom "Mommy I'm going home to God on my birthday. I wanted to pick out my own dress because you're going to have too many other things to do." Her mom said, "Inside she was all torn up and she didn't know how to address what her daughter had just confessed to her."

So, she had blown it off and proceeded to find everything that her little girl wanted from the mall. The next day she was so eager to wake up and greet her daughter to tell her happy birthday and to inform her that she was wrong about her dying today.

As soon as she had crossed the doorway she said, "I had noticed my baby was not breathing." She ran and called the ambulance. However, there was nothing they could do for the little girl. She already passed on. She was only five years old and till this day I still miss her.

I felt her mother's pain. Then I wondered if her daughter knew how much she had touched my heart. I was not exactly looking forward to having the whole church hear my life story. I felt that if he was a prophet of God, I had needed the message more than worrying about the church judging me. I needed to hear the special message from God again. I needed some divine guidance.

That Sunday I was going to go see him. My divorce court date was that Monday. I had been practicing how to disarm the bailiff and shoot him then everyone else in the courtroom. I really didn't want to carry the mass shooting out. I just could not take the proceedings anymore. I wanted it to just go away.

I went to the church to see the prophet. Right before I went into the church I said a prayer then asked for understanding and for his blessing.

Most importantly I wanted God to see that I was a fallen angel who needed help. I wanted to find my way back to his flock. The choir was into a song, the whole place was dancing and humming all as one. I went to join my family. Just as I was going to sit down, the prophet rose to his feet.

Then he stopped and told me to stand. He then pointed to the young lady that came with me and said "The spot on your breast exam will be just that a mistake on the film." She looked a little scared. At first, she did not want to come. She had been forced as a child to attend church daily. She too had her own evil demons that she was working on. It scared her to think about them in her life.

Then he pointed to me and told me "My mom had a nine-pound tumor in her stomach. He wanted me to tell her to have the operation to have it removed. That she will be fine and to tell her that God was watching over her as a daughter." He had begun to mumble to himself then it became louder until he fell out of his trance.

He told me all the glorious things he had seen. In his vision he saw me surrounded with all of God's angels, but first he told me God said, "no more jail!" He began to cry and said "he has shown me so many riches for you. The only way for me to obtain them was to get rid of all my demons." He fell silent and the head lady covered him until he rose again. He sat down to regain his strength. When it was time for offering to come around, I placed a few dollars in the tray. In front of the whole church, he said "God had riches for you." I said "Well they had nine hundred ninety-nine thousand nine hundred and ninety-nine dollars more to come once the second half of my blessing arrived."

The next week the girl I was staying with had to go for her second screening. This was to decide what they were going to do about the test results. However, when the doctor reviewed the test, he was shocked. He came to her room and said the x-ray had gotten dirt on it somehow and it turned out you were fine. It was just like the prophet said it would go. Now the big day came for me and just as he said I hadn't got incarcerated as I had in the past. I stayed in South Jersey until my Lil brother had graduated high school. He attended one year of college as well. I was proud of his accomplishments.

He wanted to go home back to Norfolk. After reasoning with him to see if he was ready to be on his own. We talked and he told me he was ready to hold his own. It was hard but finally I had to let go. I did what I promised to my mom. Now it was time to get me straight.

Before leaving South Jersey, I crossed paths with my wife's lawyer. She had the nerve to ask me "If I knew my ex-wife's whereabouts?" I was going to tell her about herself. Until she had gone on to say "Oh by the way did you hear your lawyer ran off with a settlement from one of his clients accident cases?" I was stunted.

As she walked away from me, I thought to myself is this why God had granted me no more jail time because I didn't take her life as the lawyer had suggested to me. I knew that killing her was not right. I was glad I didn't because just think if I had followed his advice, I would be telling you this story from prison.

Not here right now smoking on some sour diesel, that's for fucking sure. Huh? I'm glad now. I have four girls and three boys. I was now ready to go back to school and get my cosmetology degree, but before I went back to Norfolk I had some loose ends to tie up.

I had an investor that was a real young millionaire. I really do not want to mention him too much. He had given me sixty thousand to open my own shop. In return I had built him a state-of-the-art recording studio complete with hidden gun and full body compartments.

Just in case the boys wanted to interrupt the recording sessions. It was sixteen feet by eight feet by eight feet. It was badass for my first time and I did it all by myself. Well, anyway he was into some heavy shit. So heavy that it took a task force from Newark to bring him down. They used one of his home boys from the feds. I told him I did not trust the whole thing.

They called it "Operation Life." I mean they named the operation after that dude named Life. That's how bad they wanted him. The cops would not be able to get my boy on dope charges. So, they had got that dude to get him to talk about the murder he committed when they were kids.

Evidently no one saw him do it. It was him and Life there at the time of the murder. It was said "he was responsible for the murder of a guy that use to rob them when they were younger and it stuck."

What I did not understand was "Why did they ask him if he told them where the safe was hidden?" They would drop the cold case on him?" So right there that told everyone that it was about the cream. It was reported that the head man was worth fifteen million and my people were said to have about two to three million.

I know for sure it was close. I never had a chance to count it all, but believe me it was in there at least three million easy. He sent me to count out one hundred and eighty-five dollars one time. Well after about fifty grand my hands had cramped up and I told him to come and count it his damn self.

I never thought the day would come that I would get tired of counting cash but when I met that nigga... I hated to count cash. Before they got him, he was on his way to confront this dude who somehow got his new necklace and watch that we just picked up from Jacobs in New York.

I know for a fact because I was with him. He spent at least a half million on that necklace alone; the watch was over two hundred grand by itself. That day we were there Cameron was in the store. The big-time rapper from Harlem who came to D.C and his Lambo got shot up yeah him. Jacob had taken me and big Cuz to the basement to the safe. No one went down there at all, unless you were spending big bank.

He locked the front doors and left Cam, Jules and their newest artist standing in the store. Back in New Jersey I had tried to tell him that "I was selling everything in the shop and going to Norfolk. He didn't want to leave. I had tied all my loose ends and was on my way to the bus station.

I was told they "Had him" in custody. Only if he would have left with me. Then I thought he was one of those guys I did not want to be like. He had a good heart, don't get me wrong. I just did not want to be that nigga that died at home. You know the guy that gets so caught up in his own business that the bigger he gets the less time he spends on the outside of their hood. Until the bull shit, you're in now it's too much to bear. Then end up in jail or dead. I'm just saying that I did not want my life ending that way. If he had only listened to me, we would have been in Norfolk living like kings. Well after that situation I started to listen to myself more often. I realized I started to love myself again and I was going home.

CHAPTER 19

Learning Norfolk again

On the bus ride back to Norfolk. I played everything out in my head from the beginning to the end. I concluded that out of it all the best thing that I had done was break the chain with my brother. I gave him a start in life that I had always wanted. The whole time he was with me I owned my own businesses.

I didn't hustle nor did I allow him to hustle either. We had not bonded like I wanted to but we survived the storm. He turned out good. I hear now he works for the railroad, clearing off the tracks in shit. I don't hear from him much. I guess this is how parents feel. You give your children your all. In return you ask for them to just live happily and use that gift of life wisely.

I gave it to him to do well with this blessing. Try and help another person if you can. Always thank God because without him helping me to raise you it wouldn't have been possible. I said that to say this I hope he will get the time to read this book so he can see what I had to endure while raising him.

I had to raise him as a parent and not as a brother. I wanted his respect, not his approval. Then I thought my mom must have disliked me because I had to take him and make him finish school. I did what she asked me to do. It took a long time for me to forgive her for putting me through that at such an early age, but 2 Pac came out with a song that had a phrase that went like this "Even as a crack fiend mama, you'll always be my black queen mama."

That song touched me to the point that it made me realize that you only get one mom. It did not matter how fucked up that individual was she was mom. Now it was time for me to see my mom again after being gone for over eighteen years.

Without leaving in a few days, yes, I had come home to stay after so many years had passed. School was one year long and it lasted from May to May. I made sure I paid for school in advance before I even came back to Norfolk. I knew if I had not done so, I would have fallen deep into the world that I had tried so hard in the past to avoid for so many years.

I had for one lost my grandfather. When he passed, Norfolk to me had passed as well. But this was going to work for me, it had too. It was scary for the first time being back in Norfolk. I had no one with me to have to take care of and it felt strange but at the same time it felt comforting.

I would be so far in life if I only had to worry about myself. If I did not have to think about any kids or my little brother's needs for a stable life. I would be rich as hell right now. I'm glad I did not pride myself on shit like that. I was not materialistic at all. The thought of having all the money back kind of made me feel selfish.

I mean if I had every dime I ever spent on them I would have been well to do in life. However, that was foolish thinking. They all were a part of me and I was glad to have helped them. Now this outro of my life belongs to me.

Life has taught me how to deal with the bullshit. I needed to learn how to say no. The next time God decides to give me another chance at wealth I will not for any reason let anyone bring me down again. That goes for family or friends. Well now if things didn't work then I know I was the one that dropped the ball. I had no one else to blame. I was the reason if anything went wrong. I will know I was the one holding myself back.

For the most part I was my own and I loved it. My Cuz Big Boy told me I could crash at his place. It was in a good location between the school and the barbershop where I worked. I thought this was going to work. The only thing he told me was that the dude that I told you about in the beginning of the book wanted to hustle. That same night he got busted.

Well, he was a sergeant on the police force's drug unit now. He was going around busting all the kids of the people he went to school with that he knew that had sold drugs. Now how low could you get? I thought. Then he said "You'll get to see him, his mom lives next door."

I said "what?" Not to alarm my cousin because he did not know I had half a pound of weed with me. I kept it in his house. Between all the roaches in here and that crooked ass Narco visiting every other day I needed to find a new place to lay low. I had to have a steady income and being the new barber on the block I had to get popping.

When I first moved back home, I paid for school with the money left over. I bought me a half pound of mid-grade weed. When I found out my old friend Narco was a regular here, I knew this was not going to end well if I overstayed my welcome. He was on the same side of town where I was staying. This was not a good look.

I see the meeting between us already unfolding. He'll ask me "Where I was staying?" "How long I'm in town for?" "Where was I working at?" All of which are questions I did not feel comfortable discussing with the fucking cops. Especially with a Narc. I stopped going there completely, that was all I had needed to hear.

As a backup plan B, I also arranged to stay with an old high school sweetheart. She lived behind Hardee's on Princess Anne Road in Norfolk. Now the plan with her was for me to go to school and work. I could stay there with her and her kids with the understanding that we were strictly friends.

No more we fucked but it was no commitments made from either side. Everything was fine for the first six months we had fun. She had reintroduced Norfolk and all that I had missed. At one moment I thought that if she did not put too much pressure on me about a commitment it may have worked out.

I did stay out at times but understood that I had not been home for thirty years. And as I saw family and old friends the moment caused for a celebration drank. For the ex's (an old flame) I felt like they had to see me. I guess they wanted to see if the fire was still there. It was hard to say no to all the temptation. I stayed out. I wanted to see where this ride would take me.

This one chick from Seattle was blond, short and had a nice rack. She was married to this navy dude. I think they were married for the convenience of extra money from the allotment checks.

Why do I say that? Well for one on his leave he'll go hang with the boys and I'll be at his house fucking his wife. She used to have the bomb ass bud and head OMG. We would fuck all over the house all the time, until she wanted me to leave the chick I was with and move in with her. I wanted her and she knew it as well. However, I did not want to be tied down with no one chick at all.

She knew how I felt. One day she wanted me to leave and not contact her ever again. She started dating another black dude. It was fucked up because we were in the same class.

She would still pick me up and drop me off to and from school. Now at the same time the girl I was staying with gives me the same ultimatum. Only because my first cousin married her first cousin. She wanted to have a double wedding.

That conversation had gone on for about three more months. I could not take it anymore. I now wished I had waited until graduation before calling our relationship off. With six months left until graduation it would have been worth the nagging and bitching.

I remember it as if it was yesterday. December two thousand nine during the blizzard she asked me one last time to marry her and I said "no!" Then I went to the neighbor's house for a few drinks. Well, when I got in from the next-door neighbor's house all my things were in her hallway. I knocked on the door and she would not open it for me. Then she said through the door that she had wanted me to leave her alone.

It was starting to snow badly. I could not see two feet in front of me. Halfway walking to God only knows I stopped and realized I did not know where I was walking too. I had nowhere to go. If I did there were no cabs running anyway.

I had to stop. I was running out of steam. It was so cold. I could not believe it, all the family I had and I was out here on the streets. In a damn blizzard freezing my ass off. I was for the first time in my life homeless and by myself with no one or no where to rest my head. Just as I was about to give up and lay down in the street. I thought to just sit here and wait for death to catch me. I was cold. I was hoping to get run over by a car.

At least they would take me to the hospital. It was better than the position I was in now. At the last minute as my teeth chattered and my knees knocked. I suddenly heard a voice say "Dummy you have a key to the shop you work at!" The voice was right, the shop was only five blocks away from where I had stopped to get my bearings.

I began to summon all my strength. I grabbed all my bags with my blistered fingers and hands at once and pushed on. I could not help to think of Erica Campbell and how her songs had encouraged me. They have helped me embrace my life and appreciate it more.

A lot of people were not here to fight for their life at all. In my head all I could think about was Missy the shop owner. She lived in Chesapeake. I'm going to ask her if I could use that back storage room for my things. I know it would be ok but she was still a girl and they talk.

That arrangement must be only temporary too. I wondered how she would feel about me staying in the shop. I'll just leave work when she does and return afterwards and stay the night just until I can get it together. It was not as bad as it looked.

I had an uncle in South Norfolk. I can rent a room from him. However, he had bed bugs in his house. He said that he was not aware of them being in the home and one night they tore my ass up.

I kept the room just in case I needed a fallback place. They had me itching all over. I had bumps everywhere now thinking about it, that shit was not funny at all. Shit after that I just kept my weed there. Only returning there to pay him rent and to re-up.

That's how a stash house is supposed to be used. As it neared graduation my teacher asked me "Why were my grades dropping?" Then she said "It was not too much to hurt my gpa. She was just a little concerned." I told her "After the school year to ask me that again."

She nodded and returned to the lesson. My mom would visit me from time to time. I had promised to visit on graduation day no matter what came up. She had repeated herself until the car had faded out of view. I made it to the shop and I was happy to be inside somewhere safe.

She did not have an alarm on the place so that was a plus. Inside I was tired and scared but most of all I had shelter. I kept that up for two more days and it was unknown to anyone that I was sleeping in the shop after hours. Until that one night I was there with a few girls from school. We had started drinking and once the group had died down to only me and Blondie. We christened the whole place.

She started on the sofa sucking my dick. I put a couple towels on the sofa so, if the owner did walk in on us the sofa would not get nut on it. After she had sucked me off on the couch I took her by the hand and led her to the shampoo area. I started to eat her out and play with her clit until she had squirted all over the chair.

We lasted all night! That white bitch was bad and she knew it too. The owner used to say "she liked me" but I would deny it simply because the girl I used to see still came by the shop. I did not want them to meet.

I still let her suck my dick whenever she brought her son to the shop for a haircut. I didn't want what I had with both of them to get fucked up. The shop owner knew that too and she tried to hold that fact over my head. I had to act as if I didn't even care. Eventually I met a couple of chicks that I could stay with each a few days throughout the week.

I had to do that to have a place to rest my head. They all had to live off the bus route. This was just in case one of them would act flakey. I had a way to move around without asking them for a ride or try some old controlling shit. This was my first time being single in a long time. I wanted to embrace the feeling as if it was my lost child.

Being in the shop had brought a lot of old friend's by. Some I had wanted to catch and some I wish I could have made vanish. They're just coming around to keep tabs on me not to help or assist. These friends just wanted to look down on you and criticize your every move.

In the meantime they would share nothing but negative things about you. I went to the Roberts Park reunion. Let me tell you man it was not pretty. My cousin had picked me up from school. It was a nice July day. As we were walking to the cookout site, we saw everybody we knew from childhood there.

We saw Ju-Ju who studded all the time. He could play some basketball. Everytime he dunked on a nigga; he would always have the crowed dying when he would say "I ggggooot thhhhat asssss!" He was a little older now. All his boyish features were long gone now.

Damn there was our old next-door neighbors. They were still hot, one was red and one was redder. They both could get the dick. Oh no, there goes the one person I've been ducking since my return. Shit it was the police sergeant from school.

I heard that he worked for the narcotics squad now. I did not believe it. "Yo, is that you Tee?" I heard as I turned away. I tried to fake like I didn't hear him calling out to me. Then it happened my cousin reached over and tapped my shoulder. He said "I think that officer is calling you?"

I looked over and yep it was him standing in the flesh with a tight ass biker short set on asking me "How long I was in town for?" Then he said "We have to catch up." I nodded my head as if I was eating, then I waved and grabbed my crotch as a sign I had to go to the restroom badly.

Then I ran in the direction of the portable johns. Ssshhhh my cousin didn't know I had brought weed with me. It was only a blunt but I wasn't throwing it away. Not because of deputy dog. Seven was like he did shit without thinking. Why would he tell me to stop when I told him I didn't want to see that cop if we ran into him here.

Once I got to the portable johns, I lit the smoke and took a long pull, it all made since now. I had seen an old girlfriend of Sevens and she had asked me "When did I get out of jail?" I said, "I've been out for a year now." She said "Well that's not what your cousin told me."

I said "come again." She had gone on to say "Yeah I just saw him last week. I asked him when the last time was, he saw you?" and he was like "you know that nigga likes to be in jail." I looked at her in disbelief like my own blood said that to you. He was my first cousin. I thought to myself that haters come in all shades, even the family color.

After I left the portal john, I went to Seven and told him "I had enough and I was leaving the cookout." He called out to me but I walked to the bus stop. It's different when the hater is on the outside looking in at you. You can see him and laugh, but when he is right up on you. You have no idea why all your business is in the street.

The untrue version always hits the street first. I knew he saw it in my face. I no longer tried to pretend I wanted to be in his company. His hating could have made the cops want to search me or run my name you never know. I wasn't trying to stand by to find out either way. I need to hurry up and graduate and get the fuck out of Norfolk.

At the time I was staying back and forth between my stash house which was in South Norfolk and my job which was in Norfolk. My cousin's sister-in-law was my sweetheart. I called her brown sugar. She was my female counterpart. I'd come over to her house because she stayed by my job. I would either come by in the morning or come that night after work. We would all eat dinner together. It was fun as hell.

I really enjoyed being with her and her kids. I guessed being on my own until now I didn't know how much I missed hearing kids laughing and playing all over the house. If things were different, I would be with her and we would have had a good life. The one that they deserved to have and live.

Me and her when the kids were sleeping would always sneak off just to be alone in private. I'll have a little something rolled up and we would just talk and hold hands enjoying the time we were together.

Out of all my lady friends she was the best because she never fussed or argued with me for not coming or calling her on the regular. She knew how I felt about her. Whenever I had the time where no one was on my heels I'd be up under her all the time. We came together no matter how long our separations had lasted.

We would just pick up right from where we were at the time of our last departure. The feelings I had for her were strong; she had four kids and was doing it by herself. I respected that so whenever I did come to dinner, I would bring whatever the kids wanted to eat. The entertainment was on her to provide. It was the least I could do to show her that I really cared and appreciated how she made me feel.

I always left her at least a dub or better just for after school treats for the kids. I left her something to smoke too. It was enough to last her until the next time I came over. We had a good time whenever we could hook up but with my busy ass life it wasn't as often as we liked.

But when we did get together it was magic. Right now, I only got to see her maybe three days a week. I would stay overnight twice a week if I had money to make it back on her side of town. She never harassed me or provoked me to see her again. I know she is in Texas now. When I get myself together, I would like to visit her. Whether she is single or not. I'm going to see her and thank her just for being there for me in my time of need.

Once I had left the cookout my girl hit me up on my cell phone. She was cute as hell and she drove a silver two thousand ten BMW with the spoiler kit. It had a shark fin too it was fucking hot. No matter where I was, she came and scooped a nigga up.

Believe it or not we never fucked. It was mentioned one time but we laughed it off. We realized that we're the same and it wouldn't work. We had just like all the attention we received from the opposite sex but that didn't necessarily mean we had to fuck.

See we had more fun letting people think we were having sex then actually having sex. It was crazy. We both thought that the girl I worked with had a thing for her. I would call her on my cell phone to meet me so we can go smoke. I would meet her around the block from the beauty shop. I'd get in her car and she'd either have the blunt ready or I already have one to go.

Either way we were good. After the blunt was dead she'd drop me off and I would enter the shop and go back to work. Then she'd enter a few moments later. The girl would say wow you too sure smell like the both of you been rolling around in a weed factory. Lil Bit would burst out laughing. I would stall her out until she started bugging on me.

I had asked Lil Bit "Why didn't she go out with her (the girl I had worked with) but she would hang out with me?" Lil Bit said "she hung out with her before and she thought that the girl was coming onto her and it had made her feel uncomfortable. Since then, she did not mind her doing her hair but that was it, nothing else." "Especially if they had to be by themselves," she added.

I would refuse to be caught in the act of smoking weed with her around the shop owner. I don't like her even though she was the owner of the shop. She would get heated because she thought I was covering up me and Lil Bit's affair.

It was like a soap opera. Lil Bit was a party girl that was all she liked. She used her sex appeal to get what she wanted. I went along with them to make sure it went no farther in case she had gotten too fucked up. She would hook me up with her friends. I would let my clients know that she wasn't my girl so if they were interested in her to be my guess.

Even though I called her Lil Bit she carried a big gun. It was a .45 Cal and she wasn't afraid to use it either. They hated that we hung out so closely together. People would stare at her and she loved the attention.

She had loved it when they'd stare at her ass. She would always wear short and sexy outfits. Respectively she would have half of her ass out with a sheer top on without a bra. She was hot too and she knew it. She would invite me out with them (her and her date or at least he thought he was on a date) as her big bro. Every time she got a drink, she would say my big bro needs one too.

It was sweet and I had done the same with her. If one of her friends wanted to hang out with me, she had to accommodate

Lil Bit as well. It was nearing time to graduate from school and I was glad. I was having fun but all this bed hopping was never what I wanted to do.

I wanted to be loved and appreciated and that seemed far away. So, until then I was playing the field. My old home boy came by the shop for a cut. He was some big-time housing agent and investor now. He also had property in the area that wasn't rented. He offered me to stay in one of his townhomes on one condition, I looked him over. It's been a long time since we saw each other but he didn't seem to be gay.

I said to myself ok let's see what he's talking about. Now remember this is the same person I opened the police car door for when he got busted with four and a half ounces of crack. I asked him "what did he have in mind?" He looked at me and said, "Tee just hang out with me at night while I cruised the old neighborhood looking for chicks like old times."

Man, that's it I thought to myself. I mean I'm glad that was all he had wanted to do because he was a freak. I just couldn't image what the fuck be on his mind at times. I'm not into that man on man shit to each his own. It just wasn't my cup of tea. A problem had come up between us after maybe the tenth time of me cruising the night with him.

See he gave me a hundred dollars each time I went with him. That was in case I found a chick I wanted to trick. He did that so I would not have to interrupt him while he was fucking or whatever he was into with the chick.

The problem was that I did not trick. I mean when he had two chicks, I had to entertain the other one. I would have to spend the money. when it was just me, I kept the money for myself. I did not have to pay for pussy. I think that's why he was mad at me because he knew that and he took that to heart.

So, when he found out that I was just along to pocket the hundred dollars he stopped coming by the shop all together. I was like man you don't make sense. If you're giving me the money to have fun, I did not need to buy pussy. That showed me that's what made him mad. I knew it was the problem. He did not have to buy pussy either. He had a pretty wife at home.

That didn't look a day older than twenty-five. It made me feel like he was going out like a little kid. I was upset to the point that I could not stay in his place anymore. He was using me for his access pass to get out of the house. His wife knew it was not me. She just let him be him and it made me feel uncomfortable witnessing him cheat on her.

Plus, it was interfering with me going to school. See it goes to show you how people treat you when you are down. I did not go to his job or ride around to find him to see what he was up to. He had sorted me out to come and hang with him. Now I could not wait until I leave Norfolk.

That's when I realized that this was the same reason why I left Norfolk in the first place. He was a bad person. I should have known that from grade school. Ever since he ran up and stole my picture by jumping me in line at our graduation. I knew he was trouble. When I was in jail and I would call home, my mom would have his kids more than mine.

I would tell her "Mom, he's not going to be grateful for all you're doing for him!" She would laugh it off and say "Tee he's your friend and I'm not doing it for him I was doing it for the kids." Saga knew that my mom felt guilty because I left home and he used my absence to his advantage. She thought that watching Saga's kids in fact brought her closer to being a grandmother since my kids weren't there as often.

Now he and his wife are successful. You would think at least my mom wouldn't be homeless but that's what people do to you after they use you to get where they're going in life. You help to lift them up to see if there's any light over the other side.

And just when they find it, they push the rope down on the ones who helped them up. That angered me. He came not to look out for me even though if it wasn't for my mom watching his kids, he nor his wife wouldn't be where they are now in life. He was fucked up for that and I was so happy he showed me that side of him.

You know as kids you have that one friend that you promised that the day you get rich you would give them a million bucks just because they were your friend. That was my dream as a kid and he was that friend. No matter what we went through I was going to give him the money. I was so happy God had sent me back to my roots to see that dream was a nightmare from the start.

I know me if I wasn't there to see it for my eyes I would have given the enemy the power to take me out. Thank You God! His wife saw my post on Facebook, this new blog site. I had commented on this subject how I felt about him as a friend and how he carried my mother's love.

Well, he never answered or commented on the subject. His wife had gone off on me about the situation. I let her vent and I kept my wits even though she tried to make me feel little. No matter what, I told myself in due time just like I had to find out she will too. If she wants to know the truth about her husband. It was not my place to tell her. It hurts me the most because she had no idea. I was defending her honor and reputation the whole time.

Hopefully she will see it for herself. If not, her lost not mine. It was a very disappointing homecoming. All my family that I've helped all the years being away from home now no one came to my aid. Damn this was a cold world. I started passing out cards. I knew it was only weeks away from me getting my diploma. I was working hard on leaving Norfolk again for good this time.

And this time I'm keeping my promise to myself. I'm not coming back until I'm successful and driving in a long black car. I would act as if I was in a parade waving at these dumb ass people as I pass them by. Hell, either way I'm going to shine. Laughing out loud as I was approaching the football field across the street from the old Lafayette Shores Apartments.

Damn it was homeboy, who was my ace and partner in the Ville. The dude that was on the Good Morning America show. 'Crack cocaine: Norfolk city under siege.' Remember when the police were investigating the Ville and the video footage was thought to have been lost when the apartment was raided by the local drug dealers. Ok, yeah.

"Leak, how is it going man?" I said to him, he replied "Oh Lil Tee Yo how you been?" He looked around as if I had a TV camera crew with me. He went to say "he sponsors his son's football team and games." They are out here every weekend. "That's why I'm down here." I told him "I was cutting on Princess Ann rd."

I'm here looking to cut the home teams for a group discounted price. "So, let's hook up and I'll give your team a group rate," I said. He walked over to me, bent over a little so only I could hear him. Then he said, "man look I'm running for mayor and I'm not coming to nowhere you are nor sponsor anything you're involved with ok. So please don't come around or try to contact me from here on."

We were tight last I knew. I guess he wanted his past to be just that, the past. It was not like I was asking for shit from him. I guess he wanted to be a big shot now and old friends were not an option.

I said "Well fuck you too" and I continued to pass out the remainder of the cards I had in my hand. The nerve of people. I had more success in my life away from the people that I knew. Then I did around the people I grew up with. No matter how much I missed Norfolk once again I was ready to leave.

The time had come for rehearsals for graduation and I was excited. Me and Blondie were in an on again off again relationship but at graduation she had invited everyone back to her place for drinks. I'd hope to fuck her one last time at her get together. That would give me a chance to tell her I was leaving Norfolk.

I have not told anyone yet but my stepbrother G-boy. He had a place up in Northern Virginia and he had a few leads on a high-volume Barbershop near Potomac Mills Mall. They wanted me to come after graduation for an interview. I'll wait to tell her in the morning. Everyone had just left and we had some catching up to do, see you later.

After we walk on Friday for graduation I'm out of here first thing Saturday morning. I went to get everything packed up and waited for my mom to pick me up from Blondie's house. She was going to give me a ride to the center for the ceremony. Everything was very nice. We ate at the Azalea Garden Inn.

It was a fancy bar and grill that allowed smoking. All the girls had hit the dance floor. I was on my way to have a smoke and the teacher grabbed my arm gently. She asked me "to have a seat." I sat down right next to her so that I could hear her over the music. "Yes," I said to her. She leaned in and shouted to me "Why did your grades drop from an A plus to a B plus in the matter of four months?"

I looked her in the eyes and said "I was homeless and with the bad weather it was really hard to keep my wits about things. Especially when you had to find a safe place to secure your belongings, sleep, go to school and still pay child support it was hard." She said, "why didn't I tell her?" I told her that "she would have given me a little more leniency on my schoolwork than the other kids in the class.

I did not want to be singled out". Then I said, "I was her oldest in the class and I wanted to give them a good example." I told her "It was all my fault anyway I should have taken this course eighteen years ago." We laughed and she hugged me and said "keep on fighting son and I do believe whatever you're looking for with your determination you'll find it. Whatever you're looking for will present itself real soon." I hope so, I thought to myself because I feel as though I was running out of gas.

CHAPTER 20

New road in Life

I had a little time before my interview with the manager of Pro Cut's. My brother offered me to move in with him until I could get a place of my own. His girlfriend at the time was living with him too. It was awkward when he was not home. Well, he allowed me to use his Caddy and that was Kool as hell. His only rule was he did not want me to have any company at the house at all.

He knew it would not be no dudes so he had made sure I understood him. He was younger than me but this was his first house that he brought and I wanted him to feel comfortable that I would respect his wishes.

My other brother went with me to the interview as my model. I aced the screening. I cut his hair and edged him up in about a half an hour. The boss was impressed and asked me "When could I start?" I haven't seen my little brothers in a while. I wanted to use this weekend to catch up on old times. So "how about Monday?" "Ok Monday is fine" he said and I left to grab a drink next door at TGIF. Hell, it was happy hour and it was time to eat and celebrate.

Working there at Pro Cut's I'll be surrounded by a talented group of barbers. The shop stayed busy. It reminded me of my first shop in New Brunswick. However, the mall was right next door and when the mall got busy so did the shop. All the stars came here that had performed at that nice ass club down the street L3's. That's the hottest club in northern VA. Everyone who performed here would stop in and get a fresh cut before the show. That means all the chicks came here with their kids in hope to get a picture with a celebrity at the shop.

The first day I started I ended up with the Nationals head scout in my chair. That's when the hate from the other barber started to show. At first the shop was slowing down my flow of customers. The manager was sending them to the other barbers. I would do four cuts an hour while they laughed and joked all day.

When the shop manager picks on me, I'll pick back. He'll try to first throw me off my game by trying to get me to sweep or take out the trash hoping I would get mad. Then he'll try and make it into a joke that was on me. One thing he could not do was hit my nerves like he wanted.

He acted like he wanted to fire me. I learned people can only use against you what you tell them about yourself. That was the only way a person could hurt you. I learned not to give them fuel to hurt me. See if you don't tell people your weakness, they'll never have fuel to hurt you. No matter how much they try, they could never get under your skin.

Once he saw that he could not get to me then he went for my pockets. The other barbers feared him because he controlled the flow of customers. Plus, he knew their life story and he ran with that to the point they were wrapped around his finger. When he went in on me, I'd roast his lil ass. He hated that I did not summit like the other barbers did. His jokes were wack as hell.

I had the shop laughing at him and not with him. He had enough and the next day it showed. All in all, it was fun. I made a lot of money. I sent the majority to the kids that did not already have a security blanket in place. One of my cases made me upset the most because I had been sending money to my kids mom as directed by the court.

My youngest at the time had asked me "Daddy is it love when your spouse beats you and takes your money from your kids?" I said to her "No baby that's not love that's abuse." I asked her "Is that person putting his hands on you?" she said "oh no daddy".

I told her then "You do not have to worry about anything because your mother could handle herself." I had said to her "as long as he did not put his hands on you and your brother, me and him were Kool and the gang." She said "Well daddy I'm starting my period and my mom would not buy me what I needed. I told her she was now old enough to get her own money sent to her."

For the last ten years I sent the money through the system and my kids did not get a dime. I was very upset and I started sending the money to her ever since. Now all I had to support was her, my oldest daughter Ms. Tee and my youngest daughter Kiya in New Jersey.

The rest of the money I figured I'll pocket. Shit we made no less than two hundred dollars a day. On the weekends you could make three hundred and fifty dollars a day. It was a good job. Just too many barbers who talked like they were stylists. I finally was happy again.

With everything going well I wanted some pussy. It's been a minute not even a blow job has come my way. I had a couple prospects but I'm taking my time. I don't want to make any kids and repeat the same old bullshit with these chicks again. That's why I respected my brother's wishes. Like he said "I needed some me time" and I was enjoying it. I shopped every day. I mean the mall was right next door. I'd go to work then on lunch I'd hit the mall.

First, I started with the clothes and went from store to store. Then once I've selected my gear I went to the shoes. My shoes had to match the gear or I would go the total opposite with a whole different color scheme. Once I had the wardrobe complete, I stepped it up to the jewelry and treated myself to a new piece every other pay week.

The look was there. I had the hat for every outfit, shoes matched as if I was going to my first day of school every day. The necklace and the watch top me off like a stiff drink. The pinky ring signified that my skills in here were unmatched.

I quickly became the center attraction at the shop. The manager came to me and asked me if "I'd start working out with them at the gym across the street." I said "sure." I knew this was a stunt to get to see what made me tick. I played along just to see how far he'll take it. I'd go for a swim after our workout while they went to the sauna.

I'd do a couple laps then shower up and return to work. It just so happened that as I was walking to the beauty supply store and I saw her. She was tall and sexy. I had rarely looked twice at slim chicks but she had a smile that drew me into the store.

As I walked through the doors it occurred to me that I was in an all-women's clothing store. I had to think fast. I whipped out my cell phone and I called my oldest daughter. "You want an outfit or two for the summer baby?" I asked her once she figured out it was me on the other end of her line. "Yes daddy," she replied.

"Ok let me get some help, hold on" I told her and looked in the saleswoman's direction and waved to her for assistance. I waved to her and she smiled. I knew she saw me enter the store. She walked over and asked, "what can I help me with today?" She had a Trinidadian accent and she smelled like fresh flowers. As if she had just picked them in a tropical rainforest.

She was a little shocked I came into her place of business. I thought it would be better if I came in her place than her coming to the barber shop. Having all the wolves jumping all over her. I asked her for help with finding my daughter an outfit or two for the summer.

She happily smiled and began to show me a few nice sets. I then told Ms. Tee "outfits looked very nice and I'll be sending them to her this weekend." She was happy and said, "I love you and she'll call me later this evening."

The phone went dead. I told the pretty sales lady to "ring it all up and to write her number on the back of the receipt." She smiled and said, "how do you know I want you to have my phone number?" I did know. I replied, "Well, giving me your phone number would surely help you too get to know me right? How else are you going to know?" I asked her. "When did she get off work?"

She said "I get off at eight but out the door by nine. We do inventory every night." She knew I saw her walking from the bus stop to work in the morning.

I know she leaves with the other girl at closing to catch the bus home.

She knew a ride would be nice. I looked at her and said, "What you say, can I take you home tonight?" Before she could answer she said, "Call me at seven thirty and I'll meet you in front of my store." Yes, I said to myself then I looked at her and said, "Kool I'll see you later."

Then I turned to exit the store. While I was walking back to the shop Ms. Tee called and said, "Daddy did you just use me to get a date." I said "Yes." She said, "Daddy you a whore and when are you sending my clothes to me?" "This weekend baby." I had just told her that five minutes ago. She said ok and hung up the phone. Back at the barbershop in front of my station the guys were riding me about her age.

The youngest barber out of the group said, "Yo how old was she?" I said, "old enough" and the shop patriots went crazy. Really, I didn't know how old she was but she reminded me of this young chick from Norfolk. Shit she looked like a young Mary J. She used to walk up and down the street and cars would blow at her.

If she liked who was driving, she'd get in the car. One day I saw her and asked her "why did she do shit like that... jumping in and out of those cars?" She said, "to have fun and get weed." I asked her "was she still in school" and she said "sometimes."

I told her if she helped clean the shop for me and go to school, I'll get her a cell phone. The deal also was that she had to go to school as well, not just get good grades. I'll make sure she makes at least fifty dollars a week for herself. She agreed and she finished school. Now she's waiting on getting accepted into the Navy. This chick was a little older but only by a few years. She had to be twenty-two years old.

However, it didn't matter. I wasn't telling these niggas anything about her. The relationship lasted for a while but I felt it was not going in the direction I wanted it to.

She wanted to settle down and I was not trying to settle down with no fertile ass young chick. I could see it now she was telling me she was pregnant. After a few months of dating, I called the relationship off. I missed her but I refused to make another child with someone and had to separate from that child, no way.

Then I'll have to relocate again. It was too painful and I was not in the market for any more disappointment. I took off on Wednesday and it was slow at the shop. Plus, I just got a new batch of weed I wanted to smoke. Now two things my brother made me promise that I would not do but this chick had me since I was twelve.

Her name was Mary Jane. This time I had some sour diesel and she was my little secret. Lucky for me he had an end unit so I would act as if I was picking trash up in the yard. If a neighbor came too close to me, I would let the blunt burn out and I had a cigar on the ready to cover up the smell.

It worked all the time. I had to meet the weed dealer at the shop. It was Kool because I didn't allow dudes at my crib anyway. So, I know I was not going to have any guys at my brother's house anyway.

On my way from the shop, I remembered I needed cigarillos and a cold beer. It was the weekend of the fourth of July. After getting shot almost twenty years ago I partied alone, especially now on this holiday. Damn I need gas too. Over there was a seven eleven. I pulled up to the gas pump. I locked the doors and there she was. She just threw her hair back to clear it from her face.

When she did that, I noticed her deep blue eyes. They were popping right out at me. I had to say something but this was too fast. I wanted to approach her but my legs were not listening to me. Before I knew it, I was facing her and the only thing I could say without sounding so lame was "Who cuts your son's hair?"

Damn man you could not be any more spontaneous than that I asked myself. As I was waiting to hear a response she had said "I do." Then I went into my spiel. I'm a master barber

I.... Then she smiled and said "I cut his hair. I own my own salon in Stafford VA.

Yes, I felt it in my stomach. I came off lame but she liked it. She said, "It was nice to meet you, my name is Karen" and reached out her hand. I reached out to her and shook her hand and said "Hey the fourth is coming up. I'm new in town and I would like to take you out for a drink perhaps over dinner." She smiled and said, "since her separation she really was not looking for a mate just yet."

I agreed then said "perfect because I'm just recently out of an eighteen-year relationship and I'm definitely not looking for a long term thing just a friend. Just someone to share special moments and lonely nights with." She agreed to meet for the fourth of July.

We exchanged cards and she left. In that instant I felt like this move was going to be a positive move for the both of us. I called her out of curiosity to see how her day was going. I wanted to see her and her shop. She comes off as a very sexy and professional person.

I wanted to see them both at work. At times her phone went straight to voicemail. In no more than an hour or so she'd call back. She explained "She was busy doing a dye job or a waxing." I didn't mind, I was just making sure our first date was set. She confirmed that it was still on for tonight. She wanted me to meet her at her shop then the night was ours. To do as we pleased if we wanted too.

When I arrived at her place of work it was a little after eight. The nighttime was coming fast, so I asked her "If she would drive so I could relax?" My license was still suspended and I didn't want to get pulled over on our first date. She was like "ok" then we went outside. She had a brand-new Dodge Magnum lowered and kitted up.

I asked her "Did you have this car when we met?" She was like "yes!" I really could not remember. All I could remember was that she was from California.

When she spoke, it sounded like music to my ears. You didn't pay any attention to what she was saying at all. Her voice was hypnotizing. She sounded to me as if she was not from the east coast. She was not tainted with all that shit old white America taught for so many years about white superiority. Let me tell you I have never dated a white chick before.

I thought they dated black guys for the size of their dick and not their intellectual capabilities. Like it was a fad to date a black man. Either way it was not for me until now. I wanted to see where this relationship would take me.

When the relationship soured the white chick had always burnt the dude worse than a black chick would have burnt him. Believe me black chicks can get crazy when they are scorned. July flew by and things went well.

When my birthday came around, I was totally shocked when I went to see her. She said she "Needed my opinion on something." We got into her car and we went to lunch. At lunch she explained the situation about her divorce. Then said, "she knew that we both wanted to just be friends but her feelings were getting stronger." She wanted to see more of me and make this a full-time affair.

Then she commented on how the kids enjoyed me around. They asked "If we were going to get more time to see him?" She said, "when they asked for you, I knew they liked you from the start." With all of that said, I have a birthday gift for you. Next door to the dinner there was a car lot.

In front of the lot there was a two thousand ten Yukon XLT. The same exact one Tony drove in the Mob gangster series the sopranos but this one was money green with the lift kit.

The interior was peanut butter brown with a Bose music system and DVD player. I was like "damn that's a nice truck." She said, "I'm glad you like it because I cannot take it back. It's yours!" I looked at her and wiped my face to re-adjust my eyes. Then I said "What did you say Karen?" "You heard me!" Then she started to sing Happy Birthday baby to me.

I was speechless. No one ever brought me a truck before, let alone a Yukon XLT. I went to her side of the car, opened her door and grabbed her out of the car. I kissed her until she was fighting for air. She asked "If I wanted to move in with her and the boys?" I told my brother I was moving out to stay with Karen. At first, he was upset then he was Kool with my decision.

He gave me his blessings and said, "before I leave if you need to come back man the room will always be here for you." I weaved, then said, "thank you" and drove off. To be frank I loved being there to visit but I did not like being home when he was out.

Not that I didn't trust myself around his girl. I didn't trust his girl around me. She just had this aura about her that made me feel like I was needy or something. I did not blame her for that because I was staying under their roof. I have that feeling and when it gets to a point that I can't control it. I will be the one to leave.

Outside of that, she was a very nice person. She made my brother happy. That's all that mattered. I pulled up to the shop early with the new whip music was on sick and so was the niggas who worked at the joint. Everyone came out but a short man watched as they all paraded around the freshly cleaned truck.

I had the new leather and Black Ice incense in the air vents. Then it came, I knew it. "Yo, ok everyone has seen a new truck before. Back to work." Inside the shop everything he said were the words of a hater. He was a hater, man. I went to have lunch in the employee lounge. He came over to me while I was eating and he said, "What was the truck for?" I said "What"?

He said, "I heard your girl brought you that truck for your birthday." "I hope she can help you keep up with your payments" and he smiled. I looked at him and said "I did not have to pay them, it was a birthday gift. Oh that's right no chick ever did that for you huh? I bet you're the one buying them the trucks and shit."

He turned red as hell in the face. See he knew, I knew his little fucking mind game. I didn't care about him squeezing my pockets. Now he sees I have a sponsor. That shit doesn't affect me.

I was staying in Stafford now and dating one of the most popular hair divas in the county. It came with a lot of perks.

When I say perks, opportunities are hitting me left and right. A chance to rent a subunit in a black salon called Crayons had come across the table for me

I mean it could work. I had to do a lot of advertising and bar hoping to get the word out. I think it could work. Karen worked all day and all night. The kids were either with her or at a sitter's house. Boys will be boys and they went through a lot of sitters let me tell you. To the point I started leaving work early just to get them.

I did that so Karen didn't have to find anyone else to watch them. They did all that acting out to the sitter's so that Karen didn't have any choice but to take them to work with her. I picked them up sometimes and tried to make it back to work before that 4 o'clock traffic hits interstate ninety-five.

Man, ninety-five stays jammed and you could sit there for hours. That happened to me plenty of times. I'll just turn right around and go home. Well after that happened so many times the short man was like he wanted the keys back to the barber shop.

I knew he was going to try and have the last laugh. Karen needed me to do a few things for her at her Beauty Salon. After I get done, I'm going to make an offer to that chick that owns Crayons in Stafford. Thanksgiving was creeping up and I was just finishing up the job at Karen's shop. She was getting a new nail tech. She had a room right beside her station she was going to rent to him.

She wanted me to open the area up so I suggested cutting the wall in half all the way around and placing columns on the three exposed corners. It came out awesome and everything was perfect. I hired a guy to put on the finishing touches. That was not my strong point.

I rewired the outlets and fans. I even did the plumbing. It was loved by the clients and Karen's staff. I could not wait to get up in the morning and tell short face that I quit!

I was opening my own barber shop. I'll tell him he should try it before he is too old to enjoy the feeling. Instead of counting someone else's money every week. That morning I stopped at the Chic fil a for breakfast. Inside I was going over what I was about to tell short man. Then it hit me just to be the bigger man and wish him well.

Just think you're moving on to a better and closer location. And that's what I did. Then I turned and packed my things and left the shop. Me and Karen became an official couple.

I promised her I will do whatever it takes to make her happy. I told her there were just three things I won't put up with and that was needles because I know white people like to experiment. I wanted her to know up front how I felt I did not want to get married. We both agreed on that right away.

Lastly, no kids. The last one was optional because having unprotected sex was taking a chance of that happening. The other two were non-negotiable. She and I agreed and we all went out to eat and celebrated us becoming a family.

CHAPTER 21

Living a Lie

We were living the American dream. She had a dog named Nova that was a blue nose pit-bull. I loved to walk her around the neighborhood. She was getting old, at least that's what we thought. We were wrong. We were hoping that when she did leave us, it would be an easy transition for the kids.

I wanted to get a back up puppy as a distraction whenever Nova passed. I was lucky one of my clients had given us a boy pit bulldog. He was gray like Nova. We named him Niko. The call came that my middle son had been getting in and out of trouble doing dumb shit. A situation that he could have avoided. He did the opposite and fueled the situation. He was suspended from school.

That was the last straw for his mom. She was fed up with his shit. She had enough. I asked her "What happened?" She said a jealous ex-boyfriend of the girl he was dating pulled an AK out on him. She told him after that he had two choices: either live with me or go to an all-boys school. Allen had no intentions of going to an all-boys school. So he asked his mom "If he could come and stay with me in Stafford Virginia?"

I was all for it however, I had just moved in myself and I didn't know how Karen would adjust to my son wanting to move in too. Hell, I was in love with her, but if it was not ok for Allen to stay then I could not stay either. If push comes to shove, we will move back with my brother and take things from there.

Just as we were discussing the plans Karen walked in the room and overheard my conversation with Allen. "Not to eavesdrop but it'd be nice if Allen could stay with us. He could go to school from here. It would not be a problem."

Just as we were discussing if Allen should move in or not her boys walked into the room. They wanted to talk to Allen on the phone. They liked the fact of them having a big brother around. We looked at each other and said we were just about to bring the same subject up to you guys.

Now it was official Allen was going to come live with us. I was finally going to have another son come and stay with me. He was becoming a man and he needed a man's guidance to enter his next phase of life. His older brother had to come and stay with me for the last two years of high school too. I had nicknamed him Lil Tee after me.

He was fighting his mom and grandmother all the time. To the point his mother called me and asked me to come and get him or she was going to put his ass in jail. At this time I was already caring for my brother, and his daughter kiya. Plus, on the weekends I got my youngest son Torey from my ex-wife in New Jersey.

When I had him, I never asked his mom to stop my child support or did I ask her for any child support. However, she has the courts thinking that she had raised my kids by herself without a dime from me. That was something she will have to deal with when she crosses that road in her life. She must not know that perjury in a court of law was a motherfucker.

Lil Tee stayed with me for two years and he was an asshole the whole time. Once he graduated from school and only then I allowed him to go back home to his mother. From that story I told Allen and he knew he only had two choices: graduate or graduate. It was no in-between. Allen and the boys got along great.

Tom was the oldest and Luke was the youngest; their ages were six and nine, soon to be seven and ten. Karen had them spoiled to death but I couldn't be mad. Since I was never spoiled as a kid, I did not want to be a hater.

I enjoyed watching their faces whenever Karen went to the mall and came home with games, shoes, and toys for them. From the boys all the way to the dogs. They would all line up and eagerly wait for their gifts. She loved the attention that they gave her as she played Santa Claus weekly. The kids were the only ones getting spoiled. I promised Karen she would receive one dozen roses every weekend we're together for the first year of our union.

The roses had also included a nightly foot massage. She loved the roses at work once a week too, especially since her ex-husband had embarrassed her at the salon.

I guessed she thought being married to a government employee that made good money he would be good to her. He did have a good job (this dude worked on the machines that make the money). He made over one hundred and eighty thousand dollars a year.

It took a dude like me to show him how to treat a woman when you are in love with her. It had just so happened they had opened the beauty salon together. Well, he had started having affairs and going on long out of the country vacations. She continued to be faithful to him. Since the cheating had not stopped, she asked for a separation.

It was not his money she wanted, it was his heart. When she realized his heart was not his to give, she was hurt. She told me she wanted the marriage over. I gave her my heart and she gave me hers in return. Her heart was all I wanted.

I was going to make her happy. The hurt her ex had robbed her of was going to be replaced by me. He ran up all the business accounts to the point that she had to file for bankruptcy. At this point she had to start all over. Before the divorce she asked me "If I wanted the Mercedes or the speed boat that they owned?" I said "I did not need the things you guys had purchased together. I have you, that's all I wanted. If that's all he wants to let him have the toys. If you got the beauty salon it was a fair trade."

By this time Allen was starting his senior year of high school. Things at home were going great however, at the shop Karen had lost her star beauticians. Their mother had passed on and they had taken their inheritance and opened a beauty salon for themselves.

Karen was devastated and that was the start of her depression. Since she chose the business out of the marriage, her ex-husband Rico Sauvé went on a shopping spree with the shop's credit. He brought season tickets to the local professional football games, he paid for two vacations, purchased car upgrades and the list went on and on.

He pretty much ruined Karen's credit. If it wasn't for her thriving clientele, she would have been done. Mr. Rico also did the books and of course he did not pay the taxes. That too had fallen back on Karen. She asked for the shop and in return she assumed the debt that came along.

With the IRS on her heels, she had to work long hours every day just to keep us above water. The money that she and I brought home wasn't enough to cover our bills at home. The situation her husband had left her in had the family's finances all screwed. It was as if he knew he was leaving her. He plied on even more debt and that was why he didn't want the shop.

All she wanted was the shop, so he gave it to her alright. Real good. Now it was taking a toll on her and her body. I told her to "hold on and she will be ok." Living as a Master Barber didn't come with a 401k plan. If you live week to week like I did you have to be smart with your cash.

My retirement plan was to patent one of my ideas and live off the royalties. I was just looking for the right person to share it with. Since Karen blindly looked at my past, I figured she was the one. I told her about the patent I submitted. As long as she takes care of now, I'll have our future.

She then asked me "What did I mean?" I looked into her eyes and said, "Karen with me or not you would still have to maintain the bills and worry about your future right?" She said "Yes." I then said "Well I'll help you as much as you need me. I knew she was going through a divorce. Once I saw her house, I figured that it was going to take a lot of money to maintain this lifestyle.

I suggested that we move to a more accommodating neighborhood. Somewhere that we could afford. She insisted that we stayed in this area. I had been through two divorces and they were not good. I knew what she was going through.

The person that loses in the battle tries to hold face even if they are drowning. That was what Karen was doing but she was killing herself in the process. Then to top it all off Karen told me "She was pregnant." That was a shocker. I did not want any more damn kids. In the beginning of our union, we agreed on three things. We both agreed what we did not want to happen in our relationship; no babies, no marriage or needles. Karen broke all three now the deal was off. Well Karen had been using opiates ever since she had broken her ankle. It happened when she was pregnant with her second son.

Even though the wound had healed she still dealt with the off and on-again pain. It had become more on than off. Since the divorce she had to work long hours to pay off the debts Rico left her. Now that she was pregnant, I had hoped she would stop using.

She said "She would," but only time will tell. I was afraid she was going to get sick from the withdrawal since she was on them for so long. Then the thought came that if she stopped cold turkey, it could have bad effects on the baby. All I could do was pray for our child.

One night a person that made drug runs for her had took off with her pills. I guess Karen had pissed them off because she didn't get her money back either. One of her clients told me that "Karen had been using at least up to ten blues a day at thirty dollars a pill."

Me being a weed smoker and not a prescription drug person I did not know what she was talking about. I didn't even know what those things were but I would see them everywhere all over the house. When I first met her, I never paid any mind to them until that one night. But at thirty dollars a pill ten a day that equaled a three hundred dollar a day habit.

No wonder we were in so much fucking debt. I'll never forget she was so fucking sick. Then it came to me that she was withdrawing. I've seen that too many times before in the hood. Damn, if I wanted a fucking drug addict bitch I didn't have to come way the fuck to the country to find one. I was hurt because two of the three things that we said weren't going to happen, happened at the same time and fell on our relationship hard.

I was seeing things were starting to get out of hand. I told Allen I wanted him to get his act right or you must go back to your mom. You owe it to yourself and her so make her proud he agreed. He decided to leave anyway.

His mom always thought I had brought my kids. That was not true. What I did was help them establish a goal. Stick to their goal and I'll give them small tasks to earn the money to apply to what they are aiming to purchase. Depending on their own efforts would determine the amount they would receive.

She graduated herself to the degree of a Registered Nurse (RN) and that's why Allen was happy. She was going to spoil him and if that's what she wanted to do hey you know my motto. Things on the outside seemed to be getting better however, the lies and hiding over friends' houses had gotten worse. I had been through this shit before with my mom and that was a big reason, I left Norfolk. I felt obligated to Karen because she was pregnant.

With all that she was going through she would lose this child in the birth or from child services if her using continues at this rate. She was a friend and I wanted to see her through this hard time. The only thing was when she did not have the pills, she would have these flu-like illnesses and she would sleep all day. I hated that the most.

Her so-called friends were always in her face when she had it but when she was in need they scattered like roaches with their supply. They used her all the time.

They knew she'd have the money to support her habit and their habit when they ran for her. She was either so blind not to see it or she was so far gone that the pope could have delivered them and she would not have cared. It was a guy in particular his name was Rap he was a low life but he knew the source to any kind of drug you could name.

For some reason he would always lose Karen's package or flip hers and send her the lesser package. Like I said I did not find out this until he had already replaced what he owed her plus extra. I begged her to slow down and I told her the story of my dad. How he had died and for some reason she was another person who didn't want to listen.

I did not know this new person. For the first time in a long while I felt like I was feeling now. I was back to the age when I found out that my dad had been a user and a shooter as well. This was opening a lot of old wounds that I kept locked away for so many years.

I tried everything to wean her off until I had gotten a toothache and the first thing she offered me was a quarter piece of the pill. I had been in so much pain I never thought to look at what it was she handed me. I trusted her not to want the both of us on this shit. Then all at once it felt like the pain ran away. In a split second it made me wonder what the big deal was... boy I wrong.

We were able to keep afloat by the skin of our teeth. And by the grace of God the baby was born healthy and clean. We had weathered the storm, and now it was time to fight for freedom from these pills. Karen had broken her right ankle twice so by now she was on her feet all day. With the extra weight from having the baby her pain was worsening.

It made a big impact on whether she will continue to use the blues for the pain. So, she said "The pills helped her endure the pain and it got her through the day."

Karen said she tried drinking but the hangovers were too much to bear the following day. I suggested she see a doctor with all the money she was spending purchasing them on the street. She would always say she could not afford to waste time trying to get a doctor and the whole screening process. With Karen she always had excuse after excuse for everything. I was getting tired.

My problem was I didn't know if I had a warrant out for my arrest or not. To be honest I had written everyone off, even my brother in Woodbridge. Leavening was not an option. All my focus was on the baby and getting Karen off those blue devils.

All my emotions were resurfacing daily and it was becoming harder by the day to sit and watch everything fall. It seemed to play out in slow motion; it was surreal. A client of hers had breast cancer and had an arsenal of pain pills. Karen had gotten them for free and that's how she claims her habit started.

At least that's how Karen put it from my understanding. Up until now I don't think I ever saw her sober. Never and I really felt cheated. I refused to let the drug win her from me.

Once that same client had woken up and gotten help for her pill abuse. I had hoped Karen would get the picture and get off them too.

It left Karen to avoid it. Her client used to be her supplier. She no longer was filled with endless amounts of pills at her fingertips from her. Now she had to depend on people that steal, lie and cheat to get by daily. Let me tell you this just because she was their hairdresser, she was not exempt from their list of victims too. People like Rap, Data, and this one black man named Walter. They wanted a pill for every five she brought from them.

I told her to leave these dudes alone. She didn't listen. I had given her an ultimatum either the pills or me. I had no force behind the threat because she knew that my mom was working as a home health aide and was homeless as well.

So, she knew that I had no way out. It was not until the IRS called her and started to freeze her bank accounts. All this was from the shit her ex-husband had done when he was in control of the shop. It bit Karen in the ass to the tone of fifteen thousand dollars and that was the straw that broke the camel's back.

That broke the support in the armor of her Viking vest. All the money in the world could not fix this problem. With the IRS and the habit made it all fall at once. Her habit and poor judgment of people came in and stole the rest from her. She had gone from a one hundred and fifty thousand dollar a year woman to selling everything in her shop to the same bitches that slowly drove her into the hole.

She allowed it to happen; she couldn't blame anyone but herself. When the drugs ran out so did her so called friends. They ran just as fast. She had a few that hung around and eventually their hands were revealed of their false intentions.

Like Rosy for instance. She stayed with us and helped Karen at Crayons Beauty Salon. I gave her my space there. It worked for her and her clients. However, for Karen and Rosy it was still play time. I found out that they were now using needles.

I asked Rosy "to leave" and I stopped having any contact with Karen all together. I wondered how long she was shooting up with those pills. Was Rosy the one who showed her how to shoot up? I needed to know because I was willing to take my chances before it had gotten too deep like death. I was not going to bury one of my kid's mothers. I could not, especially from an overdose.

When I confronted her, she threw a fit and cried. Then she asked me not to leave her and I remembered our agreement. Then I said to her, "I'm not going to leave you until my promise to you has been fulfilled. You have until then to get yourself together and she agreed. I told her "I could not leave her like that anyway, she would be alone. Some of her family was in California.

The bulk of her family was still living in Germany. I would not leave her by herself. I was not going to leave my child with her under those conditions. I was the closest person to her she could depend on and I felt it was the right thing to do. Well, she never stopped and she started doing shit just as an addict would do, lie, lie, lie.

A letter had come in the mail and that's when the severity of the situation became real. It was an eviction notice and we had until November the fifteenth to move from the house or be put out on the street. The boys were at their dad's house for the holiday so that was good but we have the baby and the two dogs with us. Damn I do not want to raise my daughter like this lord please help us.

I could not wait until she got help. She acted like she was just as shocked as I was and it pissed me off. I had Lily's godparents down the street from me. I know they'll help us move with a few of my clients and a couple of her clients. It should be an easy transition. I packed the house the best way

I could because all the help had left after all the drugs Karen provided was gone.

At least all the heavy stuff was already on the truck. I had the baby and the dog's to care for while Karen worked. It was hell packing that house up practically by myself and all Karen would do was constantly ask if I got this or that item on the truck.

After my divorce I had been told to leave my house that I had owned. All I was allowed was my clippers and my personal belongings. I never had to pack a whole four-bedroom house with a two-car garage. It seemed like God either had a plan for me or I was going crazy. We rented a pet friendly hotel in Thornburg, Virginia. It was me, Karen, Lily, the two boys and the two dogs.

We were all living in a double bedroom. It was tight and neither the boys nor the dogs were comfortable. The room was a normal sized room the boys had rode to school with Karen in the mornings. I had the dogs and the baby during the day. After three weeks of her bringing the boys in at a reasonable time and her chasing those pills it started taking a toll on her mentally and physically.

To the point she could not think rationally. For example, we had received an offer on two places and Karen turned them down because she did not want to lose the dogs. I asked her if she was mad.

You would have your family on the streets for the dogs. Shit like that was taking a toll on all of us and it was pulling the very fabric of this family apart. Things had gotten so bad that I asked her to move us closer to the boy's father so that he could take them back and forward to school. They would be home at a good time and I did not have to worry about them seeing their mom in her present condition.

Karen by this point was so far gone she was in and out of conciseness. She will be talking to you then fall asleep and not remember anything when she woke up. She was in and out of the room so much that I would not eat but once a day and that's if I went to get the food myself.

It was hard because I had a newborn in the middle of the winter with me. I did not trust her with Karen or the company that she was around either. Out of all the hotels she chose to stay in she happened to pick the hotel Rosy and her boyfriend were also staying in.

No way we were staying here, I told Karen. She insisted she did not know Rosy and her boyfriend were staying at the same hotel. They were scraping old metals and at night they would lay up in the hotel and shoot up until they passed out. I was hoping Karen did not find out because she was trying to get the needle usage under control. However, I knew if she had seen the person who had introduced her to using the needle all the controlling was out the door.

Mission Impossible would seem possible compared to trying to help someone who does not want the help in the first place. It upsetted me deeply to see someone I loved to deteriorate right in front of my eyes. I was hopeless in trying to stop her from hurting herself and us. However, that night Karen told me "I am going to Rosy's room for a cigarette. I'll come right back." When she came in and walked past me, I noticed she looked pale. I asked her "what was wrong with her?" She said "Rosy and her Boyfriend had got kicked out of their room."

The police evidently were called to the hotel by the owner they ripped off early on their route today. They were picking up other people's scraps right off their property. I told her "That they were not good to hang out with anyway. Their wrong doings could affect our staying here at the hotel as well. I did not want to see her or her boyfriend around our family anymore."

Karen said that "I did not have to worry about that because they both were arrested." She had gotten worse and I begged her to go to the doctors for help for her pain. She did not listen to me.

The next day at work her first client told her "If she did not go to the hospital with her now, she was going to call an ambulance." Karen asked her to call and inform me that she was finally tired and she was going to seek help. I was so happy that I cried and thanked God. Then I fell to my knees and prayed for the best.

By the looks of Karen last night, they were going to keep her for at least a few days. I hope that slows her down. Her lips and fingertips were powder blue. She was trying to tell me she was okay. The doctor had already told her she had pneumonia in the right side of her chest. It was heading to the left side fast, if she did not slow down.

He told her to get rest and to take her antibiotics. But if it did not contain any opiates she could care less. Well, her client called me and told me that she dropped Karen off at the hospital. She said she would watch Lily for me so I could go and sit with Karen at the emergency room.

I'm glad I went because that was going to be the last time I saw Karen for two and a half months. I thought up until now all her clients did not pull for her. All they cared about was their hair and make-up. I was wrong, except this client (she knows who she is and I'm going to leave it like that) was God sent.

I witnessed how Karen treated her clients. They were pampered. You would think they felt the same towards her. Nope. It was sad. Karen had at all times put her family last. even when it had come down to her last five grand that her parents had sent for her to catch up on her house bills.

She had given that money to her business landlord instead. I thought she was mad. I asked her "why would you pay the rent on the shop and your kids did not have a roof over their heads?" Her response was "she had employees that depended on her and they had families to care for too."

I understood that but you don't put your own family out on the street to save a friend's family. I have never heard of such a thing before in my life. After her client came and got Lily from me. I went straight to the emergency room.

The front desk nurse led me to Karen's room. She looked bad. She didn't know who I was. At least she did when she was conscious enough to focus her eyes. Karen asked me to take her to the restroom.

After we made it back to her cubicle, they gave her something to relax. That was all she wrote Karen said I love you then she was out. I called her mom to tell her she had finally given in and now all we could do was wait and pray. I could not do anything but wait. I did not have the baby so I had gotten a bite to eat. It felt good to eat something.

It was like two days since I ate any real food other than chips and candy bars from the hotel lobby vending machines. Then I went back to the hotel, took the dogs out and showered. I fell asleep before the doctors could tell me any news about Karen. Lily was still with Karen's client she had called and said that I deserved a chance to get a good night's rest.

She was right between the moves to the hotel then from that hotel to this one. I had not had any time to unwind to myself. Lily was with me twenty-four hours seven days a week. This was the first time since she was born that she wasn't with me.

It felt so strange that I could not sleep. Karen was gone and now so was Lily. I cried silently to myself and fell to sleep hoping for good news in the morning. I woke up the next day after tossing and turning all night long. I really could not sleep. It didn't feel right that the boys had moved to their father's house. I had the dogs with me but the baby was not here now. I'm by myself and it felt strange.

Around two am the next morning my cell phone rang. I knew a call this time in the morning was not good news. I was right Karen had slipped into a coma. The doctors had given her only a five percent chance of surviving. My whole world had just been taken apart and reshuffled.

To the point that I wanted to scream but I knew I could not do anything at this time other than pray and cry. The next day I called Karen's client and asked her "if she could keep the baby for the weekend?" She agreed and told me "To kiss Karen for her on my visit to the hospital."

I had to figure out my next move and my license was suspended. I may have a warrant out for my arrest. With all that already over my head I still had to take care of a newborn baby. Lord, if you can hear me, I need you ASAP... I quickly called all my resources three out of the twenty phone calls came through for me. Ain't that a bitch?

I went to the first person's house and he was not home. Good thing he told his dad I was coming over because he left me a hundred dollars in his stash box. His dad was a real Kool dude. However, I was told not to let him follow me to the stash. Well, that plan did not work.

He followed me all the way to the stash box then turned his head, so as not to watch what I was doing. That was a good look. He threw in a hundred dollars for the rent on the hotel. Gus kept his word. Then Mills had come for a cut every week and he paid me double each time.

He would leave me a little bud to help with all the headaches. He knew that I was going through a lot with Karen away. Lily's god parents helped me out a lot as well. They were the third on my list. This one client Karen had used to try and keep negative shit going on between us. Well come to find out she was Karen's biggest buyer. Her husband worked for the government. All they could use was opiates.

It only stays in their system for three days. When Karen went into a coma Sue was lost without a connect. Her habit had gotten just as bad as Karen's. It was funny though because she played possum all the whole-time like she didn't use.

She was always kicking dirt on Karen. All during Karen's coma she came and sat with me and the baby. She would take me and Lily to the doctor for her checkups. I thought she was trying to mend her ways.

After three weeks passed it was getting cold as hell outside. The end of January was coming fast. I visited Karen as often as I could. She was also diagnosed with a Staph infection from her needle usage. I was afraid to get too close to her on my visits. I did not want to infect the baby. The doctors say she was improving. All the large lesions from missed injections had gotten infected.

The doctors removed all of them from her arms and hands. I thought to myself they did a good job on her. Now only if she would wake up. I kissed her on her forehead and left. Not able to look at anyone on my way to the elevators.

I did not want them to see the tears and pain that I harbored inside. Karen's mom came through for me and the baby as well. If it was not for her sending me change every couple of weeks I don't know what would have become of me and Lily. As long as I had the room paid for and the baby needs were met, I was fine.

She knew I was going days on end sometimes without eating. She made sure I did have money for food. I can hear her saying it now "if you do not eat how will you be strong enough to take care of Lily?" I thought to myself she was right and I started eating one meal a day to keep my energy level up.

All the crying had taken a toll on me and my faith. I would talk to her mom a lot. This unfortunate situation had pulled us closer. Praying and talking to her kept me sane. She was always saying to me "prepare yourself because it's going to get worse before it starts to get better."

I thanked her for all she had done for us and said, "good night." Before falling asleep I wondered what she had meant by saying "it's going to get worse before it gets better." I thought what she said was not positive at all. Only if she really knew how right she was and how wrong I was for doubting what she said to me that night.

I stayed up all night. I am praying that the lord would bring her out of this safely. I hoped this was a lesson to her. I saw it happening and I blamed myself. Then a voice said, "It's not your fault. You tried to warn her and she chose this route on her own." The voice continued "Now all you can do is stand by her while the Lord does his work."

I called the I.C.U. where Karen was located three times a day. It seemed as if every time I asked about Karen's condition the staff would say the same as yesterday. When her condition changes, we will inform you. Did they know she had a newborn? Did they know I'm in a hotel room waiting for her to wake up?

Before the next question came up, I realized that it was not their doing. It was Karen's but she was not here to vent. They were the closest ones to her. I wanted to piss them off to the point that when she did wake, they would tell her exactly how I felt. I was hurt. I told her that this was how I lost my father.

She didn't even take that into consideration. I swear when she wakes up and she gets better it's over. I'm leaving her and I'm taking Lily with me. I called the social service office the next morning. Lily's god mom told me about the emergency food stamps program. I was totally against it but I had to put my pride aside. I had to reach out because my cash was running low.

If I did get accepted, I could use the cash for Lily's dippers and personal supplies. With the food stamps they can go for her formula and snacks. I was nervous at the thought of entering the office. It brought me back to when my mom had dragged me around Norfolk. Jumping through hoops to get assistance to help take care of me.

I told myself I would do anything at this very moment to support me and Lily. I had no other options. I could not hustle at this time. If I got busted then my daughter was surely going to the state. So hustling was out of the question.

In the office the workers kept looking at her. It makes me feel like they are already trying to plot a way to take her from me as we speak. I looked around and realized I was talking to myself. "Next!" the lady behind the window said. Lily's godmother said, "That's you." Oh ok "I'm coming ma'am" I yelled. I asked her godmother to hold her while I went to the front desk. At the desk they asked a hundred questions. Then after all that I had to enter the same information into the computer.

She asked me "what program was I applying for food stamps, Medicaid or TANF?" I heard of the first two choices but the last one I was not sure of and I asked the attendant "What was the Tanf program?" Well, she said "TANF is Temporary Assistance for Needy Families. It provides temporary assistance to families with children when the parent or guardian is unable to provide the basic necessities for the child or children."

I thought to myself if I had that plan, I could keep the hotel room. But on the flip side Karen will have to be placed on child support until she pays it back. I was not going to throw her under the bus like so many of my baby mothers have done me. Don't get me wrong child support is needed for some cases but a lot of these cases are used to control the other person.

The other spouse used the system to keep tabs on the other one with the state's assistance. Sometimes they just used it as a form of payback. In my case the other person was mad that I got fed up with their bullshit and left. No matter what I put all my baby's mothers through school or gave them the opportunity to own their own business.

Except the moms that I did not know at the time they were pregnant. They already had their own thing going and I helped them to the next level. I never put them on child support. I told the lady behind the counter that "Karen was a good mother and she unfortunately had come down with pneumonia. As a result, she had fallen into a coma. The doctors had hoped her body was taking this time to recover. "I didn't need the program, just the stamps please." I responded to her.

Well, she said "if you change your mind, you can always come back here. We could switch it for you ok." I nodded and went to sit down. "Oh, ma'am" I turned and said, "I would like to enroll her into the Medicaid program too." The social worker said "sure we'll be right with you." I said "ok" and returned to my seat. As soon as my butt hit the chair my name was called Lily's god mom looked at me and said, "They're not that busy today go on in there. They just might give them to you today."

While in the back the process went rather smoothly. It wasn't as bad as I remember the process was way back then when I was younger. The social worker looked at the sign sheet that the front attendant filled out.

She asked, "So you're not currently working?" "No, ma'am," I replied. She went on to say, "where was the mother?" I guess it was not too many dudes today breaking down the door trying to take care of their child. I would have been one of them but I was not going to sell any more drugs. I felt good this was the first time I was able to have one of my children with me.

I did not have a plan but I did have my child. I was not giving her up to anyone. She asked me "who was the mother?" When I told her who she was she immediately went to the back of the office. My heart dropped. I was going to jail for sure.

No man asks for food stamps I said to myself. The thought had crossed my mind to leave get your daughter now while you can and just go. Just as I had got the heart to get out of the chair, she returned to the office with three other women. They were all looking at Lily saying, "Karen does their hair, they gave me best wishes to give her and hoped she pulled through."

Sighing in relief I thought they were coming for me. They all wanted to see Lily. One of the ladies opened the door to the lobby and called Lily's god mom. She came to the door and handed Lily to one of the ladies and they shut the door. Aww she is so cute Lily barley opening her eyes peeking and smiling at the same time.

Come talk to me in the other office. Oh boy here it comes they are going to take her from me. I bet that's before they knew it was Karen's daughter they asked if her mom was Asian or something because of Lily's slanted eyes and toffee complexion. As I followed the lady that was helping me, I had turned away from her in the direction of the social worker who was holding Lily.

The lady in front said, "Oh no please don't worry we know Karen personally and I need some more information from you." It was a lot more peaceful in here than out in the lobby. I looked at Ms. Dove and said, "she's all I have right now and if you take her, you're going to have to take me too."

It was true the business was gone, her dodge magnum was gone and half of our belongings were lost in the move. I had done most of the move by myself so a lot was left behind.

It was done half ass because I had to watch Lily while I packed the house and moved the furniture on to the truck. All I had was Lily and I could not imagine them taking her from me. That would be the nail in my coffin. All the people she helped never showed up to lend me a hand. Even the people that owed her money were refusing to pay their debt. That only showed me that they were not her friends. That made me not want any of them around us. Only if she had listened to me.

We will be a whole lot better off than we were now. As I started to tear up. I did need their help badly but not at the cost of losing Lily. I looked up to not allow the tears to fall down my face. The social worker said, "Karen did all of our hair and we will help you as much as possible." It was too late to get the stamps for the day so she told me to "come back in the morning and a debit card will be at the front desk waiting for me."

At the same time I was reaching for the door, the other social workers came into the room with Lily. She said she was "so cute and smart." I smiled and agreed with them and at the same time I was reaching for my baby. Before I left, I thanked the lady and she said, "Wait where are you and the baby staying now?"

I said, the "motel on route seventeen." She told me if my money ever runs low to call her. She knows a homeless shelter that was in the county with emergency rooms if I needed one. Then she went on to say, "it was a very nice place for you and the baby."

I looked at her and thought that it would be better than paying the rent at the motel. The rent there was two hundred and seventy-five dollars a week. That did not include an icebox or microwave. I promised Karen that I would keep the dogs and if I go to the shelter, I can't take them with me. However, I'm not going to let these dogs keep me from putting a roof over my baby's head either.

When I go see Karen, I'm going to tell her the dogs are leaving this week. I knew she might not be able to answer but at least I gave her a chance to state how she felt about giving the dogs up for adoption. Sue picked me up for Lily's doctor's appointment.

Once we were on the way back to the room, she asked me "if Karen wakes up and continues to use drugs would I leave her?" I said "after all of this shit, yes are you crazy? We lost everything. Now she is in a coma. She left me, the kids and the two dogs in a hotel room with no money. If we didn't have a child together, I would not be here now."

I knew I did not mean that because I did love her. This would teach her a lesson not to take advantage of the person closest to you. You never know when you will need that person for help. She said, "Wow! Well I have to commend you for hanging in there with her this long. I thought you would have left by now."

I was going to take Lily until Karen got out of the hospital. All I could do was look straight ahead and hold my tongue. Now it all makes sense. I told Karen that Sue was not her friend and to stay away from her.

Sue had taken it upon herself to call CPS (child protective service) on Karen. She had been highly jealous of the fact Karen was able to conceive a child doing her drug usage and she had miscarried. She had to be the one who called CPS. Social services had contacted me saying "they were told Karen was shooting up blues with heroin while leaving the kids to watch themselves.

I had a feeling it was one of Karen's closest friends that would make that shit up. I said to myself while still listening to the radio and Sue was still driving. for her to have done this to Karen.

Half the shit that Karen got Sue ordered. Sue was at our house with Karen everyday so she was just as fucked up. Sue was wrong for doing that shit, another prime example of a frenemy. I told Karen on the next visit to the hospital Sue was talking to the guest at our last cookout. She said she didn't know how Karen was able to keep her child while she had miscarried.

From that moment I knew Sue was jealous of Karen. I thanked Sue for the ride and then told her that my truck would be fixed on the next doctor's visit. It was not necessary for her to pick us up. I thanked her once more and waved until she had made that left to go on to the entrance ramp to Washington DC.

I fed Lily in her highchair since she was getting bigger and sitting up on her own. I would put the two beds together and place her in the center. She'll crawl from one end of the bed to the other until she got tired. I'll feed her then wash her up while she watches her favorite movie show.

Then I'd get her ready for bed. It had become routine until the snow hit. It went from worst to hell. I had to get her dressed then walk the dogs. Then come back, take her and get breakfast and pay the room rent. I did all of that while holding her in one arm. I had to walk one dog at a time. I swore if one of those dogs made me drop my baby, I would have gone crazy.

Karen's mom was doing what she could for me and Lily. She sent Karen five thousand dollars and that would have saved the house and the shop but Karen used that money to finish herself off. I begged her to let me handle the funds. Damn I wished she would have listened to me.

I started crying. I know Lord, crying is showing I have little faith in your works. I assure you it's from the pain I felt in my heart for Karen. I thought I was being tested and punished at the same time. My cousin found me on Facebook and asked me "If I am ok?" I told her. "The situation I was in is trying to bring me down."

She asked me "how can she help?" I told her "I need the motel to be paid for a few days." She sent me enough for three days. I put that to what Karen's mom sent me and I had enough to pay the motel room for the week. I did not have anything on hand for gas or dog food.

I must give the dogs up. That was the only way out that I could see. Then we could go to the homeless shelter. I'm tired now. I'll pray on it tonight. I put Lily to bed then I called the hospital again. Once the nurse answered the phone, I asked her "Wow Karen was doing?" It was the fourth time I had called today. I was now exhausted, my mind and strength were drained. It felt like I was starting to unravel and fall apart.

Lily finally fell asleep. So I took a shower and told the dogs I was sorry but, in the morning we were all leaving this room for good. I wanted to call the shelter but first I had to kick this addiction Karen had introduced me to first.

I tried to wean her off by hiding her pills but now since she's been gone, I haven't had anything for my toothache. I did not call anyone for anything either. I thought to myself I can do it. I have too for Lily's sake. She deserves a fair chance in life and I'm going to give it to her if it kills me.

I hated Karen again for allowing me to get hooked on that shit as well but I am used to the pain. I must get clean because I can't kick in the shelter. They would surely take Lily away from me then. It was hard and I would get chills. I would cover up then I would get extremely hot. It felt like hell and I was next up to fry. After two long nights of shitting and throwing up I felt better. I had nothing left inside of me. Even water was hard to keep down.

This opiate shit was powerful and once it was in your system. To get rid of the pain you either had to get the dope or deal with the flu like illness until it passed. One of the dudes who owed Karen money called me on her phone. When I saw the name, I knew he could educate me on what to do to push this shit out of my system.

He offered me either the pills or the money he owed Karen. He would call after I have been clean for two days and not only that I must stay clean to get into the shelter. "No, I told him I needed the money instead of the pills.

He told me "He could bring it in the morning." "Yo Walter, wait." Then I asked him "If a person was withdrawing from opiates what can they take to help with the pain?" No one else but Karen had known I was taking a piece of the pill here and there for my toothache. I did not want anyone to know either. We still were not sure who had called child protective services on us, so I kept everything to myself about me using.

He said "They could take night or day cold medicine." "What's that?" He said, "The medicine helps with the flu symptoms and takes away the pain." That was the most helpful free thing I think he ever has done in his life for anyone.

However, I did not care. All I knew is I was going to beat this addiction now! I had to for the family's sake. On the third day I felt better and I was ready to call the shelter. I made plans for Nova to go to a pit-bull retirement home for dogs. It was close to our old house in Stafford. Now Niko was adopted out to a family that lived near the kid's father. I did that to help the kids with their displacement. At least they could still see him while they are staying with their father.

CHAPTER 22

Frist time for Everything

Once I called the shelter, they had given me the address then told me to come on down so I could fill out the paperwork. I had to call them several times for directions to the facility. I had never been to this part of Fredericksburg before, it was far.

The staff was helpful and had me wait at the check in station until I was interviewed. I was waiting for the staff member to come over to check for errors. She helped me finish the process. Then after I handed the paperwork back she reached out and placed it on the desk in front of us.

As I turned around to look at the time there were two officers walking over towards our direction. One of them had asked me, "To pass them the baby." I could not believe this shit. They called the police on me. I was hesitant at first. The idea had entered my mind to run, get in your truck and don't look back. Then I thought about how far I would get.

One of the lady officers said "Come on man I'll tell the magistrate you were very cooperative." I looked at the other female officer and she had asked me "If this was Karen's baby?" I thought to myself damn we were all the way in Fredericksburg, Virginia. "How in the hell did people know Karen all the way out here?"

She heard through social services that we were going to be at this shelter. Once I heard that she went to school with Karen I was a little bit relieved. I did not know whether to run or give up. A voice said, "You're not giving up. Your following your destiny."

I turned to Lily and said, with tears rolling down my face I will be right back baby. She was looking at me with her big brown eyes sucking her binky and smiled with her hands reaching towards my face. The officers led me to the front doors of the shelter. All I could think about was where were they going to take Lilly if I got looked up? Then the older of the two had placed me in the back of her car.

We waited for her to get clearance to bring me into the office. Once she was Ok'd to proceed, she took me down to the sheriff office. On the way I had a talk with God and my grandfather. At first, I said "Lord, I know what you promised me so I do not fault them for not knowing your true plans for me."

No matter how long they keep me I'll never forsake you father. Now to you grand dad I'm sorry for falling short of your wishes and your dreams you had for me.

Please don't forget me. The car came to a complete stop when we arrived at the magistrate office. We sat there for an hour. Then she exited the car and opened my door. She led me to the magistrate and she asked me my name and date of birth. Then she asked me "why didn't I go to the court date?"

I told her "I had been living in a motel for about eight weeks now until I ran out of funds. I was referred to the homeless shelter. I could not receive any mail at the hotel." The officer said "ma'am he did not resist in any way. His girlfriend is in a coma, that's how he ended up in the homeless shelter."

The magistrate looked over her glasses at me. Then she asked, "Would I be able to make a new court date in two months from today." Ma'am I said, "If you let me out of here today, I know I can make it to court in two months". She made a phone call to whom I did not care. I just wanted to get back to Lilly.

I didn't know if it had anything to do with me or not. She hung up the phone. She then wrote something down and said to me "Wait here." After twenty minutes they both returned to the room and she told the officer to return me back to the shelter.

She said, "Please do not make me regret this and go take care of that baby." "Thank you, ma'am," I repeated twice and I waited for the officer in the lobby. Once she got my paperwork with my new court date, we left the magistrate office.

I was so happy that I couldn't put it into words. I could not wait to get back and hug Lily. Squeeze her and most important teach her all about God. If it was not for his promise he made to me I would not be here with you right now.

He never forgot me or his promise. I was glad for that, in fact I was crying tears of joy. I thanked my grandfather for being with God and telling him that I needed to be with my baby. The sheriff allowed me to ride back without the handcuffs on my wrist. I was thankful for her act of kindness.

They made them so small. They were starting to cut off my blood flow. She threw the lights on when we headed back to the shelter. Once inside the shelter Ms. Tashia who did my interview saw me walk back into the building. She said to me crying "I'm so sorry." Then went on saying "I have to call them if anyone that we consider taking in has a warrant for their arrest. We ran a check on everyone; it was nothing personal. When we ran your background check yours came back that you had a warrant in Virginia Beach. I wanted to tell you but I could have lost my job. It hurt the most when I saw your facial expression."

I was praying you did not hurt yourself or anyone else. I could not get mad at her. To myself I was very upset the warrant was from that bitch from Norview. I could have lost my child. Even worse, I could have gotten locked up and lost my child. I can't wait until the court date. She knows that I paid her and she was just trying to get seconds. I hope she rots in hell for what she's been taking me through.

The only thing that mattered was me and Lily were back together. God saved us. This just reinforced my faith even more. That was fine with me. I told her no "Harm done" I did not know about the warrant. The magistrate gave me a new court date.

The officer said she would put a good word in for you if you were cooperative with her while in custody. The intake person said "Well let's get you into orientation so I can get you a room."

I repeated what she said and she looked at me and smiled, "Yes, your own room since you are a single father with a daughter, you get your own room." For me to get a roommate the person would have to be a single father with a daughter as well. If not, the room will remain yours for the whole stay here.

She ran down the rules of the facility. The most important thing was not to get busted with drugs or alcohol. Never go into a female's room. If the three of those were done you were fine. She led me to my room. It was twice the size of the hotel room and I had my own shower.

That was good because Lily loved her baths. It helped relax her before snack time and bed. I gave the room a complete cleaning from top to bottom. Then I got Lily ready for her bath. No matter what she was going to have structure in her life. Dinner was at seven and bath was at eight. Then snack and bedtime follows.

I went into the lobby of the center and I told Tashia that I had spoken with the doctors and Karen was showing signs of progress. Which meant she would probably come out of her coma at any time. She looked at me as if to say well spit it out. I said, "I was hoping since she did not have anywhere to go as well would it be possible for her to come here?" She said, "In the morning, talk to your counselor and let her know your situation."

I think she already has a clue to what is going on with your case already. I said, "thank you" and went back to my room. The center was sort of a clean place. I would never let her crawl on these floors though they were filthy. We both had fallen asleep after Lily's bath. Today was traumatizing for the both of us.

This was the first night I forgot to call Karen. It was too late to reach the nurses station. I will call her in the morning. Once I woke up, I got myself together. Then I got Lily up, changed, wiped her down then dressed her for breakfast. On the way to breakfast hall, I called the ICU. I heard the best news ever. "Today Karen moved her arm!" I told the doctor "Tomorrow I hope she wakes up".

Lord, I thank you today for all your blessings and keeping me free and strong. Thank you for looking over, Karen, thank you father, thank you father please continue to walk and talk to me dear lord in your name I pray amen.

Valentine's Day was right around the corner and the visit to see Karen was great. She has not woken up completely but the doctors said "that was good because they had to drain the fluid off her other lung. This way she will not feel the pain. In a couple of days, they had hoped for her to have a full recovery. Then she will be released from the ICU to a regular floor soon."

I could not wait to call her mom and tell her the good news. My baby's mother was coming home. It was a huge relief God had spared her life. I never had a child of mine's mother come this close to being deceased. It was a real eye opener to really see who was in your corner when times got hard.

Or not at times like this one. It did not bother me, I had faith in God. What people thought did not matter to me at all. I still had my truck thank God for that because in the morning I must go visit Karen. Today she was coming home.

It's almost been fifty days since she's been in a coma now, she had awoken from that near death situation. I really hope she gets it together so we can get our lives back on track. I had gotten this lady who lived at the shelter with me to keep Lily for me while I went to pick Karen up from the hospital.

She was delighted to keep her. She, like everyone else in the shelter, was eager to meet Karen. I talked so much about her that she was partially a little celebrity for making a comeback from pneumonia (that's what I told the people who had lived there). I went outside after getting Lily's bag ready for the sitter. The truck was gone.

I looked all over the parking lot everywhere for it. Just my luck the day I had to pick Karen up they towed the truck damn. If it wasn't for bad luck, I would not have any is all I had thought to myself.

I went back into the shelter and I called a cab. It arrived there a little late but it did not matter because she still had not been discharged yet. Once at the hospital I got some of her favorite roses then proceeded to her room. "Good morning hi mama how do you feel?" I asked Karen.

She replied, "good baby" and hugged me hard. She looked a mess but I guess that's how you looked after sleeping for almost two and a half months. She and I had laughed and we gathered her things and headed to the discharge desk. She set down to discuss what she had to do to her wounds.

She had four holes from them draining her lungs. She had to follow up on her rehabilitation three days a week. The same cab I called earlier was waiting for us out front. We arrived at the shelter and Karen had done her check in wow she had two pills in her purse. No one saw them well; they did not really pat us down here. At least I have not seen them do that since I've been here. I cut all the staff members' hair. I was even cutting most of the male residents' hair too. I charged ten dollars a cut if you didn't have a job. If you had a job, it was fifteen dollars a haircut. So, they cut me a lot of slack when it came to the rules. I hide the pills and continue to help Karen to unpack.

We finished right before lunch. I went through the line and prepared our plates. Lilly was happy that her mommy was here with her. She was seven going on eight months at the time. Being inside the shelter Lily was able to see that the other kids had moms but no dads. She was happy for me being with her but I also noticed that she saw all the kids had their moms and she'd give me that look as if to say daddy "where is my mom?"

Even though she had me deep down inside I knew she had missed Karen as well as I missed her. After lunch Karen, me and Lily sat down to enjoy one another's company. In the midst of the conversation, I had to tell her about the cps agent Ms. Tallymen. Karen, I said "She told me that someone you knew told her you were neglecting your kids shooting heroin and opiates."

It was funny she told me that because on the way back from Lily's doctor appointment Sue slipped up and mentioned that she had not thought I was going to hang in there with you. She figured she'll get Lily from us. Karen was pissed and she cursed herself and Sue.

She said, "Sue was like my sister and when I came here from Iceland Sue was the first friend I made." Then she said, "Why would Sue do that to me?" I told her "Sue was jealous of her for us having Lilly."

When she told Karen that she had walked in on me and her adopted sister kissing. Karen knew that was a lie because I did not like skinny women and I was not into doing family members. She watched Sue from that point on. It had taken us three more weeks and we finally saved the money to move from the shelter.

I was happy to leave the shelter. I was happy it was here to help us. The program that was set up to help you move was no longer available anymore. Low funds had been the cause for a lot of programs to be shut down. We still had to deposit the money earned into an account in the shelter. I did not like that because if you found something you could afford, they had to approve it.

I felt like this, if they no longer matched what you deposited into your account why did they have to approve my place? That was the last straw we're leaving, pack your shit Karen. We went back to the hotel we rented before Karen went to the hospital.

We saved about twenty-five hundred dollars. In the morning we'll go apartment and car hunting. Karen let's say our prayer. Once we finished our prayers, we both said "amen". I looked over at both her and Lilly then I said "good night baby I kissed them and went to sleep.

I hugged her again then lightly said "Goodnight, Lily" and thank you Lord. When I woke up, I looked over at them and saw that they were still beside me asleep. Wow, last night I felt good and slept well. For the first time we all three stayed together in the same room and slept in the same bed.

I let them sleep. Lily had gotten up first then Karen. Get dressed baby we are going to eat breakfast then look at this van at Albert's auto on route seventeen. Her kid's father had rented a car for us to move around to go house and car hunting. While I was driving, she wondered how I knew about this auto sales place. I told her that I heard the staff member talking about how he stood behind his cars and it was a buy here pay here set up.

As we turned into the car lot, we were kind of amazed. He did have a nice selection of vans, jeeps, and trucks. The cars on the other hand were not as promising though. We were not here to be some high and mighty customers, we just wanted a fair deal on a reliable vehicle.

"We were here to get a dependable vehicle for you to travel back and forth to work safely with the kids," I said to Karen. The owner had come out to greet us. He saw the color difference then backed up a little. Then he embraced us like old friends. He introduced himself as "Albert Jr Hi!" he said. His father was Albert Sr. He had stepped out but how can I help you today?

"What can I do for you he asked?" Karen led the conversation. "Yes sir, we're looking for a nice truck or van." I let her talk because she loved to haggle the prices. I was hoping it would also help her feel good spending her money on something other than drugs. Sort of like her seeing the rewards of hard work.

Not by throwing it away on getting high. I came back over and after hearing the spiel about the trucks. I said, "baby why not look at the vans in the front?" She looked at Albert and pointed to the gray van and said, "how much are your vans and what was your newest model?"

Albert looked at me and then Karen and back at me. speaking in my direction he said, "how much were we looking to spend?" I had thirty-six on me. I needed twelve fifty for the apartment. I said, "I had eleven on me now." He stopped me and started to turn away. I told him to wait a second. Karen hold Lily for a moment listen Mr. Albert. I asked him "Did he think I had just driven here because you had nice colors on your signs?" "No," I answered for him. I overheard Ms. Tashia saying how good of a deal you can get here and that you were a people's person. A real family man. Is that true sir? He said "Well I am, I'm selling these two vans for forty-eight hundred dollars. The third one for fifty-five hundred dollars. Then said he'll finance it for eighteen hundred dollars down, no less."

I said "Fine." I no longer stayed at the shelter and I thank God for that but when I see Ms. Tashia, I'm going to tell her she had been wrong about you.

We started walking back to the rental car and he said, "Wait one minute Ms. Tashia that works at the homeless shelter? That's who you were talking about?" "Yes, we were there for two and a half months. We needed a car and I remembered your name had come up as a good person to get a car from."

We wanted to come and give you a shot. We had owned our business before becoming homeless. One thing we know is that word of mouth was the best advertisement of all. I told him and he agreed. He had placed his hand on my shoulder and asked me to join him in his office to fill out the papers on my new van.

He allowed us to keep the van and we could pay the difference on the deposit in two months. God is good all the time. We drove from the dealership and she was happy. It felt good seeing her this way. As we were driving, I asked her "What is this area called?" I saw that there were apartment complexes on all corners when I drove up here.

There were three more complexes on the other end of the highway. I was in a haircut heaven. Look, pull over there I saw a barber shop. It was a Latino barbershop and there were two Spanish people working. One lady's name was Lucie and the man's name was Taco. It seemed like these people needed some lessons on how to speak English.

When I entered the barber shop everyone fell silent. I was the only person that spoke English here I thought to myself. I asked, "Who is the manager here?" Lucie was standing by her station finishing up a client. She asked, "Do you want a haircut?" I shook my head no." I am here about the help wanted sign in the window."

She asked, "How long have I been a barber and if I could cut straight hair?" I answered "twenty-five years of cutting hair and yes, I can cut straight hair." She asked me, "When can I start?" I told her as soon as I got approved for the apartment across the street.

Other than that, "I'll start as soon as we move in, I will be in touch" I said to the owner. Karen was still working at Crayons and she was slowly picking up even though those shifty bitches that used to work for her snaked a lot of her clients. "I told her the real ones will stay and the ones that left were making room for new clients that will appreciate your talents even more."

I tried to boost her spirits every chance I could get. Sometimes it seemed as if she was getting too strong too fast. I started to wonder null not that because she knows if I even think her looking at the Kelly blue book, blue cheese dressing, hell the blue sky I was leaving her in a heartbeat.

She better be focusing on staying clean or I'm out. I love the internet. While she filled out all the paperwork, I had to check my email to see if the application was approved. Yes, we got approved for the place right across the street from that Spanish barbershop. The unit will be ready by Friday, great! Karen "let's turn around we have to go pass Best look apartments.

They had emailed us and we were approved for a two-bedroom apartment." I told her she turned the van around and headed for the apartment office. Things really started to look up again. I thanked God for each of them too. Karen was like you, sure you did not want your old shop back at Crayons.

I said "no I did not want to be back there. That place was always full of chicks. All they did was talk all day long about everyone except themselves." I did not want another barber shop right now.

I told her to take it and I did not mind her being there. I had a plan. I was going to work at the Spanish barber shop. They rented me a space. I want to rent the building. Until then I'll stay there and get to know the neighborhood. I had time because meanwhile I'll cut everyone who does not come to the shop at their house either way I win.

Back at the room I let the girls rekindle their relationship while I took a break and summarized all the recent events in my head. It felt good to see them rolling around in the bed together. I was glad I waited for her. Like I told my divorce attorney every child needs their mother.

Then I fell asleep. That Sunday we picked the boys up and went to church. Karen remembered the pastor was the same man that preached here when she was a young girl. I told her that was wonderful. I wondered if he still recognized her?" After church we went for a walk along the Rappahannock River.

It was a nice day, the sun was bright and the rapids were moving fast. It was beautiful. We told the boys that we found an apartment. We should be moving in by the end of the week. They were excited and full of joy knowing that they would be back with their mother again. We had to get a lot of things together at the storage. I needed to get the beds to the front of the unit along with our clothing.

The kitchen ware was important too. By Friday we got up early and went to the apartment to meet Cindy. She was a tall lady with a funky shape. She talked with a hiss and to me she needed some mints too. I was trying to not laugh. I found out she was the property manager. I did not want to piss her off.

Other than that, she had been very polite despite her deformities. We had to go and get money orders for the first month's rent and the deposit. I went to the store. Karen and Cindy finished up the paperwork.

They waited for me to return with the money orders. I was happy that we were finally moving into a place. Lily had not had time to be a baby yet. She never crawled on the floor nor did I let her practice walking either. The place was just not clean enough.

That had handicapped her from trying to walk. When I returned to the office Lily was all over the place. I was about to cry not in pain or from being hurt. It was from picturing my daughter crawling and seeing her on a clean carpet. It felt good seeing her be a normal toddler. I was amazed watching her having fun finally acting like a baby.

That CPS lady said "If we moved back to Stafford, she was going to make Karen go to an in-house detox program." That's another person I did not want to run into at all. Moving back to Stafford is crazy. I have my clients from Stafford come here. With the Spanish and other minorities already here, that means Mo money, Mo money.

I must go to court next month so I really needed to get cracking setting up some appointments real soon. My client from the last shop had gotten signed with Timberland and the dude he duets with had won a Grammy, so I had that under my belt as being their barber. It would be helpful because he was Spanish too. I could not wait to show the pictures of me cutting their hair to the shop owner.

CHAPTER 23

New Start

I was so happy with the new place it had been like taking in a breath of fresh air. It was a sunny day out with patches of snow littering the landscape of the complex. It was slightly chilly but otherwise it was nice today. All we had to move in with us was the clothes that we had been hauling around for the last five months.

We had all our things in the storage. To get our belongings out was two hundred and four dollars. So, Karen had some friends who told us that the best look was a good community to live in. From the outside it was. It came time to see the apartment manager again to return some last-minute paperwork. Karen told her that Rita referred us and she should get the three hundred dollars for the finder's fee.

The manager looked at Karen and said, "You had to put her name on the application at the time of signing the lease." I could not go to the office because I was not on the lease. Rita's daughter Leah started keeping Lily for us. Karen was in no shape to care for her and take care of her clients.

I started working to pay the storage off. In the meantime, walking to the barber shop. I began to think about all the people that came through for us in our time of need. I wanted to get them all together for a nice dinner my treat. Who was I fooling all the money I was making went to child support?

At court even though I've been sending my child support directly to my kids. The judge was not trying to hear it. Only if she knew my kid's mother did not want to commit perjury by admitting that I had in fact been sending the payments to her. I might have not sent it to where it was supposed to go first however, I was sending it to my kids. That had gone against the court wishes.

Since our daughter was eleven, she called me about her monthly female thing. I was shocked to have been having that conversation with her but she said "that when she had attempted to tell her mom she refused to leave work to help her." So ever since then I've sent all the child support to her and she did what she needed to do with the money.

So, for the first ten years I paid it the way the court ordered me to. But when the money was not reaching my kids, I had gotten upset and felt let down by the system. So, for the last ten years I have been sending it to my daughter. I hoped the judge would understand but she did not. I was ordered to pay one hundred and twelve hundred dollars in back pay every week.

At the rate of three hundred a month from here on until it's paid in full or I die. Ain't that a bitch! It was not fair. I sent her three thousand dollars two summers ago for her late mortgage and I was staying with a friend. She was working the system. I wish they would give her a lie detector test. That would prove I was not being a dead-beat father.

Man, it's crowded in here, yes Mr. Celebrity Barber, they all have been waiting for you. So, all the advertising I did by passing out these cards and flyers paid off. I had gone to the mall and every spot I saw young people hanging out and having a good time I gave them cards and flyers. I picked out the quits too. One out of each group and told them to pass out all the cards and to put their names on the backs. That way I knew who to give a free haircut and twenty dollars too.

One of the guys was excited and yelled out loud a free haircut and twenty bucks that's what's up!! Who's next? Over here a dude with a head full of hair and hair all over his face stood up and walked over to my station.

Ok this was the first cut of the day. It's showtime. I prompted him to sit in my chair. He did and I started draping him. Then I asked, "How was he doing today?" As he went on telling me how his day went.

I was going to work on his hair cut. Only agreeing and disagreeing while I was focusing on the task at hand. Fifteen minutes later I was starting his edge up. "Would you like your neck tapered or squared sir?" "Square please," he answered. "Ok" I handed him the mirror and he was gasping for air saying in a low to medium voice "Where have you been young man? This town needed a man of your talents in this community" he had added. That's exactly what I wanted to hear. Now I'm going to infect this entire community until everyone has my cut on their head. I want my name to ring out in all seven apartment complexes.

Time was flying so fast that the days had blended with the weeks and then into months. Before you knew it was Lily's birthday. The house still had not been furnished yet. Karen decided to do the birthday party at Crayon's. The owner did not mind. She had a party there almost every month, sometimes twice a month.

Depending on the occasion. Things were progressing but I was having a gut feeling and it did not sit well with me. I had to tell Karen how I felt because if she even thinks of dragging this family through that bullshit again, I'm going to jail. Once the party decorations were all into place the guests began to arrive. That's when the dude Walter showed up but he didn't come into the shop. He looks as if he was waiting for someone. Right at that second, I had a flashback of how he felt guilty for taking advantage of Karen.

He would always meet her a block or two from the house to avoid seeing me. I'm going to just see who he is waiting for because his girl did not work here anymore. So, what was his story? I thought to myself as I walked over to him. Once his girl had got caught stealing out of Karen's register Karen fired her. I know he was not waiting for Pam. Karen was not anywhere to be found and I was getting worried.

It was time to start the party. I was running out of things to entertain the kids with while we waited for her to sing happy birthday to Lilly. There she is turning into the complex now.

Wonder if she's high. If she is when I ask her, she'll get loud and withdraw from the subject and that's how I'll know if she is high or not.

I asked her "where were you?" She was like "I told the lady in there I had to drop some of the guests off and I was coming right back." "Why didn't you tell me Karen?" I asked her. The music had gotten louder and over the volume she said "She didn't want to talk about this around the kids." "I agreed" but I was fuming mad.

I never intended to have a kid and get this deeply involved but it happened and I was going to give Lily the same chance I had given all my other kids. So now the game plan is to sit and wait until she has missed Walter. She's going to need that dosage from him and when she goes to leave I will take the keys and act as if they were missing. she will not dare have him come to this shop because I told him if he ever sold her anything else her death will be on his hands. I told him he can wait by her bedside the next time she overdoses. I was done. I meant every word too.

We went to drop the boys off because they had school in the morning. I told them "I would cut their hair when they come back." Then waved to them once they were at the front door. Karen yelled "see you guys late," they screamed "goodnight!" and went inside their father's house. On the way home she was panicking as if she had to use the restroom. She was turning away from the house.

"Where are you going?" I asked her. "Pass the hotel Sam owed me money. It was not Sam, it was Walter and she was not doing this to me again." "Go to the house now" I said to her and she turned around because the cat was out of the bag. She knew she had some explaining to do starting from when she started using again until now.

She had denied it to the very end and I left it alone. That night the flu symptoms were back and because she tried to start at the same dose she was on before the hospital it made her go into cardiac arrest. She turned blue and she was shaking violently. Lilly was crying at the sight of her mother laying on the floor foaming at the mouth. All she wanted to do was to hold her mom. I had to separate the two of them because she almost fell on Lily when she collapsed.

I put Lily in her stroller and I was able to drag Karen into the front room. This is it. The doctor told her that since she had a heart murmur her heart could not take another shocker from the withdrawal again.

He said the next time she could die from heart failure. Now it was here. I laid her on her side and made sure she was still breathing. I called nine one one and told them the situation. The operator asked, "If her condition was from drug usage?" I said, "no but it may be from the withdrawals."

The operator then told me to make sure she was on her side and I told "her she was" and she assured me that the E.M.S would be here in eight minutes. I heard the trucks pulling in and then a loud knock came on the door. I called Karen's client and she came over to help with Lily. Her boyfriend came too, his name was Travis. He was a Winnie ass nigga.

I called him Remix. You know he's that dude that loves to spread bad news and tell stories about how bad he treated women. He treated women cruelly and he had some shortcomings that just gave me a bad vibe about him. I did not like him around. From the first look you would think he was a Kool dude until something happens or goes wrong in his life. Or God forbid something in your life happens, then you'll hear it all over town in a thousand different ways other than the right way. He would act as if he was helping you but the whole time, he's gathering information on you.

As soon as his data banks were full with all the details he would leave and serve it up to everyone he knew. At times I would stop him before he would finish his sentences because I was not a gossiper. I'm a barber. We keep shit told to us tight. That was another reason he rubbed me the wrong way.

He was Karen's friend so I dealt with him on the strength of her. If I could get away from him popping up on the scene like now, that would be nice. Travis looked in and said, "How can I help?" I wanted to say by going back where the hell you had crawled from.

They had to put her on a transport bed and strap her down. Then they rolled her away and she did it again. I'm not staying for the outcome of this one. When they drive off, I'm going to pay the rent and go to Norfolk for a break. On the road everything rewinded to when she started coming home late again. The money started not adding up to the time she was claiming she was at work.

Some check's had bounced. I knew those stories had no merit to them. Karen thought that she was hurting me by using again. It was not just me she was hurting most of all she was killing herself, but now look she was back in the hospital. I'm not sticking around to watch her die. I'm gone.

When she comes around and gets released from the hospital this time, I will not be there to pick her up. I called my mom and told her Karen was using again.

I needed to get the right phone number to the attorney. My mother had cared for his mother-in-law. He wanted to meet me, so this freed me up to see what this dude was all about. I was hoping he would assist me in obtaining my patent. I know I can't keep making up excuses for Karen but I tried to tell her mom. Karen was using again and I was afraid of what might happen to her. She was all the way in California and she could not have done anything to deter Karen from there.

I just wanted to let her know in case she asked her for any money. She said, "She would not help her if she called this time for anything." I told her I'm leaving here because I can't sit here and watch her kill herself. I'm not. Not this time! My heart was hurt because I was always the dysfunctional one in the family. This was a first for me. It had me to the point where I was jerking off all the time for the simple fact, I was too afraid to fuck her.

I did not want to meet another crazy bitch like the one I had stayed with in Norfolk. The one that all she wanted was to get married. Just because our cousins were tying the knot. Fuck that shit. I was now Halfway to Norfolk. Karen called and said "Am I on my way to see her?" I said "No!" She started crying asking "Why I was leaving her?"

I asked her to tell the charge nurse to give you your wallet and you can catch the cab. "Where are you?" she mumbled to me over her crying. "On my way to Norfolk," I said.

She fell silent. Then replied, "you're really leaving me." I said, "look around and tell me why I should be there?" She stopped crying and said to me "If I get into a program that gives out methadone would I come back home?" I paused and replied "Yes" Lily was the only reason. I would go back because on the meth she would not spend all her money. Then she could rebuild herself faster and have Lily full time.

See I have a warrant and no driver's license. No matter how much I wanted to leave Karen alone and keep Lily I don't think our run would last too long on our own. The thought of me coming home and I getting stopped had crossed my mind. I would go to jail and Lily will have no one to sign for her. I could not think negatively.

The lord said no more jail so that's what it was going to be. Hell, I'm not out here hurting anyone. Being on my own now is not what I wanted either. However, I do not want her being raised by a bitch that was only interested in me for my ability to get the bag.

I ignored that thought and knew that my child needed Karen to get better. In Norfolk the family was happy to meet Lily. She was the second mixed child in the family. She was gorgeous. The family loved her so much that everyone we stayed with wanted me to stay the night with them. I was happy to be away from all that drama. I just wanted to let my hair down even though I was bald.

When I was in the hotel with Lily I could have come home. I enjoyed watching Lily play with her dark-skinned family members. In the hotel and the shelter, I could have come home but Norfolk was ruff and unforgiving. I'll give Lily until she can walk and talk a lot better before we move here full time, I thought to myself. Definitely talking better was the deal breaker for me moving back home.

Ever since a family member raped my mixed cousin. Not only did I have to watch for the public but now you tell me I have to watch the family too. Until she can do those two things Norfolk was out of the picture.

Well, I had to meet the lawyer and he wanted to see how far I was in the patent process. We discussed that he would follow up with the patent office and we will get things rolling. He would keep me posted on every step of the way. I felt good about the meeting and if I got anything from this it was that my step grandmother must be loaded. I'll be there soon yawl, just hold my spot for me.

Karen called when I was in the meeting. I hit the silence button and finished the conversation with the lawyer. I'll call her back once I get Lily ready for her nap. I made a note to myself. I laid Lily down and the phone rang again. It was Karen. She was the only person I gave the fire alarm ringer to because it was always danger when she called me. Everything was an emergency. If she saw a bug, she called me to kill it. She can't find something OMG the world is coming to an end and guess what she calls me.

Hence why she has the fire alarm ringer. "Yes, I was just about to call you." Lily just fell asleep twenty minutes ago. I was laying beside her till I knew she was out for sure. "Oh, ok look I'm truly sorry about everything" she said. It was all my fault this time "The pain" Karen said, "hurts so much." In the shelter "I told you I thought I needed to get some kind of treatment." she went on saying "I tried to push forward because of you. I thought I could. Only because You said you believed in me." What I did not know at the time was that she was still using. I couldn't believe in her lies anymore.

I told her "It was ok to start over, I've lost way more." It was her I was interested in. I said "You took me in with seven kids and six ex's." Today's women would have crossed their legs while trying to run away. You didn't and I respected you for that. But it seems you think because you make the most money you should run shit at home. You can do whatever you want while I must jump at your every beck and call.

Well, she said "I just wanted to prove to you and the kids I was accepted into an outpatient program right in Fredericksburg, VA." Ok I was happy for Lily because Karen showed me, she was not trying to be like how she was before. Hell we all relapse right? And with the meth it's all the punch with no bite. I could deal with those odds and the prices.

Plus, at the shop I had everything going for me. The customers knew I was just new to the shop but not the hair cutting game. I lived right across the street. A lot of the clients were happy to let me cut them after seeing the end results of the previous customer.

If they wanted an after hours cut it was good to know they did not have to leave the neighborhood either. I had locked the area down to all seven complexes. The money was just getting to where I needed it. I was almost up to a hundred dollars a day.

Just as I was getting the home front on point Karen started withholding again. Money started to come up missing two hundred here a hundred there. When I would confront her, she would always say she forgot the money at work. That she'll bring it home the following night.

I am surely getting tired of her shit. When I get back home, we have to talk. The shop owner is now acting grimy towards me. After work I'm giving her a choice: either let me pay her to rent a chair or I'm leaving.

I worked from the house before. The community knows me already. I made sure of that once I locked the shop down. She was acting like she was jealous of my talents. She was a good barber as well. I could just feel the tension when her clients waited to sit in my chair. I just used the same tactics as I did when I was hustling. Pass out cards and flyers. It always paid off to advertise.

The plan worked. My name was in the air as a master barber. It was done. I got my chair from storage and now it's time to open shop at home. It started off slow. Then boom I was booked up and getting new clients every day. Things started to look up for Karen as well. She and the owner of Crayons had a falling out. By that time Karen had received an offer to open a new shop of her own.

Like I told Karen the lady that owned the building had come to you and she would allow you three months to set up without a deposit. She would have been crazy not to take the offer. The owner of Crayon's was mad at the fact Karen wanted to move on. She told Karen how she really felt about her then they parted ways. That had to be a no brainer God was giving you another chance at a better life. Your reward for not giving up on your life. *Lily starts crying.* I told Karen to let Lilly cry. She'll get over it one day. I was teaching Lilly that life will make you cry all the time. It was up to you to bear it and push on. Things are somewhat returning to normal. Thank you God!

CHAPTER 24

Back in the Saddle

The more Karen's clients started to return, her confidence grew. And soon the methadone had fully kicked in and had been filling her need to get high. It was leaving a big void for the pain though. Daily she would complain of the pain in her ankles. That's where all her drug use had stemmed from when she broke her ankles.

When she made those comments, it touched a nerve with me. To think all that she put the family through not to say what she put her body through. Her mind should be on other things. I guess that's what people go through after they have truly awakened from all the haze on their brain from years of drug use.

They see things in their mind clearly. Things she said, "seemed totally different from what she thought she was seeing in her coma." In her mind she may have seen things as being ok. But in all reality that was far from the truth, things were not fine. My daughter by that Norview bitch called me and told me her mom put her out of the house again.

This time she was with a child. This is why I sent the money home to her. Her mom let her husband's habit get the best of her. He was fighting her over the kids' support money for drugs. She took it out on my kids to the point she had told them and the courts I never paid child support. Whenever he took the check.

So now the money I saved for my patent, I have to give it once again to the court system. After my daughter had the baby, I told her since I had to pay the back child support order. I could not keep sending money to you and your mother.

I could only do so much for her and the baby. I thought she was happy. That boy needs to play his part. Was I wrong for thinking like that? My grandson was a very handsome baby and I wanted to do more for them both. So, I decided to go to Norfolk a day early so that I could spend some extra time with them.

Last week she told me that he might have to have a minor operation on one of his lungs. The doctor said, "that it looked a little abnormal and they wanted to remove it before it got too big." He went on to say, "that the procedure was normal and it would take about two hours." He assured us "it was nothing to be at wits end over and he would be fine." I was still concerned because he was so young.

Now here is where things become crazy. I was like could it get any worse? And it did let me tell you. It did exactly that. All the time up until the day I was to leave for Norfolk for my grandson's operation Karen was acting worried.

She would argue over the smallest of things. I knew she was better and I was feeling the pressure of her being sober. Then it dawned on me that I don't know this person here at all in the background. In the midst of her getting better the thought of me leaving kept repeating itself in my head. It influenced me that I could not seem to shake or break.

All the relationships I tried my hardest to make it work. Only to be left broken hearted and financially depleted. I guess I was putting myself in my child's shoes by staying with their moms. Seeing me not growing up with my father and that would overrule any thoughts of me abandoning them.

I would endure the pain of not being happy for any of my kids. This voice was like the others. It was intense just as the voice told me to leave my marriage in New Jersey after the airplanes hit the building in New York.

I was getting ready to go to New York. I will never forget this day. My wife at the time was mad because I had not offered her to go with me. Before today I had always asked if she wanted to come along and her answer was "this was the only day I had off, I do not want to spend it on no train in New York City."

After that I never asked her to go again. She was driving me to the train station. Suddenly over the radio it came that the World Trade Center was hit. We looked at each other and returned to the house in fear of the country being under attack.

See if she did not start an argument with me, I would have been right in the middle of the crisis. I may have even died in the aftermath with the other unexpected citizens of N.Y.C. that day. When I didn't listen to the voice inside of me, I felt as if I could have died. I was a little disturb about the whole ordeal. When the voice told me to leave her alone, I should have just left.

She was not into the relationship any longer anyway as I was. Since I did not read the signs, I was trying to force the marriage to work. She was getting a divorce behind my back. See if I would have left, I would have seen the divorce coming. She was a frenemy and not my wife. The signs were there from the start but I was too naive to see them. And the same signs were coming back now and since I was going to Norfolk anyway now may be the time to listen to that voice.

If I leave, I'm never coming back. I immediately thought about Lily. Should I take her or should I leave her with Karen? I had a babysitter in Norfolk. Her oldest sister would watch her while I worked. That was the greatest concern of mine. I did not want to separate them and have Lily getting used to another sitter.

The best thing about this was this babysitter she has now had family all over the seven cities. She had come down to Norfolk weekly or the family went to the Burg. That meant I had transportation whenever I wanted to see her. If I decide to leave her with Karen. I'll make up my mind in the morning. I'm going to Norfolk to stay, that's for sure. Karen had thought this was another threat and when she saw all of my things packed away, she had begun the same old story.

Don't leave, everyone has problems and if you leave don't come back. To me when she said that it didn't bother me like it had in the past. It was like she had her body but as the words were leaving her lips the heads of all my kids' mothers appeared on top of her shoulders the whole time she was talking to me. Listen, maybe my intentions were wrong in the beginning of these relationships. At first, I just wanted them to watch my brother while I worked and ran the streets.

Once I educated them, they then thought that they were better than me. So now instead of a relationship it turned into a challenge to see who will achieve more than the other. At first, I would either find a new girlfriend or deal with the madness until my child had gotten old enough to understand that it was not their fault, I was leaving them.

The shit repeated itself so many times that I refuse to go through that again. I said to myself it stops now. When Karen went to work, I told the sitter of my intentions and assured her I was still going to pay for Lily's day care. She was not happy about the situation but she was glad that Lily was staying here.

The operation was Tuesday. Since I had gotten in a day early, I did what I wanted to do, which was to spend the day prior to the procedure with Tie, my grandson. We laughed and played for three or four hours. I wanted him to get ready for the big day he had coming up.

I kissed him on the forehead and said goodnight to them both then left. I went back to my mom's house to sleep. My mom got me up at five in the morning. Even though the operation was to start at seven thirty. She wanted to be there early. I could not sleep at all last night. The argument I had with Karen before I left kept rewinding in my head.

This had been the first time she said "She wanted me to leave." Then she changed her mind. Who does she think she was trying to control my wellbeing at the drop of a dime? Without me she would be lost. She only works on everything else she needs help with. Not that she can't do shit on her own. She was just spoiled.

It was time for me to change that! At the hospital the doctor had taken him to the back. After a long three hours he came in with the news. We did not operate on him today. In his test the doctor said they wanted to monitor the area further before they decide to proceed with the operation.

They rescheduled him for a follow update. "Thank you, God," I said aloud. With all the other shit that was on my mind I was happy to put this on the back burner. I did not want my grandson cut on. This had been a good day. I left the hospital and my mom and her husband went to work.

Later that day I planned to move back to Norfolk. I set up an interview for this new shop out Ghent to cut hair. It had gone well except the owner's attitude was shitty and demanding. After she handed me an application, I refused the job. Then I told her "Because of her bad aura I could not work in that kind of environment." Then I kindly excused myself.

One good thing that came from the interview was that I caught up with my old homebody Eater. He swore he was God's gift to women especially when it came to eating them out. We went to the local Go-Go bar, it was on the other side of town. We wanted to catch up and have a couple of beers.

The Go-Go bar was two blocks from my mom's house, so if we got drunk we did not have far to walk home. The bar was dead. There were plenty of people buying up that ice cold beer though but as far as the selection of women it was horrible. To top it off this skinny ass black stripper kept dancing at the end of our pool table. She acted like somebody was interested in what she had to offer. We just wanted to shoot some pool and have a laugh or two over the old times.

She put her nose up and got off the stage pissed as hell. I called Karen the very next day to tell her I was leaving on the one o'clock bus. All I heard in the background was Lily crying and the sound of water gushing. Karen said "She accidently hit the sprinkler in the laundry room and it was coming out too fast to stop it by myself.

"Call the rent office for help." I cut the head maintenance man's hair. I hung up with Karen. Then I called him. He was at the door as we spoke. He told me that the house had flooded and it was about two feet deep in water. Well guess we must keep what we can and throw the rest away. At least none of the kid's electronics were damaged.

We still had all of our jewelry so I had guessed that we had gotten off pretty safe. The housing clean up team came over to help while the fire department turned the water off. They had placed heaters and humidifiers throughout the apartment.

Karen said, "I cancould not stay at the place because everything is still drying." I told her "I'll leave on Friday and just stay with our neighbor until I get home." She was from New York and I think that's what attracted me to her. By me being in a relationship I would not approach her in that manner. Plus, you'll have to wife her up. She was a total package. She was half Indian and half Chinese.

She wore both very well. She was five foot five inches tall. Her weight was around a nice one hundred and maybe sixty-five pounds give or take a pound or two. She had long bleach blond hair with brown highlights and a body that made your old lady say damn she looks hot.

Well since we knew that we were attracted to each other but as neighbors we kept it just as that. We never touched, hugged or even kissed but that could all change if we were not living in Best Look Apartments. She agreed to sleep over at the neighbor's house and I told her I'll leave Saturday morning. Now since it was nowhere to sleep there anyway I told her to just call me when she got off work.

That night when Karen called, she was balling. I was like to myself for someone who wanted me to be out of her life she sure does call me a fucking lot! "Stop crying in shit. What now?" I said it in anger because this all could have been avoided if she was not acting like an asshole before I left.

Someone must have heard us fussing and knew I was leaving her ass. She said, "We've been robbed!" "What the fuck is going on Karen?" I asked her and she said, "we've been robbed!" I was like "huh, robbed?" She said, "Yes when I came home, I had to use the restroom. So, I didn't turn on the lights when I first came into the house. I felt something was crunching under my feet." Then she says "She reached for the light switch then noticed the place was torn up.

The back bedroom window was up with the screen missing. I told her to "Hang up with me and call the police. I'll be there tonight." She agreed and said, "We'll figure out the next move once you get back." I'm calling the police and I'll call you back she said. Then hung up the phone.

It was Friday eleven o'clock at night. Why had it taken so long for her to get home? I wondered to myself. In my heart I wondered if she had gone and sold our valuables. Was she using again? Was the break in a cover up to hide the shit from me? I hoped she hadn't started using again.

The fussing I could put up with on the count I wanted to be in Lily's life, as long as I can. If she is using again, that's some shit I will not tolerate. I'll be returning to get my daughter if that's the case because she doesn't seem capable enough to handle her by herself. I'll take my chances on having a warrant. So now I want to go back ASAP. I told my mom about the robbery. With her being an ex-addict she even thought it sounded strange the house flooded, then robbed. It was just too close and she did not want me to get into any trouble going back there fooling with Karen. She knew Lily was there and I was not going to leave her there with Karen alone. "I didn't leave my brother behind. I'm not going to leave her behind either." I told my mom.

She agreed with me and told my cousin to come back with me just in case it was some bull shit going on. Good, I had thought to myself. I'll have a person to have my back since I was not from that part of VA. She told her husband "Dickey to see if he could take off then they could drive us there." He said "I have a vacation day I could use and it should not be a problem. I just had to call in to notify them that I will not be able to work today. I just had to run some errands for my mother and afterwards we could leave." He then asked "If me and Eater wanted to ride along to save time on returning back to pick us up?"

We both agreed to wait for them to return. After the trip we jumped on ninety-five south heading to Fredericksburg, VA. On the way there he stopped at every liquor store he saw. The last one was right before we got on the road to go through the Hampton tunnel. He stopped and now I was mad as hell.

"Yo Dickey. Do you have to stop at every abc store? Are you going to be able to drive, man?" I asked him. "Sure, I can," he said as he stumbled into the driver's seat. My mom wanted to say something he quickly told her "To shut the fuck up bitch men are talking." Now I've been staying with them for a week now. He's not once called her out of her name or anything like that so now I see what he was up to.

He wanted to get drunk and provoke me by cussing at my mother. This was her thing and I stayed out of it. We all got back into the car and Eater said, "I don't want you playing with my life. I think we should leave in the morning." Dickey said, "Man I got this.'. Then I stepped in and said "look man let's just go to the house and work on your facebook page. Hopefully he would fall asleep and sleep the alcohol off.

Dickey's mom opened a business for him and he offered me to organize it for him by getting it off the ground. I explained to him that the world was run by technology now and for starters we must get you set up in the computer world. Just like in your personal life, it would be easier to teach you. However, in the business world it was mandatory to be plugged into social media.

That was the aspect of using the computer for maintaining your business affairs. My cousin was on the phone with Dickey's son, so we could set him up a facebook page. When I could not teach him, his son would be able to step in and assist. Dickey went to the kitchen, me and Eater were at the dining room table and my mom was in the front room. As we were talking to Dickey's son, he was in the kitchen talking out loud saying "fuck your son he don't know everything." repeatedly to himself.

I told him you asked for my help. Even though I left the businesses I opened to my children's mothers, that was for the kids' sake more than for the mothers. I considered myself knowledgeable of the basics on starting a business. I saw it like this after me and their mother's relationships were over, I knew the bills, my kid's lifestyles and housing still needed to be a priority.I did not want it to change. I had come from the gutter.

I could survive it again if I had too. They have never been to the hood and I was not going to let them go either. Whenever it was time to leave, I did not fight for anything. That did not make me unsuccessful just caring for my kids. I said to him "but you had to get your mom to open your shit so I don't want to help you and fuck you too. As a matter of fact I want my clippers out of your truck and I'll leave."

His response to that "was you are not getting shit and you not leaving now." He had crossed the line, I thought to myself. "She is your wife and if she wants to let you degrade her and talk to her any kind of way you want too, that's on her. But fuck with me if you want too, I got your ass" I said. Eater said, "his son hung up the phone from embarrassment of his dad".

He said "he was going to leave too. I told him to "Wait." Then I heard a drawer open and you could hear silverware slamming first to the front of the drawer then settling back into place. Then you could hear them slamming to the back of the drawer again after he slammed the drawer closed. With my back still to him I said, "If you come out that kitchen with anything other than a spoon to eat with, I'm going to fuck you up." I saw a shadow move quickly behind me. At the same time, I turned and Dickey had a long ass knife in his hand. He was going to stab me from behind with a fucking cutting knife. I did not know how many he had in his hand. I just know I've been shot before. However, letting him stab me in the back was not about to go down. I placed the chair between him and me. My mom ended up being just a little bit slower than I was because I had her path to him in the kitchen blocked.

The seat of my chair was the only thing I had to defend myself with. She screamed to him "Dickey you're not going to stab my son." Up until that point I had known the seriousness behind the situation. It had been funny to me because we all had been drinking since seven am. I guess he was at his wits end. With the chair between the both of us he looked at me and I stared back at him. Then he said, "I'm going to get your mother fucking ass." Right at that moment I had a flashback to when I was eight and everyone was against me then a little kid said to me, he is serious Tee defend yourself I don't want to die.

I threw the chair to the side and said, "come and get me then bitch." He charged at me. Now he came at me with the knife in his right hand. I had reached into the kitchen drawer. It must have come back open when he slammed it. I reached in with one quick swoop and we collided. His knife had struck me on my side and I felt the pain surge through my body. It burned and angered me to the point that I curled my left arm to shield me from another swing.

As he tried to grab me with his left hand, he reached out for me then I stabbed him eight times under his armpit. I was going to stab him in the face but as I looked over to my mom she was still in love with this fool. I stopped and she started screaming "Dickey no Dickey no." At that moment I was not eight years old anymore I was a forty-one-year-old man alive. After realizing what had just happened, I looked at Dickey and my mom. I threw the knife down soon after my mom passed by me to stand between me and him.

It all happened so fast that Eater was telling me to come on before last call at the club. I looked at him and said, "Ok, I'm coming." I turned back to investigate the kitchen. Dickey was still standing up with the knife in one hand and his other fist balled up shouting "you punk ass mother fucker." Other cuss words were used as my mom was standing with him. Her arm was around his waist and her other hand was on his mouth. She said, "yeah go to the club and call me when the club closes." I said, "I'll call you but if he is still up fussing and shit, I'm getting a room." She said "fine."

We left for the bar. The club was only two blocks from their house. We cut through the neighborhood and got on to Diamond Springs Rd. I saw like ten Virginia Beach police cars fly by us at mind blowing speed. Eater looked at me and said, "What happened in the kitchen between you and Dickey?" Before he finished his sentence two helicopters hovered overhead.

I saw all of it play threw my head and said to myself Dickey had charged at me first. If I had not seen my mom's shadow streak past my back, I'd be dead now. I turned in slow motion. I'm seeing this play out scene by scene. When he charged it gave me only two options: run out the apartment with him on my heels or fight. So that left me nothing else to do but defend my life. The chair stopped him only for a moment.

I jumped into the lion's den. I felt a sharp pinch in my left side and it had gotten blurred from there. That's when I looked up and saw my mom hugging Dickey and trying to cover his mouth. She tried to calm him down from cussing and pumping his arm with the knife. I looked down into my hands and there was no blood. None was on my clothes either. I felt a pain in my side and I looked for any cuts. Damn, I did get a small cut?

So, I guessed we must have missed each other. From that point I had said to Eater "nothing happened let's just go to the bar," I needed a beer. Damn the first person I saw was that black bitch from the other night lmao. She rolled her eyes at me. Funny I thought to myself because her eyes were the biggest thing on her body. I went to the bar and ordered two Coronas.

Eater was in the corner at the bar. He repeated the same question that he asked me on the way here. "Man, you sure your mom was going to be ok with him?" With all the arguing that Dickey and I was doing, someone had to have called the police. With no blood on me. I figured that when we had locked up my hand with the knife had to have gotten entangled in his tee shirt. What I had taken for blood on my hands must have been his sweat? While walking to the bar it was a thick film on my hands. It had to have been his sweat I kept repeating to myself. Which had led me to believe he was ok.

In fact, he was still standing on his own cussing when I left the house. He seemed to be fine. Eater said "Look man with all of those cops down by the house she'll be ok." When he said that it made me think what if he did try to get her. I did say I was going to call her after the bar closed. Eater I said "I'm going to the restroom. I looked at my cell phones and saw that both of my cell phones were dead.

I'll just walk back down to check on them." "Ok" he said. I went off to the restroom. While in there things just did not feel right. My life had begun to speed by in a blur in my mind's eye. The last time this had happened I could not remember what came next. I hoped to myself that Dickey was ok. After I peed and zipped up my pants, I grabbed the beer and washed my hands. Hoping that when the lights go on that no one tries to hassle me.

I didn't want another situation on my hands. At this point I could not take any more bull shit in my life. As I passed by the first pool table, I took a swig of beer as the bottle returned to the ready position. I was just about to drain the last of it. That's when I saw them there had to have been at least twenty police officers. They were in the front lobby of the club.

They were casually looking around for anything out of the ordinary. I looked to see if there was a rear door. I could not run because they were everywhere. It was, I guess, out of habit. One officer turned to me and I finished off the last drop of beer not knowing from this point on if I would ever have another beer for the rest of my life.

I locked eyes with him so as not to alarm the rest of the police. I said to him "you must be looking for me." I had placed my beer bottle on the front desk then turned to the wall. I placed my hands so he could see them. Then in a blink of an eye they were all over me before I could even react. They were pulling on me and tugging at my arms to get me on the ground. I was not going down and let them stomp me to death. They struggled with me until a voice from the crowd broke their concentration. "Shut up" was constantly repeated by the police until silence fell over the bar. The skinny bitch that rolled her eyes at me made it her business to walk out in front of the officers while I was in handcuffs.

Then she looked over at me and said aloud "huh, that's good they got your ass good for you." Then she twisted her little, tiny ass out the door and into an awaiting cab. As they tried to continue to rough me up a stronger voice came from out the crowd and yelled saying "the fucking man came up to you and you surrendered without any problems all that bull shit is not necessary."

The fifteen cops that were behind the five that held me in place turned in and about face. Then shielded the officers and me from the mob. The strip club was owned by white people and the dancers were mostly white with two or three sisters there but all the patrons were black. The officers were outnumbered at least three to one. So they were right to face the mob. I did not want the situation to escalate to more than it already had become. Inside a voice told me to start to fight back. So they could jump me and let that rage the crowd to a fighting frenzy. I only protected myself.

At the time I was not getting the support that I needed to propel me or her to the next level at home, it felt like a prison. I had two patents sitting on the fucking desk in the patent office in Alexandria. A book I wanted to write and several other pet peas I wanted to invest my time towards. Now look at me arrested for attempted murder... shit. Lord please, you know I never asked for anything before. There are way more people who need so much more than me, but just this one-time watch over my kids in your name I pray amen.

CHAPTER 25

Let God judge Me

The police had Eater on the car. I was in handcuffs in the back seat of another police car. I was calm and I asked the officer "if he could loosen the handcuffs just a little?" His young ass comes to the car and says, "they weren't made for comfort." I replied, "If I ran from you, I can see this type of ruff housing but now you're just being unreasonable."

His eyes bugged out his head and he said "What?" Then he continued to say, "You ran from the scene of the crime". I said to the young officer "You were not there so whatever young blood." He slammed the car door. See that's why I did not go back to the apartment for that simple reason. To him and the rest of the officers I was just another nigga that stab someone and fled the scene.

They were here to tame me and then cage me that's all. Believe me they were willing to do it at any cost. Once the door slammed shut, he stood by the window and said, "how do the cuffs feel now?" I said, "I can tell you were never in the Armed Services." He said, "What does that have to do with anything?" I replied, "You would have had to serve to understand what I mean?"

I said "From the way it looks I don't have the time now to teach you. So run off and go play with yourself." he was pissed. He turned red and started to say something back but the sergeant walked over and asked me "If I was ok?"

"I replied no the cuffs were too tight." he asked the officer did anyone check his hand cuffs and he nodded yes.

His sergeant said "we'll be at the station soon," then closed the door. When the driver returned to the car, he turned on the camera and asked me my side of the story. I thought for a second and remembered the episodes from the first forty-eight hours where this guy told his story to the person that he surrendered to. They used his answers from the car against his answers at the station. That was how they tripped him up in his own story. I gave my side of events that led them to arrest me. He turned the camera off then hit his lights and we left for the detective's office.

The ride had been longer than I remembered. He had the fucking window down the whole damn ride. Now it was back to my military training mind over matter. That was a Marine Corps saying. Translation meaning if the shit you go through don't mind then it won't matter going through it. Once you let it out of your mind then whatever you were going through now doesn't matter. It was cold as hell plus I had to piss. Finally, I said to myself I have never been so happy to see a jail before. By now I had to piss like a racehorse and to him it did not matter.

I told him I had to go ten lights ago. "Please officer, I have to use the restroom." I'm awake so I'm not going to pee on myself. "Ok" the officer replied and then went on to say, "we will be inside the office shortly then you can go to the restroom ok." In the office I was directed to an interrogation room. The doors locked behind me. I could hear the discussion that was going on outside in the office.

A voice said, "He has to use the head" are they on the way?" he asked the detective on duty. The dick had said "as we speak." The police who brought me in said "ok, well have them photograph him first and then he'll be allowed to go to the restroom." "Ok" the officer answered. As I waited for the chance to use the restroom I realized that I was not as upset about jail as I had been before in the past. I guessed after fighting all my life, raising a brother up till this point I have eight children all together. To myself I felt that I had a good run.

Then I said to myself while I'm in prison if a motherfucker gets it twisted, I'm going in his mouth as soon as they finish saying one thing I did not like. That's how I felt because I did not ask for what happened. He came at me and the way I saw it, it was self-defense. I was in prison at home in Fredericksburg, VA. If I had to pick my poison of living instead of dying my choice was living in prison then being buried. That was my answer so the trading of the prisons here or with Karen were not chosen anymore. I had picked gladiator school over living with Karen. My home life that I had fought for so Lily could have both parents was all lost now. Something I had been trying ever since I had to care for my Lil brother. Just because he left the nest, I still wanted it for myself. That was to have a family. Karen was always arguing all the time over anything and it was getting to the point that I wanted to move back to the seven cities anyway.

The place of my birth any way. Just I did not have this in mind. I left at the age of seventeen years old. I told my mom that I was not coming back until I was rich. I should have stayed away. Now I'm in the Virginia Beach jail house being charge with another attempted murder case. Damn what is it about these city streets? Everywhere you go you must be ready for anything that jumps out at you. As a barber clients ask me all the time why did I leave Norfolk? I told them every chance I got "that if you did not have a plan and you moved to Norfolk, Norfolk will have a plan for your ass."

Then the door opened "Stand up. Look at me. *snap* Turn right *snap*. Turn left *snap* ok. Now hold out your hands *snap*. Turn them over *snap*. Now get undressed." I asked "How far down?" "To your boxers *snap* Turn around *snap*. You can get dressed and the restroom is around the corner, the second door on the left." The officer said, then left me in the room to get dressed. One of the other detectives followed me to the bathroom. As I was entering the room to turn on the lights a voice said out aloud "keep the door open." Wow I knew he was a watcher. They took pictures of everything except a nude shot. He walked me back to the room where there were two detectives already sitting there waiting for me to return.

"Have a seat," the older of the two said. Then he turned to the younger detective and said "you ready," he shook his head.

He prepared himself to take notes as well. First thing first he read me my rights and as soon as he got to where they say, "you have the right to remain silent". Well, I stopped him there and said, "I'm not talking". He looked up from the card he was reading from and said, "whether or not you want to speak to us I still have to read you your rights."

I nodded my head and listened to the rest. Once he finally finished, I looked at him and his partner. To myself I said really, they can't do a damn thing for my ass but they want me to talk to them. They must think I'm going to be dumb enough to say anything. I'm drunk, I'm hungry and I'm tired. I'll tell my story to the judge. I looked at them, waiting for them to say stand up you're going to jail.

I was ready too. They can take me to jail. Then I looked up and said "I want an attorney present before I say anything to anyone. They recorded my statement and left the room. Outside the door again I could hear them talking about me. The officer that I rode back in the car with was like "I don't think he was the aggressor in this case."

The female from CSI said she looked at all the pictures and there was no blood on him or on his belongings. Then one of them said maybe "he changed clothes." Someone said we need to pay "more attention to the pictures of his hands. We looked at them too, but there was nothing there either" the CSI said. They were both in denial that he did not hit a person that would have done this. If he was the suspect. It just does not add up. All the blood was everywhere in the house. If he had not changed his clothes and there was no blood anywhere on him. I don't think he did the crime.

After the conversation between the two officers was over the sergeant on duty came back into the room. He looked at me then closed the door. Maybe three and a half hours had passed and the door reopened. The detective said, "you can go now." I was puzzled and half asleep. I stood up and I faced the wall he said, "you're free to go." Huh? I looked at him to size him up as to see if this was some act to make me fuck around and get shot. I did not trust any police and especially Virginia

Beach police. Ever since the oceanfront had that riot the beach had never been the same.

I was very worried if this was going to be a revenge thing. They bought me a change of clothes and I grabbed the bag. They said this is the clothing my mom sent me. She thought that they were going to take my clothes from me. I did not need to change but I had grabbed the bag off the table anyway and gave the old clothes to them and walked to the door. While walking to the door I was still watching the detective the whole time. I guess I was anticipating him to stop me. By using force or something. To my surprise he did not even budge. When I passed him, I asked, "if I could use the restroom before I leave." He said "yes."

I entered the restroom and turned on the lights. This time I left the door open to beat him to the punch. Just as I had started to piss, he shouted "hey shut the damn door shit people do not want to see what you got." I was laughing my ass off. I had done that to be funny and he fell face first in it. I washed my hands and, on the way, out the door. I had asked him if "Dickey was all right." He had asked me "what did I care that I had stabbed him?" I looked at him and said, "it was either him or me and I chose me." He said, "well you did not want to talk to me then so you're free to go have a nice night."

I placed the batteries in my phones and called Eater to meet me in the parking lot. They were letting me go. He said, "that they questioned him and had him walk back the way we went to the club." I asked him, "What did they find?" I did not have to ask Eater what he found. One thing I did know about him, my mom or Dickey did not see what I did with the knife. It all happened so fast I did not even realize what I did until I was arrested.

"Yo Eater it's ok where are you at now?" They just released me and it's cold as hell out here. We're at the Va. Beach General hospital your mom said, "catch a cab here." "Ok" I said and hung up the phone.

I arrived at the hospital and my mom met me downstairs. She said "he dropped the charges. So, are you willing to apologize to him?" I thought long and hard and I was sorry for what happened but not for what I had done to him. Life has taught me that with every action there is a reaction. And if I did not react I would be in here laid up and not him. She saw where I was going with the situation but had asked me if I could go and say something to him "please baby or I'm going to leave him." I did not want her to leave him because I could not give her what she wanted from a mate. I damn sure could not see what she got from him either. I told her I would go and see how he was and she led me to his room. As I neared the room my heart started pumping fast and the whole thing started replaying in my head.

I went over to his bed and he slowly turned to me and said "man I'm sorry for what had gone down earlier. I looked at all the tubes he had hooked up to him and tears filled my eyes not because I stabbed him. It was because I really liked him and he felt like the closet thing I had to a real father. I said that was all gone. "Are you all right now man?" "Yeah, I'm ok son." I thought I'm not your son, not anymore. Anyways, I held my tongue and said, "thanks for dropping the charges" he replied, "yeah man no problem." "I should not have drunk so much," he said. "Yeah, you did drink too much and if we do talk again, I want it to be without drinking," he agreed.

My mom asked me "if I could go back and clean up the blood in the house." I said goodbye to Dickey and my mom. She told me "How much damage had been done to him." She said "he had a punctured left lung and he lost eight pints of blood. The doctors told him he was lucky that I was there to apply pressure on the wounds. He would have died for sure if he was alone."

She went on to say "when he had woken up, he had realized the same thing and he told the detectives he was not going to press charges. I told him if he did press charges on you and you got locked up, I was going to leave him."

Mom, thank you. She passed me the car keys and gave me a kiss. I kissed her back, me and Eater left for her house. When we got there the front door had blood everywhere. I turned the key and as we entered the house you were overwhelmed with the smell of iron in the air.

I left the front door open, so I could see my way to the light switch in the kitchen. When I cut the light on it was blood everywhere. On the table, under the table. The kitchen floor was covered as if he tried to clean the floor while he was laying on his back. There was a blood trail from the kitchen to the bathroom and back to the front door. It was going to be a long night.

Karen was coming to get me as soon as the banks opened. She had checks that she wanted cashed because Sunday the banks would have been closed for the whole weekend. Eater wanted to help but little did he know he had helped me enough just by being with me from the start of all this shit. I told him to go to sleep. I had the cleanup job to myself. I sat down alone in the bedroom and fell to my knees and I thanked God.

For not allowing me to be in jail for the rest of my life. For yet another day to be free and I cried. Once I felt as if the Lord had healed me and made me feel whole once more. I began to clean up. I had taken a box of gloves from the hospital so I put on three pairs on each hand.

I went to the bathroom and started running hot water in the tub and put pine sol and bleach in it. Then I retrieved all the rugs that had blood on them and placed them in the hot soapy water. I then made a bleach solution and I wiped all the walls and the furniture off. I went outside and cleaned the front door and porch. I changed my gloves and jumped in the kitchen. It was the worst of all the rooms. That's why I left it for last. All together it took me four hours to clean up all that blood. It's now been almost two days of no sleep and I can't wait for this week to end. I had gotten like an hour worth of sleep when the phone rang.

Damn time flew by. I remembered throwing out the trash, smoking a cigarette and sitting in this chair. Karen was coming through the Hampton tunnel. I had to start getting ready now. She was pushing it because she had appointments early the next morning. Eater drove my mom's car to the hospital and he gave my mom the keys to her car. She jumped on me and said, "I love you baby."

I told her that "I never stopped loving you mom." Lily got out of the car and all you could hear was "grandma grandma." She walked over to us and hugged our legs. My mom told me to "leave Norfolk, that's when you have the most peace in your life."

I thought to myself that she was right, my life had been a good one. It had a lot of ups and downs. It has mostly been filled with a bunch of lows here lately but it always happens when I'm home. However, the reality of it was I only became more stable. When I was not around the people who said "they were friends," but they always turned out to be my biggest foes.

So, after the thought had passed, I looked at Eater and told him "to stay in contact." Then I said to Karen, let's go and get ourselves back to the Burg. On the drive back Karen was sleepy. Long drives did that to her but it was a nice day out. The sun was very bright, the grass seemed a lot greener than usual and the sky was a brilliant blue. Then I wondered to myself did the things around me seem to be a lot more colorful or did I just enjoy viewing them live and up close. In its true form because just the night before I was on the verge of never seeing these wonderful things in real life again. For the rest of my life or if I did see it would've been on television or in a magazine. That would have been bullshit.

"Pull over at the next rest stop." Karen did not like for me to drive but since we were on the interstate, I did not think she would mind. I liked driving long distances. It was better than her driving. She agreed to let me take over the trip for the rest of the way to Fredericksburg, VA. While driving I reflected on all the events that had gone down in my life in the last week. Sunday me and Karen had a serious argument to the point she had asked "me to leave." I agreed and since I was going to be in Norfolk anyway for my grandson's operation I decided to return to Norfolk for good.

Tuesday the day of the operation the doctor told us that they decided to put off the procedure until further testing. I thought that was excellent. My blood line was for the most part saved. He was my first grandson and the operation was not that serious but anything can happen with those types of procedures. He is only six months old so I had been worried but hopeful. Thursday the house flooded and I found out my insurance on the place had lapsed. So, four thousand dollars' worth of water damage was gone with no compensation.

Karen called me on Friday and what we did not lose in the flood was stolen when the apartment was robbed. Now what was on my mind had Karen relapsed after the flood and pawned the things that did not get damaged to get drugs. That did not make sense because she had money now. Maybe not as much as before but enough to hide her habit. Especially without having to go through so much extra to hide her using. Now that night I almost lost my life then almost took a life only to be arrested and held for attempted murder and aggravated assault. It was a long week. I just could not help to wonder if this is what the prophet in New Jersey said "That I would never see the inside of a jail again." This was the fifth time I evaded a serious charge without even going pass booking. I never went out to test his prophecy. I just did not understand how five times since he told me that I would not be incarcerated again and it had come to pass.

He said God told him I would never go to jail again and that riches will follow me and my blood line for the rest of time. "What was I doing wrong?" He also mentioned for me to get rid of my demons. I thought my moving home would change that, but it had not changed a thing.

I went for my patents only to fall short on making it pass the approval department due to lack of funds. So, I wondered where the riches were? What did I have to do to obtain them? Karen had gone back to sleep after we stopped to feed and change Lily.

She was asleep until the car stopped. Lily loved driving, I had thought or was it because she had loved sleeping while being driven. Either way it was a delight to watch her look at the landscape while going sixty-five miles an hour. Her little eyes are looking crossed eyed after a while then she'll fall asleep. She looked so pretty sleeping. We got to the house around four or five o'clock and Karen was right the place was a mess. There were heaters, humidifiers, and evaporators everywhere. First Karen I said, "I'm going to clear the machines up and clear the front room, so we can have a place to sleep." After she and Lily laid down, I was so upset at myself. Not for what had happened but for the direction that my life was going.

I wanted a change. I met someone who in the beginning would be perfect. After the baby they would see my commitment to being a family man and they take that and run. They end up messing up a good thing and who suffers in the end the baby and me. I was the only caretaker so their whole world would become rearranged. And as for me I would also have avoided it in my heart as well. I knew deep down that to relieve the pain I would have to move away and send money. The loss of my time with them was all I would regret. Then a voice said, "don't be sad just be grateful that you're free with these problems and not in jail."

You can change your problems out here but in jail your problems become a part of you forever. Well, I know one thing when I wake up on Sunday, I'm going to church for sure to thank God for all of his blessings. Amen.

CHAPTER 26

Getting an understanding

I knew what I had promised to myself that I was going to church but Sunday was Karen's only day off. She worked hard all week long as she always did since I had known her. So, asking her to take me and Lily to church would be out of the question. I still had gotten up anyway as if I had a way for us to go to church. Then out of the blue a client called and asked, "if I would cut her son's hair before church service?"

Right then I knew that God was listening to my heart because I wanted to go to church badly. I told her "To bring Zap over and I'll cut his hair for her before church." She asked me every Sunday if I wanted to go to church with them to the services. I wonder if today she would do the same. I wanted to take Lily with me but she was not feeling too well, so I had to leave her home with Karen. If Ty asked me to go with them that was if I got invited to tag along. Sure, as summer follows spring, she asked me "if I would like to attend the morning service with her and the kids?" I said "sure," and we left after I cleaned Zap up and wiped his hairline off with the neck strip.

It felt strange she was telling me not to be scared if I see people in the church shouting and dancing. Or if they start to jump and scream, she said. "They do what they feel when the spirit hits them." I told her "My mom had me in every church in Norfolk and the spirit was in all the people who attended those churches" then we laughed.

Rest assured that it will not offend me none the least. Service was the same as in any other church. I had seen the members as they flowed in to be seated. The closer it came for the church the place ended up packed. Service was about to start. Once everyone was in attendance and had filled the room the prophet came in and was seated. Then everyone started to get louder and louder until she stood in front of the pedestal and raised her arms. Then as she slowly lowered them the crowd began to lower its volume. She greeted the Sunday worshipers with a hardy "Good morning people have we come to praise God today, amen"

The crow answered "yes ma'am" in a huge roar. Ok then let's start by greeting all the visitors today. If you're a visitor please stand up and say your names. She said, "this was how we can welcome you into the flock this beautiful morning." I was the only visitor that day so after I stated my name and where I was from. The group greeted me and service announcements had begun right afterwards. A new pastor was coming for the second service and there was a meet and greet next Sunday. That's all the functions that will be held for today thank you and thank God for such a great day amen.

The speaker sat down, the crowd said "amen" and the prophet retook the stage. "Let the church say amen" she said as she approached the podium. The group responded in unison. She then began to speak about no matter what your life state is in, you still owe God time. He can direct you to your life's purposes.

And as she had taken in a deep breath to continue on that subject all of a sudden, she leveled her head and began to speak in tongues. She then lifted her head and out loud she repeated what she calmed was being sent to her in a divine message. She stated that God said, "for you to look to your left say I've been shot." The crowd did as they were instructed. Then she said, "turn to your right and say I've been stabbed and I've been falsely jailed but no matter what I'm still coming." At that point I felt a feeling of being whole again but once the feeling faded, I felt honestly that she had that message for me.

I was so excited as if I had hit the power ball number. All my worries were going to be solved. After the service the prophet had a guess that had given a reading to the onlookers and then she vowed to take a young lady shopping for her unborn child. The church went into prayer then we were dismissed. Everyone lined up to thank the prophet for her preaching. We left but on the way home Ty asked, "if I enjoyed the service?" I said "yes, it was very moving." She asked me "Did I want to go to the other two services?"

I could not say anything. My main focus was on the message from God. She asked us to repeat the three things that happened to me in the same order as they occurred in my life. I know how the saying goes when you go to church the guilt of not fully being a faithful follower that every message that's preached for the day you take it as the preacher was pointing at you. For all your shortcomings when instead the preacher plans their service days in advance. That's not always the case. So that's why today's message to me was God's way of telling me he's still watching over me. I did not have to worry but to just continue to focus and I'll receive what I was looking for.

I felt that the key to getting the full message from God was to open my heart and receive him. Ty asked me "before I closed the car door "did I want to come back again?" I said, "I would love too but Lily did not feel too well and I wanted to nurse her back to health." Especially since I had just received my healing for the day. I wanted to pass it along to my baby.

I cleaned up and Karen left for the day. I never asked where she was going or when she'd be back. I really did not think I would get an honest answer, so it did not bother me. In church I had a divine state of mind and when the prophet had us repeat the situation it fit me to a T.

I needed more answers and I knew just who to ask Mr. J. Mr. J was one of my clients that was a car dealer during the day and devoted Christian by night. He also was a deacon in his church, so he would be more than eligible to help me or at least to steer me in the right direction. I prepared a big dinner on Sunday. I wanted to be full so that after I said my prayers, I would fall right asleep.

I wanted to rest well through the night just in case God wanted to send me a message. I wanted to receive it without any interruption. I slept through the night and I did not feel any different in the morning. I thought deeply and I did not see any road maps to the promise land that I had hoped for. Then I just fell into my regular routine. Once I had taken Lily to the sitter. I helped Karen to get out of the house on time.

I sat down on the sofa and took a deep breath. After sitting there for a minute, I got up and made myself a cup of coffee. I set up for my first client as I sipped and thought about my day. Once I cleaned the combs, I heard a knock at the front door. it was Mr. J right on time. The house was clean and my workstation was open for business.

I said "Have a seat Mr. J.'" "Good morning master barber" as he had liked to call me. I greeted him and I continued to allow him to have the floor while I retrieved a neck strip. I grabbed my cape and placed it around his neck. Then asked him "how did he want his hair cut today?" He was about sixty-five years old but he looked no older than fifty. He wore his hair in a skintight high top box fade. While I started to cut his hair I asked him for his understanding of the events of what had occurred to me last week in detail.

I did not want to scare him away from me but I needed to know the truth. I wanted to know what he got from the message. From the first prophet reading back in two thousand three and the one from Sunday. The message I told him I received back in two thousand three was that "I was never going to jail again." "Secondly I was going to be wealthy beyond belief." The first part of the prophets testimony came true several times

However, the second part has not yet revealed itself to me. He said to me "It seems as if there is a message for you, but the only way for you to receive the meaning is to first go to God and ask him what direction he wanted you to go in? Ask him what he wants you to do?" That made sense to me but I never asked for anything from God before. I did not know where to start. I felt as though there were other people in the world more worthy of his blessings than me, I said to myself.

I told him that "I never prayed for anything from God before other than to take my soul if I did not wake up from my sleep." I just knew that it was people who had way less than me that needed way more than me. Asking God for anything seemed wrong. I felt he knew it all. I figured "why ask for anything from him?" Especially when he knew I did not need it to live. That night I took his advice and in my prayers, (it's been a long time since) I saw I was a little kid and I prayed. I kneeled as if my existence had depended on it. I had started by thanking God for all his blessings and for all the things he created in the world. I felt he accepted my offerings. Then I went on to ask, "him for wisdom and understanding of what these messages he keeps sending me meant?" The next thing I asked God for was the riches he had shown the prophet from Atlanta."

I wanted to right the wrongs in my life before I left to join him with my grandfather in heaven. See he (God) knew how much I wanted to leave my children a nice nest egg. I wanted them to have a life without all the pitfalls as I had dealt with in my life. At least they would have an opportunity, education, or the means to lead a somewhat normal life of their own.

I learned that from my real father. He really killed himself for my sister and brother to have a secured future. Killing myself so they can live well was out of the question. I'd rather work myself to death and take that chance that if I stayed focused enough, I would be able to be here to enjoy it with them.

That was my secret prayer to God. And that's all I wanted in life, nothing else mattered. I did not wait for an immediate response at that moment. I knew it did not work that fast. It could but I never tempt my God so I laid down and went to sleep.

The very next day I got a phone call from my cousin and he told me that my father's dad had been taken to the hospital in DC. I told him that I had just been robbed and I'd definitely try to make it out to see him. He then asked me about my progress on the patent.

I told him "It was in the office and it was going to sit there until I get up thirty-five hundred dollars for the lawyer to finish the project for me." "What?" He said. That really made me think. He said, "what do you need thirty-five hundred dollars for?" If you stop giving your money away to everybody you would probably have that ten times over by now. He was right and a recipient of my generosity several times but now he has his business going. All he can do is boast and brag about his success. It did not matter anyway because they treated me as an outcast until they needed some dirt done. My sister was the same way I supported her all the way through college and the one time I did not come to her like I was her dog she cut me off.

I even tried to put my patient in her name. She said no and cussed me out for asking her to do that for me at the last minute. Well, I had a warrant out for my arrest and before I went to court, I wanted to transfer the ownership so I could continue the work. However, she must not see it that way and refused to help.

That was my life's story. They all just used me but see here's the thing. I was the oldest and the oldest is supposed to support his siblings no matter what they did to you in return. Our father was dead so I felt obligated to fill his shoes. I told him "Ok then I'll see you soon." He said "ok" and we hung up.

Later that night while laying in bed I thought to myself "why was he so concerned about my patent?" If he was so interested "why doesn't he contribute to the research and development? I was upset. Everyone hoped it went through but no one wanted to help. It made me mad as hell because if the patent was completed, I would have shared it with everyone.

Now I see why people close their circle once they get their plan in play. I did not want to be rich, I just wanted to be remembered. Somehow, I knew I'd be the first person they would call when shit got tough but I never have anyone to just pick up the phone and say hi. The next day I was still perplexed about my place here on earth. I lived a good life so lord if you do want me to receive the blessings you've shown me it was fine by me. Either way I'll die waiting to see it.

I've always pictured my riches in heaven where the thieves and the moths can't reach them. I figured if I died I would still obtain the riches anyway thru Christ from my beliefs. I was more interested in the riches waiting on me in heaven than hoarding them here on earth.

Either way I was finally at peace in my heart and with my life. At that moment my phone rang and it was my daughter. She told me "That my grandson was fine and that her mom had gone to court for the child support case."

I told her "Why doesn't your mom just drop that shit because she doesn't know that she is messing with the money that I'm sending to you and the baby?" She said, "my mom can't change the order, the state has picked up the case." I knew that was not true because she never received welfare.

I took care of her even though I did not live with her. I asked my daughter "if she would just write me a letter to state that I have been in her life financially and that she has known since she was eleven." Her response was that her "mom promised her a car and that she was not going to do that and jeopardize her getting a new car."

Then she went on further to say, "why didn't I get my other kids to write the letter?" I was crushed she said some hurtful shit to me before but this time it was like a stake in the heart. I thought we had a special relationship. Once I left her mom for the bullshit... She told her new boyfriend that he was her father. My daughter believed that up until she was eight and they had a daughter of their own.

One night my daughter called me and she asked me "Is beating up your wife love?" I said, "Well no baby. Then I asked her "Has anyone been hitting on her?" She said, "no but he is fighting with mommy all the time." I knew from there what they were saying about him beating her up for my baby's child support.

From then on, she knew who her father was and I told her that we'll be together soon. I then started sending the money through Money depot to whoever had the kids for that weekend for the next ten years. See I was breaking the court order so her mother's husband did not take my baby's money. I told her "I'm breaking the court order to give you the money because your mom wasn't giving you anything I was sending to you guys. All these years I've risked my freedom for you and now you tell me you can care less if I get locked up or not.

I wanted to go back and forth with her but at that point I was already disappointed in her reply and I was done with her too. It did not matter what she had to say, I knew she would need me before I needed her ass. I said to her "I see you don't care if I have to pay child support twice, as long as you get a car out of the deal? I'm sorry you feel that way," I told her. Then I said "my phone was getting low and I hung up."

I knew she needed a lot of things. She was with a child now and in school. I sent her money for a new cell phone and I paid the bill. Plus sent money weekly for her and my grandson. I could not understand why she would not care if I'm in jail or not. I was hurt but also relieved because she was that daughter that if I did not send her what she wanted when she had wanted it, the first thing that came out of her face next would be" I wish I was dead."

That was my saying all the time as a kid and no one ever listened to me. I wanted to be that person to listen to her. I could have given my kids anything they wanted but that would not solve anything. Look at these kids now shooting up schools and malls in shit. It was because they had everything they could have ever wanted except love. That's what I wanted them to get from me, love and understanding. That material shit doesn't make you.

You define who you are when all else is said and done. I had thought to myself that she did not care if I'm in jail. Then I was going to treat her as if I was there and not return any of her calls and send any more money to her. Now let's see her drive that car. Who was going to pay for the things that I was already paying for her huh? I had asked myself. I was a barber and all the cash I made I invested it into my kids and their mothers.

It has gotten to the point that I've been homeless and still was keeping up with my obligation to them. Only for them to grow up and be a bunch of selfish brats. And right at that second it hit me like a ton of bricks. You're not the only one son. I was like huh? That was the message I've been waiting for so long to hear from my father.

NO, you dummy you're not the only person who the system is not seeing the whole story behind the money situations in these child support cases. Then when I thought about it, it didn't make sense to me right away. I was upset for being made to pay back my child support twice but who cared.

I was not the only person this happened too. I had gone to bed that night and I could not sleep. Something was on my mind and it was heavy, so that I had awoken from my sleep twice now. Then it happened I got out my laptop and began typing. Title: Get off the bus (The bull shit under minding your stride to success). The biggest ride of my life has ended and I felt relieved. All my life I had placed my kids first, no matter what it took except for theft. I made it happen for them. Even if it meant my freedom or my life. Not seeing them over the years I turned into a dollar sign to them. I'm not leaving them anything now. It made me feel as if I was buying their love. I did not want to no longer expose the wrongs of the court. Now my eyes were open to the fact that whether my children's mothers give them the money or not I should have just followed the court order and sent the money to the state.

It was set out for me from the start but because my children asked me for the money I disobeyed the courts. Now it was time to right that ASAP. As I got to the fourth chapter of my book my grandson's mother called me. She asked if I was still mad at her. I said to her "Baby I don't get mad at my kids because my kids did not do anything for me. That showed me why I should not let what you'll do affect my decisions. When in fact you all did not even know where you were heading."

I was allowing the guilt from not being with them to impair my thought process. She sighed and said, "Well you don't have to worry about me calling you anymore because my cell phone is going to be off."

I said, "no it will not, I have a money order right here. I'm sending it to your mom and she can give it to you for your bill," I finished. She knew I always paid her bill no matter what she had done or said to me in the past. I felt she knew that this time things were a whole lot different. She replied by saying "now I know my phone is going to get cut off." Well, I'll talk to you when you get it back on" and I hung up the phone.

She knew just as well as I did that her mother was not going to pay her bill. I really feel-good today and I hope that God continues to show me favor in my future endeavors. Now I realized I just got off the bus and it felt good (next stop please). It felt strange that it took forty-two years of my life to realize that whether it be a drug, best friend, job, child, or anything that interferes with your goals you have set out for yourself in life.

To be the fulfillment you deemed to conquer. Then my friend that is your bus (Bullshit under minding your stride to success). People get on the bus just so you miss your destination. It's up to you to know when your stop in life comes up. Some people get on the bus to pace you and once they see you're about to get off, they jump off ahead of you and leave you behind. Just stay sharp and remember you're in control of your own destination. Learn your stop and never look back. You may have to leave some people behind. They'll have to find their own stop in life. Trust and believe me, you will find yourself following the same bull shit that got you on that bus all over again.

If I had not identified my stop was my children that would have been my downfall. I was out in the world taking life threatening chances just for them to have a cell phone and necessities that they told me they needed. All along they didn't care if I went to jail or not. That really changed my plans in life but now I did not feel as obligated to them as I did before the confession. My whole life was based on my kids and leaving them a chance in life. I was robbed of my childhood. Well that still is going to be a goal of mine but it will not be the top priority in my life, as it has been for so many years.

Over that time, I've lost and gained weight a hundred times over and had been willing to do it a hundred times for all of them. If it was for my kids but now the situation has changed. When my daughter said that to me it felt like a string was cut. I fell to my knees as if a big burden was lifted. This made me free of all my worries. Now at the conclusion of this book I tell you the same. We have a black president and we can't say oh the white man did this or because the white man I can't get ahead in life. The United States has now shown us if you work hard and keep a clean record you too can be president. You have to want to achieve it.

You don't have to blame God, your best friend, your mom, or your teachers, it's you. The bus ride represents life's and all of its twists and turns. Now on this bus there are a lot of people that's happily ready to sell you, teach you or just fuck you over just to keep you down on this ride. You keep seeing your stop but you were so involved in the shit that's going on that now your stop has passed you. The driver has no idea if that stop will ever be on the schedule again. Now you're stuck up here until you see the next opportunity that suits you on the way. The more stops you pass become less opportunities you will pass. The longer you're on this bus you begin to see that all the people on the bus physically change. Except your situation stays the same.

All the stories of these people stay the same. It was the same, it's just being looped. This is to keep you distracted from your stop. The old shit that like me had landed you back here. I just needed clarity. I had a feeling my kids felt some type of way about me. I never thought it would end up like this.

It was painful for me to find my stop but who said life was pain free? Now that I have identified my stop, what do you think your stop will be? Will your story be one of the same old stories that will play out forever on that same bus in your same neighborhood? Like it was for a long time driving mine.

I say to you "Be strong and be alert because misery loves company." While on that bus know why you're there and understand that there's no man that can make you stay on that bus but you. Only you! Remember your stop and when you see it slowly approaching you get off the bus and never look back again.

Thank you for your time and I hope that you were able to get something from my bus ride (my life). I hoped that in writing about my trip it would help the next passenger find a way to wake up and get off that bus!

AUTOBIOGRAPHY

I am an African American aged forty-one and a half. I have five girls and three boys and about a hundred stepchildren and I love and support them all. I grew up in Norfolk, Virginia. Life there was hell, especially when the adults you look up to don't care if you make it or not. It was and still is a place of despair but its home and I'll see you soon Dear old Norfolk. To my kids I say please continue to reach for your goals and as always daddy will be looking over your every move, I love you all. I just want to start by thanking God for being just and hard on me to not just complete this book but also for giving me the strength and knowledge to see that I was a leader trapped amongst followers. The only way to understand that was for me to pray for clarity and from there I had to pick my own path. The same can happen for you, just pray and ask for what you need and he'll see you through. I thank you for taking time to read my story, take me and my tribulations and use it as a reference. Maybe my life's lesson can give clarity to you or someone else you love. Please pass it on and may God bless you and God Bless America.

Purging in the Form of Poetry

A-Z Volume 1

Written By

LEONARD A. WALLACE

INTRO

The beginning of Knowledge
"The proverbs of Solomon, son of David king of Israel:
To know wisdom and instruction,
To understand words of insight, to receive instruction in wise dealing; In righteousness, justice, and equity; Knowledge and discretion to the youth. Let the wise hear and increase in learning,
And the one who understands obtain guidance, to understand a proverb and saying, the words and their riddles.

King Solomom

SUMMARY

This is my fifth book I've written to date. I planned on writing this book on an island somewhere in the south pacific. Well, that didn't happen. I was locked up for three months in the Virginia Beach Jail on charges of purgery. Hint: that's where the title of this book was born. My mother always told me to use my time wisely.

Remember to follow only your Dreams. They do come true. As a matter of fact, you're reading one of mine now. Thank you and enjoy. Here's a small collection of thoughts and ideas that I hope will lift your spirits. I hope these poems help to spread joy, laughter, and healing. Something that's greatly needed today. Stay safe and blessed!

DEDICATION

Of course, if it wasn't for the Heavenly Father there would be no me, thank you God. My grandfather for giving me someone to look up to as a strong Black Male role model when others fell short of the plate.

Friends and family that helped shape and form who I've become in life. And then to all the haters I told this day was coming but just like the thief in the night you never see them coming. Did you honestly?

To my seeds daddy did it all for you. The generational curse is over, Amen. Invest wisely because this will be your inheritance.

TABLE OF CONTENTS

Ascending After All

Looking at the birds as they dance high in the sky, oh how I wondered and wished that I could fly...

As a kid I extend my arms and run fast then pretend to take off. I'm flying at last...

Once exhaustion invades my lungs; I'd open my eyes, look around then see my feet never left the ground...

Heartbroken, I wondered why my dream never came true; only learning of Jesus, as long as I believed in him my dreams were obtainable...

Through living righteous and being true I would be rewarded wings to fly, transforming into an angel living in heavens up in the blue sky...

By keeping his commandments living in him day to day "Ascending After All" will no longer be a dream of yesterday fulfilled by his holiness...

Blissful thinking

If I could change the world, I would say live, love, and laugh would be the graceful way. Oh, how I only wish it was possible for me.

I feel my life was a very big waste. Being a young man stuck in an old man's place, watching from the sideline feeling disgraced.

Feeling hopelessly alone, my hair turning all gray wondering at times is this the end for me. Nonsense I'd think while waiting and praying for a life changing sign to blow my way.

I'll look up to the sky with tears in my eyes was this negative thinking will life for me remain on this course until I die. Well, I'm a cheerful person and positivity has been one of my qualities I possess inside.

I'd rather be alone than sinning or living a lie. Calmly waiting for an invitation from my savior Jesus Christ. If that is "Blissful Thinking" I will caress it until I fly...

Coming to Reality

Out of all the places I could be I'm happy to be approaching life stage number three. Stage one and two were great just the same; However, I know all things inside of us will not remain the same.

In my life I worked so hard to change the game, no matter what or who we are we all must return from that in which we came. Understand we need to take a different way if you want to make a difference in the world before our bodies fade away.

It's not going to be easy to break your old training. Replace old habits with positive things and Blissful thinking. Distractions from your past will try to derail you; Stay focused and others will see than mimic these actions. This is setting the bar higher. By doing so you secure a bed in heaven for your soul's eternal resting.

Thank you, father, for blessing the knowledge of

"Coming To Reality".

Dreaming for Dummies

Living in America I was told that dreaming was free but growing up in poverty through my eyes that I didn't see. Here was the land you can be whoever you choose to be and at bedtime I would lay back and visualize the journey life was going to take me...

For some reason I'd always dream of me taking flight but who was I fooling. Round in size and lacking in height. Books became my true-blue passion dreaming of becoming an Author. That would be great then fast forwarding to acting.

My standards were set high. I knew schooling was the only way to achieve these goals of mine. At a young age I was scraping and struggling just to survive. I'll take my chances you know why, if 'Dreaming is for Dummies' then I must be as dumb as they come. One thing life has taught me is that nothing is given so I'm never giving up......

Effusion Vs. Efficiency

At our start as a child, we're foreign to bills, when life's plentiful we as children unintentionally don't use efficiency abusing resources not realizing it's hurting mother earth's protective layers. Our elders always told us waste not want not was the way to live; our parents would blame it on us being young and not knowing any better.

I'd leave the water running or a light on not caring about consumption. The thought of efficiency didn't matter, effusion had seemed to be always on my platter. Effusing food, time, or money whatever in my reach as a young venomous snake would use his venom in his very first bite.

He would dispense his entire supply in his first fight. As I got older, I learned in time the resources I had abused as a child weren't abundant without a price. Just as that venomous snake learned to conserve his strikes, limiting his venom for that one bite.

Effusion vs. Efficiency learn how to control your resources in life...

Foreshadowing

Being human beings we're born with five senses; not me I always felt different like I had six through prenatal intervention. I could see things before it happened or speak it into existence. As a child I used to think of this as a power that only I possessed.

Sometimes I would pretend I was a superhero from another planet. This feeling made me feel special as if receiving love from somewhere else looking over me when no one else bothered. It felt as if the sun had always followed me. On the gloomiest days the sky still seemed sunny. Not having much made me feel protected. I know it was God sending his angel to comfort me. Now that I'm older I see it as "Foreshadowing."

Guilty Plea

I'm living, laughing, and loving my life; Coming and going, not doing for myself. I'm not selfish, that's okay and It's fine with me; On sunny days I'll visit the park and lay down under a shaded tree. Visualizing this was a great life that I led. Helping others was the only way for my soul to be free; If it was up to me, I'd travel the world assisting the elderly, overseeing the babies, and supporting those who were in trouble. When I die remember that all I wanted to do was rebuild the world's communities. That's my "Guilty Plea."

Honor Higher Than I

Hoping to reach heaven is my only goal in life...

Oppressed by my family made me strong. I don't cry...

N od is what my father did oh how he loved heroin...

Omitting he loved me I can't agree, not one hug I received...

Reading people's thoughts comes freely to my third eye see...

Halcyon is what I prayed for when I lost my granddaddy.

Infinity x Infinity is how many times God has forgave me.

God is my king through him I shall live eternally...

Heaven is the place I want to see united with loved ones...

Expropriating my belongings to charity giving back...

Rapture at this age I feel free at last to do as I please...

Titanium is my thought engraved in my.

Heart no harboring regret look into my eye see that,

Everlasting love made me rise above the rest ...

Novocain my pain dealing with stress overall blessed...

Infiltration never faded made me the best. Whoever did it believe me I'm a winner!

Induce In Infancy

From day one I never had a chance to play or do anything for fun. As a youth lacking in everything was my middle name. In the back of my heart aiming at the top.

After I started walking, I learned to run looking back only to remember where I came from, slum. Developed tunnel vision visualizing what's needed for my empire to grow.

No family, friends, mother, or Dad hardened my heart refusing to get sidetracked. I steadfastly pushing ahead. Sometimes feeling alone, I still wouldn't allow myself room to get mad looking at the sand seeing double footprints, I felt Jesus' presence.

Guess this is why I will never give in Blessed by the best promise land, new plan. "Induced In Infancy" now I see it was God's Plan. He was with me from seed to a man...

Joining The Race

Life is a game and you must play like you want to win. The pieces you have don't forget the movements. Making moves in your mind before you apply them keeps you ten steps ahead. Watch the other opponents like you were in making the band. If you're not careful they'll pass you, never extending a helping hand. Fall to the wayside is where you'll land.

Once you reach the age of being grown, life becomes school. No plan, one wrong move will take yours from you. Never forget to guard your strategies, remember the rules; always keep that poker face when "Joining the race." Then all the right moves will be revealed like in the Billie Jean video the his Will will light up the way!

Keystone

A pillar in life I was made to be giving kibitz to my friends and family. Since infancy I felt it was my kismet to be in kilter to my surroundings in all walks of life. As the oldest fruit from my family tree staying upright trying not to keel over was a big deal to me.

Being keen using my third eye and depending on God made me strong. Having positive kinetics helps me to keep my kleptomania focused and sharpens my mind. Keeping this process in play became my "Key Stone" for life.

Living Life Legacy

By this time, I had planned to have it all. Now forty-seven here stands an old man only time I've acquired. Life's dreams lost in the sand; all possessions I gave to the mothers of my children. Objects that I can easily replace.

The biggest challenge to me was leaving life without a legacy. Those material items were so mindlessly obtained. I only wished that at least one of my kids' mothers would have chosen me over the earthly things.

However, that wasn't the case without a thought I gave it all away. With or without them I had to remain focused, keep up the pace and finish the race. Every time I had to leave and start all over again it was my decision, I didn't get mad.

They had it all except for my faith. I still had Jesus on my side leading the way.

A man's sacrifice leaving a "Living Life Legacy".

Making Change

Brainstorming is a natural process that comes easy to me. Modified thinking as a guide to success on the journey to being the best. This gives my cerebral time to digest all the info people throw at my bullet proof vest.

Choosing to respond this way helps me to stay focused all the while keeping my stride in order. At the same time positioning my priorities in proper perspectives to accomplish world domination or whatever comes in my direction. Tailoring life's situations to fit my purpose of personal design, mental alterations.

Problems come in all shapes, forms, and sizes, recreate your steps making sure you stay to what you're trying to establish. Ideas are the process of the brain staying on top, always creating new conceptions to keep you in touch with your thoughts.

None The Lesser

You can't base your existence on material things, certain people's job in life is to acquire your possessions. Social media makes it easy, stop bragging and blogging everything.

I never could imagine this happening to me, but posting my accomplishments helped them carry out their negative theme. It felt unreal like a kid wanting to see cartoons but his parents instead tuned into the daily news, confused.

It taught me one lesson not to post anything until I return home. You never know how many eyes are on your prize. Ever since then None the Lesser has been my motto.

Open Heart

Days are like candy, some are sweet and some will be tart; I wish people would be like days instead they conceal their true thoughts. It would be nice to know their inner purposes; Like the weatherman in the mornings giving us Weatherby overcast.

Observing the seasons, we can see and feel the change. It would be splinted if we as humans would display our emotions the same. We now have a machine to influence the weather. It would be nice to have one so we can reach each other. Who am I fooling? We can't find a way to stop using dinosaur blubber.

Well, if not that, we should build a machine to open our hearts. Then we would remember to shelter the homeless, feed the hungry, and save our people from living in poverty. If it could be done it will stop all the violence laying low in our society. It's my dream but it will never happen in today's world because doing so there's no profit.

No one's even willing to solve these problems but they'll hold debates on subjects to build walls to keep out terrorist. Is this just; Congress discussing the salaries of those who are supposed to represent us. Solely to use them to mislead and control the masses. We can't even enjoy our dwellings; they even pull the strings of the ones whose job is to protect and provide services.

We are hip to the news about the singers, sport players, and actors. Always reporting about their houses, money, and latest fashions to distract us. Speaking on their choices of vacations, and bad habits. None of us really care what Kanye says or where Diddy lives. All the long you're confusing the public while using these foolish tactics to cover your wrong doings and foul practices.

I wonder what would've become of Bill Cosby. He should've done what President Trump did paying those girls he touched by using a dummy accountant. Oh, he thinks he's the smart one behind the U.S.'s back sleeping with Mother Russia. Being a double agent is just hurting us. Now even shutting down the federal government. In due time his impeachment will catch him.

Or like Paris Hilton's father the judge said no to her release, he gave the sheriff a million dollars. See I learned their game by doing the same thing, but instead of fake news I'm giving you the real play by play. Now that you hear the actual facts. We must wake up and tell them to give us a break or more lost rights will follow if we continue this way.

Now sit back a minute and take a deep breath and ask yourself what do you think? Will they come after me since I spilled their beans? I'm not worried. Last time I looked, freedom of speech is still on the books. I'm living my dream doing my thing with nothing to hide. I'm just living out my dreams with an "Open heart" join me. It's not too late I challenge you, so the next generation will have a brand-new slate.

Purging Poem

You think bad thoughts when the word purge is brought up. Oh, how closed minded we're in our teachings. This title for the poem was just pure luck when the child support judge didn't believe me. As a result, I was sentenced to three months or pay double the court fees.

You may say that's not luck. Who's this guy he must be nuts? Just pay the court fee so you can remain free! Look not to sound selfish but I refused to get railroad again by the judicial system. A scorned Baby mom cheated on me, so I moved on. In order to see my children, she demanded I pay cash or I'll never get to see them again.

Reluctant, I agreed I needed to see my kids. When it came to graduation for both of them the funds were sent to her, I stopped. Listening to her girlfriends she took me to court. I pleaded to your honor that in fact I paid weekly support. Then the judge replied that since it didn't go through the state in their eyes, I was the bad guy.

The judge's name I will not mention in fear of infractions her lacking a sense of humor only God knows what her reactions would be. To say anything to her that day would've been pointless. Here's a hint: she's a Shark in all ways and when she smiles you can see her jagged fangs. Leading all her victims to the Virginia Beach Juvenile and Domestic Court System. Then it's off with your head. The halls steadily ring, bailiff who's next!

Last hint I'll give, so listen very closely please don't hesitate one moment to be late. This Poem I now dedicate to that great white shark who swims in courtroom eight. That's where I received my three-month break. I said to myself why not write a book titled by my sentencing.

Purgy in the form of poems A-Z vols. 1,2, and 3.

This poem was all written in fun. I will send her a copy in hopes she'll stop and listen instead of taking a bite out of everyone..... As if you all are clean without any blemishes, some of us are innocent, a few may be guilty but before judging a person at least hear both sides of the story!

Quarrel or Quell

Fight or flight is a question of old; Like life's riddle once said which came first the chicken or the egg? Human nature is to run or face your fears. Whatever one you make to others make sure it's clear.

Some choose to be the hero and quarrel it out. They take their problems head on. Win or lose it's always best to stand up for your respect.

That's the thing that makes bullies stand back. Others will Quell not concerned with the outcome. Never solving anything, always on the run. This offense that's used sometimes is ok until they find themselves between a rock and a hard place.

Well step back and let's see both sides of the coin. Running away sometimes saves the day but if you cut off a corn on your foot they come back unexpectedly with more pain. Pick and choose the destiny, it's all up to you but in this world to be a survivor at times you must "Quarrel or Quell".

Restless For Resurrection

I used to worry where my soul would end up in heaven or hell. I often grieved. Being uncaring yesterday changed my whole life a hundred and eighty degrees. I wanted to see the pearly gates, get my halo and wings.

The outcome of my life left me guessing, restless for rebirth while constantly praying for the lord's blessings. Living on earth I did my best but people here change so much I chose eternal rest instead of dealing with this stress.

It is said energy never dies, it just passes into other lives. If that is the case, I want my life's force to be passed to a bird. I can fly away and not worry about what to take or what should stay. I'm happy to have had the chance to enjoy this planet. Here was only a test, now that I'm older I understand it. We were given a choice to see who will get invited to the new world under God's order.

Ever since I lost my grandfather, I have been working harder to receive forgiveness from the Lord. At all times walking in total balance with my good and bad side focusing on harmony. Sometimes the distance will get too hard to see. So, when it gets difficult I close my eyes and ask God to forgive me. I know it's only a test and these are tough times in life's sessions. Missing my grandpa just leaves me Restless for Resurrection.

Secede or Salute

Large, I was picked on by others in grade school. Back then there were no cameras to rewind to see the truth. Having them around today helps the ones being bullied to have proof. To prevent it from happening to me I stayed in the teachers face. I guess I did it so much she began to ignore me.

Her as a defender must not have been a part of her curriculum. I'd wave my hand to bring my situation to her attention but she'll slowly wave me off. The bullying was persistent. Today this problem is consistent running away choosing to remain silent committing suicide as the answer.

We need to be more hands on with our kids by asking questions while looking out for depression. There's always two sides to every story while some kids choose to salute and join the bullies. This way isn't good either, this gives them time to plan an ambush. All that pinned up anger inside is why we in return have all the school shootings.

Both sides need to come together with the victims and the bullies if we want to resolve this unnecessary matter. This will break the chain and only then we'll have peace.

Testimony

Thank you, Father,....

For all that you are and done for me. For loving me like only you can, and for the footprints you left in the sand. All the years supplying support, comfort, and compassion. And showing me daily how much you care for me. Holding me down when my heart was so full of rage coming to me with blessings freeing me from my cage. Through meditation and prayers, you've given me vision which lifted my despair. This has been my

"T testimony" please father continue to rain peace all over me.

Universal Choice
Ultimate Sacrifice

We're heading towards a one world government, the signs are all around us. Look closely, their systems are all over with messages on the money In God we trust translation using religion to mislead us.

As people living in a free nation our Liberties are slowly dissipating. Just like our freedoms are vanishing too. If we don't address this, we'll become batteries like the movie Matrix. Tied down act now or end up supplying the machinery. If not you or me what would be the future for our seeds.

The constitution clearly states this country was founded to say what we want and to act how we may. The right to bear arms and to live where we want but today, they are all going to waste. Bet the forefathers are turning over in their graves seeing all their hard work being washed away.

We as a nation need to take a stand against "Universal Choice." Support one another instead of not allowing them to make a division between each other. Billions of dollars are spent daily to make America remember slavery.

This is done to keep us divided and people choose sides. Especially people of the same races killing each other in our own communities.

This can't be the plot for a country that has the name "The Melting Pot." Step back and look at what I'm telling you twice. Let's come together and unite.

Let us Put down the guns to make it right!

"Ultimate Sacrifice"

Virtue Becomes Victory

Death before dishonor our heroes shouted. Never cheat to win if you lose, be courteous, shake hands and walk away as friends. Display good merit, honor, and integrity when going up against the enemy. Donating patience my mind is still off in the races. All the while not trying to lose my face.

I thank God for all his grace. He saved my soul so many times that I can say man I feel great. Wish I could've been the lamb and taken his place. Crucified on the cross that would've secured my seat in heaven's gates.

Let "Virtue Become Victory" the reward will be your weight in gold. Follow through his plan he'll light up the way. Pray and God will show you, just wait.

Walking Tall, Watching All

Keep your head held up to the sky, never forget where you come from, always give back for the next generation. Set the stage so they can follow your footprints and do the same thing. I call it breaking the chain. Treat others how you want to be treated best, believe all eyes are watching. If life's a game, then there are rules: God is the judge recording your every move. Be careful, watch what you're doing. He is the coach that hands out the tools to assist us in life so they're not to be abused. Watch who's around you. If they're not on your side, they'll want you to lose. It's for us to be true to the light, so we don't stray away. Always remaining on the straight cause some of us want to win and use you at any expense. People like that without us will not make it because their values and hearts are in all the wrong places. Doing whatever they want, hurting whoever is in their way for all the wealth in the world except for heaven's gates. Not to be stuck on earth, respect one another. Walk Tall. Watch all. Be the one who makes a difference.

X-acute Then Pursue

Most of us start out in life with a lot of great plans. Somewhere we want to be when we become our own boss staying in the pursuit of happiness. We wait until the stars give a sign. Others hesitate not wanting to leave old habits, lifestyles, and friends behind.

Prayers were made and sacrifices were paid. Our insecurities repelled us from receiving the way. It's a good thing he gave us saints watching over us glory be to God. He is awesome. In my heart he will always live. At times helping friends and family I almost lost my bearings. He knew that wasn't me and put my dreams back in my sight.

Dear father, you really know my heart. I'll help anyone without a second thought. Always ready to lend a helping hand not expecting anything in return. Anything for my fellow man. I learned to X-acute my own dreams becoming strong and he'll still protect me.

Yearning For Results

Lord, I've been longing for a change in my life. I feel like a vampire never staying in the same place twice. Everywhere I wake it's strange. Being around new people, places, and things. Oh father, how long will you keep me here away from your grace. May I ask what the reason or the game plan is?

I'm here on bending knees praying help me please. I have no one here but me. At times Lord, it seems as if you're not with me. It's all my fault I promise I'll change, just give me a sign that you'll visit me again.

Father, I apologize for all my sins I committed don't leave me lord can you hear my repentance? For your love and grace, you can have my whole life. My mind, body, and soul is already yours dear Lord. I just ask for the opportunity to sit at the foot of your throne. To give you praise till eternity like David in the book of Psalms.

Oh Lord, I hear your commands, you say "wake up" then my eyes are reopened. He sat me down by green pastures. I hear water flowing. I turned to see then he placed me in a trance. Anointing me with oils is soothing as it covers my head. It's so refreshing, overflowing my cup. I now wonder if I'm alive or dead. He laid me down and I fell asleep. I felt great as if I was a computer rebooting my spirit and he uploaded me once again. I woke up with new energy and the same program to help my fellow man.

He knew my purpose before anyone else and gave me a new body cause the other one was through. Upon realizing he blessed me then said, "I want you to be the leader of the Orchestra Band." Then he blew life back into me while I was still swimming in his hands. In a blink of his eye, I was attached to my mother's uterus once again.

Nine months he educated me while I was inside of her womb like superman's father did for him. When I fully matured, I could hear words that sounded as if I was in a room. Then with one big push I fell back into the world renewed, but I had the same old plans. To do his will, lead his people, and uplift his name. "Yearning for Result" I now have the plan I'm reborn, a new man...

Zero To Zeal

Before I had no ambition my life wasn't clear. Being a son without a father and a mother who didn't care. I felt useless. My mind was unfocused, food so hopelessly rare. I only went to school for the free meals. Then one day Lord while contemplating suicidal thoughts I hear your voice. You renewed my faith and opened my heart.

After hearing you I fell to the floor. You told me to always pray and there would be no more closed doors. Father, I give you praise for making my path clear to me. Then my life seem to change overnight from "Zero to Zeal". I know when you're near the introduction for trumpets I'll hear.

Now I found the true purpose of my life. It feels wonderful going from nothing to having you on my side. Now all is abundant no more how's, who's, and when's. I just call on you my Lord and whatever I yearn for you make it appear. Thank you, father, for your glory. You're the real reason I went from "Zero to Zeal" true story.

David's Prayer

The Lord is my shepherd; I shall not want. He maketh me lie down in green pastures: he leadeth me beside still waters.

He restoreth my soul: he leadeth me in the path of righteousness for his name's sake.

Yea, though I walk through the valley of the shadow of death, I will fear no evil for thou art with me; thy rod and staff they comfort me.

Thou preparest a table before me in the presence of mine enemies: thou anointest my head with oil; my cup runneth over.

Surely goodness and mercy shall follow me all the days of my life: and I will dwell in the house of the lord forever.

THE END